The American History Series

SERIES EDITORS

John Hope Franklin, *Duke University*

Abraham S. Eisenstadt, *Brooklyn College*

Arthur S. Link

GENERAL EDITOR FOR HISTORY

Donald R. Wright

State University of New York
College at Cortland

African Americans in the Early Republic

1789–1831

Harlan Davidson, Inc.
Wheeling, Illinois 60090-6000

Library of Congress Cataloging-in-Publication Data

Wright, Donald R.
African Americans in the early republic, 1789–1831/Donald R. Wright
p. cm.—(The American history series)
Includes bibliographical references and index.
ISBN 0-88295-897-6
1. Afro-Americans—History—To 1863. I. Title II. Series: American history series (Arlington Heights, Ill.)
E185.W944 1993
973′.0496073—dc20 92-27210
CIP

Cover photo: Nat Turner and his confederates in conference.
Culver Pictures, Inc.

Manufactured in the United States of America
97 96 2 3 4 5 EB

For Wilma S. Wright
and
In Memory of Richard M. Wright

FOREWORD

Every generation writes its own history for the reason that it sees the past in the foreshortened perspective of its own experience. This has surely been true of the writing of American history. The practical aim of our historiography is to give us a more informed sense of where we are going by helping us understand the road we took in getting where we are. As the nature and dimensions of American life are changing, so too are the themes of our historical writing. Today's scholars are hard at work reconsidering every major aspect of the nation's past: its politics, diplomacy, economy, society, recreation, mores and values, as well as status, ethnic, race, sexual, and family relations. The lists of series titles that appear at the back of this book will show at once that our historians are ever broadening the range of their studies.

The aim of this series is to offer our readers a survey of what today's historians are saying about the central themes and aspects of the American past. To do this, we have invited to write for the series only scholars who have made notable contributions to the respective fields in which they are working. Drawing on primary and secondary materials, each volume presents a factual and narrative account of its particular subject, one that affords readers a basis for perceiving its larger dimensions and importance. Conscious that readers respond to the closeness and immediacy of a subject, each of our authors seeks to restore the past as an actual present, to revive it as a living reality. The individuals and groups who figure in the pages of our books appear as real people who once were looking for survival and fulfillment. Aware that historical subjects are often matters of controversy, our authors present their own findings and conclusions. Each volume closes with an extensive critical essay on the writings of the major authorities on its particular theme.

The books in this series are designed for use in both basic and advanced courses in American history, on the undergraduate and graduate levels. Such a series has a particular value these days, when the format of American history courses is being altered to accommodate a greater diversity of reading materials. The series offers a number of distinct advantages. It extends the dimensions of regular course work. Going well beyond the confines of the textbook, it makes clear that the study of our past is, more than the student might otherwise understand, at once complex, profound, and absorbing. It presents that past as a subject of continuing interest and fresh investigation. The work of experts in their respective fields, the series, moreover, puts at the disposal of the reader the rich findings of historical inquiry. It invites the reader to join, in major fields of research, those who are pondering anew the central themes and aspects of our past. And it reminds the reader that in each successive generation of the ever-changing American adventure, men and women and children were attempting, as we are now, to live their lives and to make their way.

John Hope Franklin
A. S. Eisenstadt

CONTENTS

ACKNOWLEDGMENTS

Above all, I wish to acknowledge the scores of historians whose scholarship, mostly from the past twenty years, provides the foundation for this book.

A number of persons were important in the book's formative stages. Abraham S. Eisenstadt first suggested that I take on this project. He offered encouragement and sound advice on several occasions. He and his coeditor of the American History Series, John Hope Franklin, and two anonymous reviewers provided useful comments and suggestions on the manuscript.

Several people at Cortland College of the State University of New York have been particularly supportive of my work. Frank Czerwinski and Berchie Rafferty in the History Department have been helpful with everything from bibliographic references to assistance with word processing; Len Cohen, Tom Bonn, and Lauren Stiles have kept the college's African-American history collection current through times of austerity; and Eileen Williams never failed to obtain the materials I needed through the college's interlibrary loan network.

Two exceptional students assisted me with this project. Andrea Thomas spent a good part of one summer compiling a basic bibliography on the topic, and Mary Beth Townsend helped throughout much of the time I spent writing, mostly with library and reference work.

Working with the editors at Harlan Davidson has been one of

the real joys of this project. I am particularly grateful to Andrew J. Davidson, who kept me to a schedule without badgering me and who copyedited the manuscript with care and skill.

As ever, Marilou Wright has been my consultant on words, sentences, paragraphs, grammar, punctuation, and, in every sense of the word, style. She has also listened to me talk about many of the ideas I include in this book, and she was able to straighten me out on a few of them.

And finally, I wish to acknowledge the never-flagging support of my mother, Wilma Wright, and my late father, Richard Wright. They were my first and best teachers about race and history—and most other things that matter.

Donald R. Wright

INTRODUCTION

On the sixteenth of April in 1789, George Washington set out from his home in Mount Vernon, Virginia, for New York City, the temporary seat of government, where he was to be inaugurated two weeks later as the first president of the United States. Washington would soon become the executive leader of the first nation on earth whose foundation rested on the ideals of liberty: of that fact he and most Americans were justly proud. Washington's trip northward was triumphant. Crowds cheered him along the way, and wherever he stopped joyful citizens staged celebrations. Many of New York's thirty thousand people turned out to greet the president-elect upon his arrival. The inauguration that followed was stately, with large crowds witnessing the events.

Traveling ahead of Washington to make arrangements for his trip was the president-elect's favorite slave, an African American named William Lee. Joining Lee in New York to begin serving the president and Mrs. Washington in their residence on Cherry Street were six other slaves from Mount Vernon. The seven African Americans helped bring order to the house, assisted Washington in his preparations for the inauguration, and thereafter helped ready the Washingtons and the residence for visits from dignitaries. Anyone attending the inauguration and catching sight of the president's slaves, or anyone simply looking about and noticing some of the city's two thousand other enslaved African-American men and women, would have recognized quickly that the blessings of liberty upon which the Republic was founded did not extend to Americans of African descent.

Just over forty-two years later, on August 22, 1831, seven different African Americans, these not owned by an American president but led by a slave preacher named Nathaniel Turner, left a meeting place in the backwoods of Southampton County, Virginia, and went on a deadly march about the county, massacring white people along the way. Over the span of thirty hours, Turner's forces, which eventually included some seventy slaves and free blacks, killed sixty white men, women, and children. Turner and his group served notice to southern slave owners that African Americans were not the contented bunch whites thought them to be. Indeed, they showed that African Americans were willing to take drastic measures to win the blessings of liberty that Washington and the other Founding Fathers had attempted to secure, at least for whites, when they established the Constitution of the Republic.

This is a study of African Americans in the early republic, which, as it is defined here, is the time beginning with Washington's inauguration in 1789 and ending with Nat Turner's rebellion in 1831. In between these two events, African Americans went through a tumultuous period of change. When Washington entered office: slavery was still legally recognized in all but two of the thirteen American states; the Atlantic slave trade was bringing thousands of Africans across the ocean every year to spend their lives in bondage in America; the centers of slave-based agriculture remained the tobacco farms of piedmont Virginia and the rice plantations of lowcountry South Carolina; fewer than 60,000 African Americans lived as "free" persons in the country; and the slave population of the United States was just under 700,000. By the summer of 1831, American slavery was a peculiar institution indeed, for: it existed only in the twelve southern states and virtually not at all in the twelve northern ones; there had been no legal importation of slaves into the United States for nearly a quarter of a century; the heart of slave-based agriculture consisted of the cotton plantations that stretched from central Georgia to the Mississippi River; there were 300,000 free African Americans, mostly in the states of the North and Upper South; and the number of slaves was something over two million.

Less obvious were other social and intellectual changes over the period. As enslaved African Americans were uprooted and moved south, they struggled under difficult circumstances to maintain or recreate the close ties to family and community that their ancestors had developed during the eighteenth century. Over the early decades of the 1800s, as the institutions of family and community matured among American slaves, they became still more important for black social, psychological, and cultural development. As slaves learned more of the ideology of the American and French revolutions, gained knowledge of the successful slave revolt on Saint Domingue (Haiti) in the Caribbean, and then watched whatever hopes they might have for gaining their own freedom come to nothing, they grew more rebellious. In addition to conspiring and rising up against authority more frequently than ever before or after, and doing so on a grander scale, during the years of the early republic enslaved African Americans continued to resist their masters and the institution of slavery in a variety of less noticeable ways.

Many more African Americans gained their freedom in the generation following the American Revolution, and those who did struggled to survive the difficult transition from slavery. Like their fellow blacks in slavery, free blacks worked through adversity to maintain family structures; then they proceeded to build the institutions that helped them coalesce into a distinct community and that would serve as the bases for free African-American society from that time onward. As these free black men and women received treatment from whites that relegated them to a lower-caste-like existence, many in the North and Upper South broadened their concept of community to include those African Americans still in slavery and began working to improve the lots of all persons of African descent living in the country. In 1831, African Americans were more united than ever before by race and more convinced that only in ending slavery could their lives be improved significantly. The most astute among them even may have suspected, as it seems Nat Turner did, that it would take the holocaust of a grand civil uprising, or some such cataclysmic event, to put an end to the institution that still held almost nine out of ten African Americans in bondage.

Like its predecessor in the American History Series, *African*

Americans in the Colonial Era: From African Origins through the American Revolution (1990), this study uses as a foundation two ideas about African Americans and their history. One is that experiences of African Americans differed considerably over the years and across the geographical space of the growing United States, even for those in the same circumstance of slavery or freedom. Ira Berlin directed historians' attention to the importance of time and space in the study of early African-American history, initially in his doctoral thesis in 1970, and he has stressed the point ever since—in *Slaves Without Masters: The Free Negro in the Antebellum South* (1974); in "Time, Space, and the Evolution of Afro-American Society on British Mainland North America," *American Historical Review*, 85 (1980); and still more recently in "Time, Space, and the Transformation of Afro-American Society in the United States: 1770–1820," in *Autre Temps, Autre Espace, An Other Time, An Other Space: Etudes sur l'Amérique pré-industrielle*, edited by Elise Marienstras and Barbara Karsky (1986). Unfortunately, not enough have listened to his call. But it is critical to understanding African-American history to recognize that the lives of African Americans changed rapidly due to new economic, political, social, intellectual, or demographic conditions—or due to such less-often-weighed factors as the introduction of new crops or growing methods, new diseases or strains thereof, changing weather patterns, technological advances, and more. The experiences of African-American men and women in piedmont Virginia in 1790, for instance, were different from the experiences of blacks in lowcountry South Carolina at the same time, and they were different still from African Americans' experiences in piedmont Virginia forty years later, in 1830. Failure to recognize this variety across space and change over time can lead to conclusions about African Americans that add weight to the racist assumptions that modern scholars have been working to overcome.

The second idea that is central to this study is that African Americans at any point in the past were neither more nor less than normal human beings, with all the variety that entails. This is contrary to the racial stereotypes and romantic exaggerations that long have been an element in the historical study of persons of African descent. Typical African Americans living during the time of the early republic, or before or after, were not merely the objects of whites' evil deeds, able to do naught but suffer; nor were they principled revolutionaries, quick to risk death to gain freedom and civil rights; nor were they wily calculators, always at work behind the scenes to fool white folks and get what they wanted. They were persons with complex characters, who, like most people then and today, were immensely practical. Most faced their lives squarely, assessed their positions as carefully as they could, and made the best decisions possible in light of the options they had. It is good to have advanced to a stage in the study of African-American history at which we can move beyond old racist notions and fanciful characterizations and focus on the fundamental humanity of persons in America of African descent.

Finally, it is important at the beginning of this study to call attention to a theme that runs throughout its pages and underlies much of the history of African Americans in the time of the early republic. It is simply the conflict between freedom and slavery: a conflict born of the American colonists' libertarian rationale for their political separation from England, which spread rapidly to all levels of the American population at the same time that slavery was expanding and becoming a still greater element in the economy and society of the Lower South.

The ideological basis of the Declaration of Independence—"that all men are created equal; that they are endowed by their Creator with certain unalienable Rights, that among these are Life, Liberty, and the pursuit of Happiness. . . ."—that was self-evident mostly in the minds of American intellectuals and patriot leaders prior to 1776, broadened its appeal in the years that followed as Americans of all classes fought to achieve independence and lived through the trying years of the new Republic. By the time the Founding Fathers sat together in Philadelphia to write the United States Constitution, broad segments of American society had indeed accepted life, liberty, and the pursuit of happiness as unalienable rights of the country's citizens. Slavery, of course, stood in the way of the sweeping application of these principles. At the Constitutional Convention, pragmatic considerations and, to be sure, a lessened concern for the personal liberties of persons of African descent, led the

Founding Fathers, through a series of compromises, to recognize slavery in the Constitution and thus lend it a legitimacy that would be difficult to overcome. Still, many of the Constitution's creators recognized how clearly slavery ran against the ideological grain of the Republic. (Indeed, many delegates believed the very word *slavery* would "stain" the Constitution, and therefore they left it out of the document, which refers to slaves as "other persons," or "such persons," or in the singular as a "person held to Service or Labour.") A number of the country's early leaders thought that, in time, the institution that had existed on the North American mainland for a century and a half would simply wither away.

There is no doubt that for decades after the country's beginning, fundamental ideas about human dignity and personal liberty worked against human bondage in the United States. These ideas: were important in effecting the end of the Atlantic slave trade into American ports; were part of the intellectual undercurrent in much of the slave unrest of the early republic; were responsible for the demise of slavery in the North and for the wave of manumission in the Upper South that provided the foundation for America's free black community; were the root of the thinking of free African Americans that freedom ought to bring something more than membership in a lowly caste; were the basis for much of the antislavery activity undertaken by whites during the early republic; underlay the fierce debates over the extension of slavery in the 1820s; and were an important element in the thinking of many free blacks outside the Lower South that prescribed that so long as any were enslaved, no African American could be a full citizen in the land of the free.

But as ideas about individual liberty were gaining broad acceptance in America, slavery was doing anything but withering away. Once the Revolutionary War ended, slavery quickly rebounded in the southern states and then spread rapidly into newly opening lands where cotton could be grown. As southern cotton production expanded to meet European demand, slavery became further entrenched as the foundation of the economy and society of that part of the country. Slaves from Africa poured into southern ports for the first eighteen years of the United States' existence. And throughout that time and afterward, American slaves were forced to leave their homes in the Upper South and to move long distances away, to the Lower South, where they had to reestablish their families, communities, and culture.

It was not until the third decade of the nineteenth century that the absolutely antithetical nature of the doctrine of personal liberty on the one hand and the entrenchment of African-American bondage on the other created profound problems in the public arena. By the 1820s it was evident to some black and white Americans that a country based on a doctrine of individual liberty could not continue to condone the enslavement of human beings within its borders. No longer was it considered to be a problem that, if ignored, would likely go away. And this would become only clearer to an increasing number of persons as the years passed toward midcentury. Abraham Lincoln's belief, which he expressed three years before the start of the Civil War in his famous "House Divided" speech, that "this government cannot endure permanently half slave and half free," was hardly novel. Through the years of the early republic, large numbers of blacks and whites were moving steadily toward recognizing this truth: a truth that became increasingly evident as the libertarian ideology of the Revolution percolated through a nation whose southern tier had become more than ever before a region in which social stability and economic well-being were incumbent upon slavery.

CHAPTER ONE

A Second Forced Migration

Between November 1834 and July 1835, a period of just eight months, two New England natives and an Englishman were traveling in different parts of the southern United States. The men did not know one another, so it was by coincidence that each encountered, at about the same time, a different part of the country's interregional slave-trading network. The records these men left provide a picture from the time of the systematic purchase, movement, and sale of African Americans that was the heart of the domestic slave trade—a traffic that had been going on with increasing volume since not long after the end of the American Revolution.

Ethan Allen Andrews was a Latin teacher in a private academy in Connecticut when the movement to abolish slavery gained strength in New England. After several years of hearing his fellow Yankees decry the traffic in human beings, Allen decided to investigate for himself. He traveled south and wrote about his experiences in *Slavery and the Domestic Slave Trade in the United States* (1836).

Andrews arrived in Alexandria, Virginia, in July of 1835 to visit the slave-trading establishment of Franklin and Armfield, one of the largest in the country at the time. Around noon, in the oppressive summertime heat, Andrews approached the high, whitewashed walls that made the place look like a penitentiary. Shown around by a clerk, Andrews first looked through grated doors and iron gates held closed by padlocks and bolts. The fifty or sixty men and boy slaves he saw in one yard, "were standing or moving in groups, some amusing themselves with rude sports, and others engaged in conversation, which was often interrupted by loud laughter, in all the varied tones peculiar to the negroes." In another yard he saw thirty or forty women slaves. Both groups "were well dresed, and everything about them had a neat and comfortable appearance," he added, "for a prison."

The hundred or so African Americans Andrews encountered were "apparently from eighteen to thirty years old, but among them were a few boys whose age did not exceed ten or fifteen years." There was only one mother with an infant. Andrews's guide informed him that the establishment preferred not to purchase women with young children, "as they were less saleable than others." Franklin and Armfield sent slaves from the Upper South to New Orleans by boat, with a shipload of 150 making the voyage about every two months. They also marched slaves overland to the states of the Lower South. The one hundred persons in the pen in Alexandria that Andrews encountered were going to walk—they were to set off, in fact, within a few days of his visit. "A train of wagons, with the provisions, tents, and other necessaries, accompanies the expedition," Andrews noted, "and at night they all encamp. Their place of destination is Natchez [Mississippi]."

Late in 1834, George Featherstonhaugh, an Englishman employed by the United States government as a geographer and surveyor, was headed south on a working trip. He had passed through the Cumberland Gap in far western Virginia and was moving southward through Tennessee when he met up with a large gang of slaves on the march toward Mississippi. "Just as we reached New River [about forty miles northwest of present-day Knoxville, Tennessee]," he writes in *Excursion Through the Slave States* (1844), in the early grey of the morning, we came up with a singular spectacle, the most striking of the kind I have ever witnessed. It was a camp of negro slave-drivers, just packing up to start; they had about three hundred slaves with them, who had bivouacked the preceding night in chains in the woods. . . . They had a caravan of nine waggons [*sic*] and single-horse carriages, for the purpose of conducting the white people, and any of the blacks that should fall lame, to which they were now putting the horses to pursue their march. The female slaves were, some of them, sitting on logs of wood, whilst others were standing, and a great many little black children were warming themselves at the fires of the bivouac. In front of them all, and prepared for the march, stood, in double files, about two hundred male slaves, manacled and chained to each other. . . . Some of the principal white slave drivers, who were tolerably well dressed, and had broad brimmed white hats on, with black crape round them, were standing near, laughing and smoking cigars.

Featherstonhaugh watched the gang set to the road before the sun was fully up. Its destination was the slave market in Natchez.

Just four months before Andrews toured the Alexandria slave pen and four months after Featherstonhaugh had encountered the large "coffle" of slaves on the road, Joseph Holt Ingraham visited the Natchez market—a place called, euphemistically, "Forks of the Road" on the outskirts of town. It was, as Ingraham called it, "one of the great slave-marts of the south-west." Only twenty-two years old at the time, Ingraham was a Maine native who moved to Mississippi and then wrote in glowing terms about his new home in books like *The South-West, by a Yankee* (1835). Ingraham and a planter companion, who was in the market for a slave, approached Forks of the Road, left their horses with a "neatly dressed yellow boy belonging to the establishment," and passed through a gate into a narrow courtyard where "a scene of novel character was at once presented. A line of negroes," he writes,

commencing at the entrance with the tallest . . . down to a little fellow about ten years of age, extended in a semicircle around the right side of the yard. There were in all about forty. With their hats in their hands, which hung down by their sides, they stood perfectly still, and in close order, while some gentlemen were passing from one to another examining for the purpose of buying.

Upon discovering that Ingraham's friend was interested in a slave to drive his carriage, one of the merchants called forth "George, . . . a light-coloured negro, with a fine figure and good face," who had been marched down the road from Virginia not long before. "Then came a series of the usual questions from the intended purchaser," Ingraham writes. "'Let me see your teeth—your tongue—open your hands—roll up your sleeves—have you a good appetite? Are you good tempered?'" The answers were apparently satisfactory, for George became the property of Ingraham's companion for $950, and soon he was off with his new owner. The African American who had spent the first twenty-three years of his life on a farm near Richmond, Virginia, who was married to a woman whom he had been forced to leave behind, would now have to begin adjusting to a new existence one thousand miles from his home, among people he had never seen, as a plantation slave in southwestern Mississippi.

What the slaves felt about all of this is not apparent in the records of the three visitors, but there are hints. While examining the slaves in the Franklin and Armfield yard in Alexandria, Andrews had a brief encounter, apparently unnoticed by anyone else, that left the Yankee school teacher perplexed. The black men in the slave pen had been lined up, single file, around three sides of the walled enclosure. Andrews and his guide were inspecting the group. He writes,

> As my conductor was expatiating on their happy condition—a discourse apparently intended for the joint benefit of the slaves and their northern visitor—I observed a young man, of an interesting and intelligent countenance, who looked earnestly at me, and as often as the keeper turned away his face, he shook his head and seemed desirous of having me understand, that he did not feel any such happiness as was described, and that he dissented from the representation made of his condition. I would have given much to hear his tale, but in my situation that was impossible. Still, in imagination, I see his countenance, anxiously and fearfully turning from the keeper to me, with an expression which seemed to say, like the ghost in Hamlet, 'I could a tale unfold.'

Two forced migrations underlie the lives of African Americans in slavery. One, longer in distance, was the initial uprooting from

Africa and the transportation to the British mainland colonies of North America, later the United States. The other was the forced movement from one state or region of the United States to another, generally from north and east to south and west, which began before the Atlantic slave trade ceased to the country's ports in 1808. The internal migration was possible because of the rapid growth of the slave population along the southern Atlantic seaboard, especially in Maryland, Virginia, and the Carolinas. It was necessitated by the white planters' need to have slave labor on their newly acquired and settled land in the Lower South, where production of cotton and sugar was booming.

The forced migration across the Atlantic to the North American mainland lasted, legally, for nearly two centuries. It is the basis for the existence of persons of African descent in the United States, and thus is more widely known. The interregional forced migration within the United States existed for about two-thirds of a century, from the 1790s through 1860. Yet, perhaps twice as many persons of African descent were uprooted and moved to new lands in the United States through the domestic slave trade as came from Africa to the British North American mainland through the Atlantic slave trade. This "great migration of slaves . . . that began after the Revolution," writes Allan Kulikoff in "Uprooted Peoples: Black Migrants in the Age of the American Revolution", in *Slavery and Freedom in the Age of the American Revolution*, edited by Ira Berlin and Ronald Hoffman (1983), "was one of the most significant events in the history of black society in the United States." One way or another, a forced interregional move became a common experience for many African-American men and women who were slaves in the decades following the American Revolution.

Before Cotton's Ascendancy

The period just before the onset of the American Revolution was one of relative stability and security for many African Americans. Nearly all persons of African descent in the British mainland colonies were enslaved, but for most blacks born in America, commonly called *creoles*, acculturation was completed by this time and slave communities existed that were composed of stable families that were able to transmit cultural values to the young. The typical creole slave of, say, the early 1770s never had been forced to move a long distance from his or her place of birth. Home stayed the same, and the family was the basis of human interaction.

If African-American society at the time of the Revolution was as stable as it ever had been, so, in a greater sense, was the institution of slavery in America. This is contrary to what historians once thought. For a time there was an idea that America's "peculiar institution" was on the wane, even in the southern states, through perhaps as much as the last third of the eighteenth century—that is until Eli Whitney's new model of a cotton gin revolutionized slave-based, southern agriculture. Ulrich B. Phillips in *American Negro Slavery* (1918), for example, cites a decade-long depression in the plantation districts and George Washington's lament over the never-ceasing problems he had with his "troublesome species of property" as evidence that slavery's future in America was bleak.

But recent, careful examination of the economic growth of particular states or regions has put that notion to rest. Most recently, Rachel N. Klein in *Unification of a Slave State: The Rise of the Planter Class in the South Carolina Backcountry, 1790–1808* (1990), has identified in South Carolina's piedmont region as early as the mid–1760s a "fledgling elite," a sizeable body of "inland entrepreneurs [who] were the core of what would later become a backcountry planter class." These enterprising settlers "were oriented toward slave acquisition and commercial agriculture." The South Carolina Regulator Movement of the late 1760s was an effort on the part of the backcountry white elite to insure their rights to property, including especially slave property, and to stifle any threats to their hierarchical dominance over slaves. "The backcountry would not be a plantation society for years to come," Klein writes, "but an emerging planter class had already [by 1770] begun to mold the frontier in its own image. Rather than simply not dying away, the slave regime was steadily perpetuating itself—or, at the least, positioning itself for a longer run.

The war of the American Revolution was disruptive for many African Americans. This was especially true for those in the southernmost colonies, Georgia and South Carolina, where fighting was most widespread. It was true also for the thousands of slaves who escaped to the backcountry or to Spanish Florida, or for those who cast their lots with the British and left the mainland with the war's end. However, it was after the hostilities had ended, as Americans fresh from the fighting began to run Indians out of lands the nation claimed on its western frontier, that still more serious disruptions to blacks' lives began. Through the 1780s, Virginians and Marylanders continued to move into the remaining unsettled areas of their states beyond the coastal plain, and in both states, but especially in southern portions of Virginia, white migrants used slave labor to carve out tobacco and grain farms and plantations. Then, in the 1780s and 1790s, a more dramatic westward and southern push began. Whites from the Chesapeake migrated to Kentucky and Tennessee, hoping to begin in the West something akin to the Chesapeake's tobacco economy. Others moved into the piedmont areas of Georgia and South Carolina, joining the earlier settlers and more migrants from the coastal lowcountry. Fundamental to all of these white migrants across the western edge of settlement was the recreation of a slave-based, agricultural economy. The crop that the slaves would grow remained a question into the 1790s. Tobacco farming was still considered by many to be the most profitable concern and, indeed, the tobacco economy seemed to have been the model for schemes of commercial agriculture from Kentucky southward. But by the close of the eighteenth century, world demand and prices for tobacco were not what they once were. What could the aspiring planters have their slaves produce?

"Webs of Woven Wind"

The continuation and, eventually, the enormous increase in the interregional migration of slaves in the United States was bound up in national and international economic forces resulting largely from the mechanization of the weaving process. At the root of it all was cotton.

In its natural state, cotton is a wispy fiber attached to the seeds of plants of the genus *Gossypium*. The fiber and seeds exist inside one of several of the plant's bolls—oblong, golf-ball-sized pods. When the plant matures the bolls open, and, again naturally, as it dies away the wind picks up the exposed, clingy fibers and blows them and the seeds about, propagating the plant. Ages ago, perhaps first in the Indus and Nile river valleys around 3,000 B.C., humans discovered that with a reasonable amount of work the seeds could be removed from the cotton fiber (or lint); the tangled mass of fibers could be straightened and made roughly parallel (a process called "carding"); the straightened fibers could be drawn out, twisted, and spun together to form thread; and then the thread could be woven into cloth. In the minds of the early producers it was "webs of woven wind"—some of the finest and most useful cloth ever known. Persons inhabiting the Indian subcontinent were long the premier weavers of the cloth. Muslim merchants carried it from there to the Mediterranean and, from the Arabic word for 'a plant found in conquered lands,' *quttan*, gave plant, fiber, and cloth their modern name.

Europeans wove cotton through the Middle Ages, but found that Indians generally did it better. It was not until the mid-eighteenth century, when a series of inventions in England enabled mechanization of the processes of cotton-cloth manufacturing (and when the British East India Company clamped down on Indian competition by limiting their exports of woven cotton), that Westerners took a major hand in cotton-cloth making. When that happened, world market demand for raw cotton soared. From about the time of the end of the American Revolution, machines in such English mill cities as Nottingham, Leeds, and Blackpool hummed away as they ate enormous mounds of raw cotton and remained unsated. Great Britain imported each year, on average, about seven million pounds of cotton fiber through the late 1770s. In 1784 it imported twelve million pounds, in 1791 twenty-six million, and in 1800 fifty-six million. By 1821 Great Britain was importing ninety-three million pounds of cotton from the United States alone, and France's budding cloth industry was importing twenty-seven million. The price of cotton rose steadily from twenty-five cents a pound in 1790 to forty-four cents a pound in 1800 (when, according to one estimate, a planter could turn a profit with cotton selling at twelve cents a pound). People with capital and ambition around the tropical and subtropical world noted the high prices for cotton fiber and cast their eyes about for fertile lands on which the crop could grow.

It is a misconception to think of cotton production beginning in the United States only in 1793 with Eli Whitney's creation of a new kind of cotton gin. Cotton production came on gradually in the American South for some years prior to Whitney's work. What the Yankee inventor did was to make the inland expansion of cotton production possible and to encourage the development and planting of different varieties of a shorter-staple cotton.

Cotton had been known to planters on the North American mainland since the first days of English settlement. Some of the earliest proprietors and trustees tried in vain to interest would-be planters in lowcountry South Carolina and Georgia in growing the crop for the export market, but that was the area in which rice production remained, as one Carolinian put it, "the slow but sure way of getting rich." Through the middle decades of the seventeenth century, individuals in the mainland colonies experimented with cotton (along with pineapples, silk, soybeans, and more) and sought information on the technology involved with its production. African Americans participated in this process on their own. Those in the lowcountry, where the task system of labor gave them free time to cultivate private plots that yielded goods for consumption or sale, found cotton a valuable crop for their own needs—extra clothing and extra money to buy frills or necessities. According to Joyce E. Chaplin in "Creating a Cotton South in Georgia and South Carolina, 1760–1815," *Journal of Southern History*, 57 (1991), on the eve of the American Revolution "most blacks and whites who lived in rural areas would have had some idea of how to clean, card, spin, and weave cotton."

Commencement of hostilities in the Revolution brought many southerners to increase cotton production. Cut off from imported cloth, colonists needed to produce their own. Cotton growing thus became at once patriotic and necessary, especially for owners of large plantations with households (including slaves) that needed clothing. Ginning the cotton—that is, removing its seeds—was not the biggest obstacle to the early cotton growers in the American South. East Indian *churka* gins that simply drew the lint through tight rollers, squeezing out the slick seeds in the process, worked well enough.

Lowcountry planters grew a long-staple variety of cotton from which the seeds fell somewhat freely (as opposed to the short-staple cottons that had seeds that clung tenaciously to the lint). With Atlantic imports greatly reduced, cotton growers were most concerned with finding equipment for carding and weaving. But find them they did. Thus, as Chaplin writes, across the southernmost colonies, through the heaviest fighting of the Revolution, "the clacking of looms accompanied the clamor of battle." By the late 1770s, there appeared in the rebellious colonies a respectable local market for raw cotton, cotton yarn, and homespun.

Not surprisingly, the skills of African Americans as cotton producers and cloth makers took on greater importance. Owners wanting to sell certain slave women began to advertise them as "carders and spinners," and it became clear from advertisements in Georgia and South Carolina newspapers that wartime runaway slaves were making their own clothes. They were often last spotted, on the run, wearing homespun.

Once the Revolution was over and the English market again beckoned, coastal planters continued producing long-staple cotton as they rebuilt their rice estates. A new variety of long-staple cotton, called "sea-island" because it could be grown most effectively on the warm, humid sea islands off the lowcountry coast, was introduced in 1785. Coastal cotton production did not lag. But it was in the South Carolina and Georgia backcountry that important changes were taking place that held the greatest implications for cotton production, plantation growth, and African-American slaves. Many settlers of the southern backcountry were midcentury or later migrants from Virginia, Maryland, and Pennsylvania as well as from the lowcountry of the southern coast. They brought with them a model of commercial agriculture and black slavery that they had learned in tobacco cultivation some time earlier. The "early cotton cultivators," writes Chaplin, "used cotton to preserve a world already shaped by commercial agriculture and slavery." Thus, before the cotton boom, before Whitney had gone south and begun work on a contraption to remove cotton seeds from lint, backcountry yeomen and budding planters had established a society that would grow crops for export, relying on African Americans to perform the labor. Once cotton cultivation became more lucrative business and once more fertile land became available, the expansion of a slave-based plantation economy into a virtual Cotton Kingdom was close at hand.

Of course, the place of Whitney's new model gin, which worked well and was inexpensive, simple, and thus open to improvement (as well as duplication), should not be underplayed. The machine with the rotating wire teeth could rip seeds from the most tenacious lint and could do it fairly rapidly. (One person could hand-seed about a pound of short-staple cotton fiber per day; the same person, with the simplest of Whitney's devices, could gin fifty pounds of the same fiber in a day's time, and workers using subsequent models could gin even more.) Thus, the short-staple cotton that grew well inland, all across the South, could now be ginned and processed for sale in quantities that made its production profitable. Soon it would become something more than merely a crop that enabled the preservation of a world already shaped by commercial agriculture and slavery. With English demand for the cotton fiber high and continuing to rise, cotton was the crop that promised ambitious farmers a quick ride to the status of "planter" and, with a certain amount of good fortune, the ultimate bonanza.

Coincidentally, new lands for cotton production became available. First it was central and western Georgia in the mid-1790s. A series of treaties with the Cherokees opened Indian lands to white settlement. Planters rushed in with African-American slaves and began producing "Georgia green-seed" cotton.

Then, at irregular intervals, various parts of the heart of the Lower South—southern Georgia, Alabama, Mississippi, and Louisiana—became United States territory and open for public settlement. By the 1798 Treaty of San Lorenzo the United States acquired the Mississippi Territory (including most of present-day Mississippi and Alabama), and in 1803, once the black rebellion in Saint Domingue had convinced Napoleon that his dreams of a New-World empire were no longer practical, the country purchased the huge tract of land known as Louisiana. Already in place around Natchez since the 1770s were English-speaking planters who, following two decades of slave-based tobacco production, were seeking a new cash crop to stave off economic ruin. When insects devoured their experimental indigo crops in 1790, they tried growing on a grander scale a crop they had been cultivating for domestic purposes, Siamese black-seed cotton. The rebellion on Saint Domingue that began in 1791 cut England off from its principal supplier of raw cotton, so there was a ready market for the fiber; Natchez planters began floating small amounts of it down the Mississippi toward the export market. These new cotton planters got wind of Whitney's gin soon after 1793; they and their slaves made modifications and improvements on the gin, and then cotton plantations grew quickly through the Natchez district. Mississippi Territory thus entered the United States in 1798 with its own budding cotton enterprise.

Southern Georgia, most of Alabama, and eastern Mississippi were opened to American settlers soon after Andrew Jackson's frontier army defeated the Creek Nation in 1814. Cessions by the Chickasaw, Choctaw, and Cherokee Indians eventually added to the available agricultural lands in Mississippi, eastern Alabama, and western Georgia.

These lands that would rapidly become the heart of American cotton production held great, if temporary, advantage over the old slave-areas from Maryland and Virginia to coastal Georgia. Some of the new lands had excellent grids of inland water transportation that, before the days of railroads, provided the quickest and least expensive way to haul bulky commodities over long distances. The Mississippi River system, in particular, was the cotton exporter's dream, but the Pearl, Tombigbee, Alabama, and Chattahoochee rivers sliced northward from the Gulf of Mexico into prime cotton-growing territory. This meant that much of the best land for growing the crop was within reasonable hauling distance of landings on navigable streams that headed toward the market.

Also, a good part of the newly opened southern region had virgin soils that were much better than those of the Carolina and Georgia piedmonts. Alluvial and wind-blown soils near the Mississippi, enriched by leaf mold, and the band of dark, rich earth that arched through the middle of Alabama and up into western Georgia (giving the region the designation "Black Belt") provided an excellent medium for cotton. Planting of row crops in this region of heavy rains would eventually erode the soils badly and remove much of their richness, but the first generations of settlers who entered the area saw and gladly exploited its potential for growing and shipping cotton.

The first region to experience a bona fide cotton boom was upcountry South Carolina and Georgia. Not long after Whitney's gin became available, in an oblong-shaped region with Columbia, South Carolina, near the east end and Atlanta near the west, white settlers with slaves flocked in and within a few years turned an area of small farms with a diversified economy into one of cotton plantations. By 1801 the region was producing thirty million of the forty million pounds of cotton grown annually in America; by 1811 sixty million of the country's eighty million pounds. Much of the remainder of American cotton, apart from the steady sea-island production along the coast, came from southeastern Virginia, central North Carolina, or middle Tennessee.

Justly angry and hostile Indians, a half-dozen years of relatively low cotton prices, and a restricted market because of the War of 1812 curtailed further cotton expansion in the Lower South before 1815. But with the war's end, cotton prices shot up, and planters were ready to use the new land to expand their output. It was in the quarter century after 1815 that the "Cotton Belt" came into being. In the late 1810s the population of Mississippi Territory grew dramatically. Mississippi achieved statehood late in 1817, and Alabama did so two years later. White settlers and African-American slaves occupied the wooded bottomlands of Alabama's central black prairies and its Tennessee River valley, and in Mississippi they filled in especially along the eastern side of the Mississippi River. Areas of central and southern Louisiana were by this time also being plowed for cotton.

The 1820s saw an even greater increase in southern cotton production. The former lands of the Creeks in western Georgia were already populated by white settlers, cleared, and planted, as were lands on the west side of the lower Mississippi and parts of western Tennessee. Other regions of Alabama and Mississippi also filled in with plantations at this time. A drop in cotton prices following the panic of 1819 lowered profits but did not deter settlers from seeking still more lands for cotton. A new variety of Mexican cotton, developed by planters living near Rodney, Mississippi, in the second decade of the nineteenth century, had large bolls full of lint that slaves could pick much faster and more easily than earlier varieties. Mississippi planters adopted the "Rodney" cotton steadily through the 1820s. The cotton crop of Mississippi was some ten million pounds in 1821, thirty million in 1826, and eighty million in 1834. Exports from New Orleans grew from 48,000 bales in 1819 (with a bale weighing, on average, just over 300 pounds in the 1820s), to 156,000 in 1822, to 426,000 in 1830. And as cotton prices began inching back up after 1830, it became all the more clear that growing cotton with slave labor was the wave of the present and the future across the southernmost part of the existing United States.

There were other factors, sometimes overlooked, that made growing cotton with slave labor good business. Cotton was a crop that, when worked with plow and hoe, required strenuous work at certain times of the growing season but did not require continual labor. Plowing and planting made early spring a busy time, and slaves had to chop and thin the cotton before it was "laid by" until harvest. Picking cotton was by far the most labor-intensive of all the efforts, since it had to be done in a fairly short time, and the amount of cotton a planter's slaves could pick over the harvest period, before rain damaged the fiber, dictated how much cotton he could plant (it being of no use, of course, to grow more cotton than could be harvested). Thus, slaves on cotton plantations had a good bit of time throughout the year during which they were not required to work on cotton. Planters believed that underuse of slaves was dangerous as well as bad business—it made their laborers profligate and provided them time to plot and scheme—and "free" time could always be spent growing other crops at practically no expense to the planter. The result throughout the Cotton South was the widespread growing of food crops, especially corn. Ultimately, a kind of symbiotic relationship between cotton and corn production came to exist. Slaves could plant, cultivate, and harvest corn around their schedules for work in the cotton. Corn thus became an inexpensive staple of the southern diet as well as the main feed for southern cattle and hogs.

If this were not enough to create considerable need for slaves in the Lower South, add to it the rise of sugar production in southeastern Louisiana. Sugar had been the crop at the heart of the Atlantic commercial network for several centuries prior to the American Revolution. First grown in the New World in Brazil in the sixteenth century, by the 1770s sugar was grown mainly on the islands of the West Indies. Wherever it was produced, slaves did the work. The French in Louisiana had grown cane for domestic use for a good part of the eighteenth century, but once Etienne de Boré brought in the technology for milling sugar, and once Louisiana became a refuge for sugar planters from revolution-torn Saint Domingue, successful sugar plantations began to appear along the lower Mississippi. When the United States acquired Louisiana in 1803, sugar production was ready to take off. As cotton boomed on a broader scale so did sugar in Louisiana.

What this meant for African Americans was obvious. Planters who were eager to make their fortunes by producing rapidly the most marketable crops would need many more slaves. So long as the Atlantic slave trade could bring more Africans into the country—that is, until January 1, 1808—the demand for human laborers, to a great extent, could be satisfied thusly. But after 1808 the supply of African-American laborers in bondage would have to be generated by those already present in the United States. Existing slaves in the regions where cotton and sugar would not grow so well, or where the land was worn out from a century and more of tobacco growing, would have to produce abundant offspring. Then, one way or another, the "excess slave population" would have to be moved from the regions where they were less productive (referred to generally in this study as the Upper South) to the promising lands of the Lower South. The result was the second forced migration in the still-short history of persons of African descent in America.

The Great Uprooting

The harbinger of the larger movement of blacks of the early nineteenth century was the passage out of the Chesapeake region of white migrants, with their slaves, to Kentucky and Tennessee on the one hand, and to the backcountry of the Carolinas and Georgia on the other, in the 1780s and 1790s. These were joined by some lowcountry migrants into the piedmont areas of the southernmost states. A smattering of these traveled on to Louisiana.

Demand for slave labor grew so rapidly in all the newly acquired areas that the Chesapeake's supply of slaves was not sufficient. Thus, soon after the Treaty of Paris was signed in 1783, ending the Revolutionary War, the Atlantic trade was reopened. What followed was, in the words of Kulikoff, "the most massive infusion of slaves that ever reached the North American mainland."

Persons brought to the United States from Africa (along with some from the West Indies) in the reopened slave trade did not enter so many different ports along America's Atlantic coast as they once did, but at the fewer ports where the slavers docked, African slaves stepped onto land in large numbers. Savannah, Georgia, was the major importing center in the 1790s—lowcountry planters in South Carolina, who had enough slaves for their rice and cotton plantations, managed to keep that state's ports closed to the trade through 1803. At different times, depending on changing laws, slavers sailed up the Mississippi and docked at New Orleans and even Natchez. Then in 1804, as the compromise date for ending the slave trade to the United States approached, and with slave-based agriculture in the southern backcountry on the rise, South Carolina reopened its ports to slave ships. Once more, Charleston, South Carolina, became the focus of slave importing—at a rate of about 10,000 per year—until January 1, 1808, when all legal importing of slaves into the country ceased. The final quarter century of slave trading, negotiated by southerners at the Constitutional Convention, had served its purpose. Between 1783 and 1808, well over 100,000 Africans—a figure that constitutes roughly 20 percent of all those brought to British mainland North America over nearly two centuries of slave trading—disembarked at one of the southern ports. Most of these persons arriving fresh from Africa ended up in the southern backcountry and participated in the extension of plantation agriculture.

A good number of the African- or West-Indian-born slaves were taken into the interior of the United States by traders, but the movement of American-born slaves into new lands was largely in the form of planter migrations through the 1780s and 1790s—perhaps even until 1808. Regularly from the 1780s and for the next half century and more, planters in the Upper South would relocate to the new, uncultivated lands of the Lower South. Some of the slave owners on the move were sons of successful Chesapeake or lowcountry planters; some were already successful men who believed their economic lots could be cast more beneficially on new ground. Planter migrants normally took with them their entire complement of slaves, from infants to aging adults. Some got together what extra money they could and added to their gangs of slaves by buying a number of additional black laborers just before leaving. The typical planter migrant moved with a small number of slaves—roughly equal numbers of men and women, and persons of all ages. Once established, the planter could hope to increase his number of laborers through purchase from the interregional trade.

James Asbury Tait was one such planter migrant, and his circumstances may have been typical of the larger group. Tait and his father left Georgia in 1818 and relocated on the southern edge of Alabama's belt of fertile black soil, near Camden on the Alabama River. The Taits traveled with all sixty of the slaves they owned at the time—twenty-five of whom were "working hands." They began with small plantings of cotton and corn. Within two years of their migration they had produced about twice as much cotton as they had grown in Georgia; by 1835, when the elder Tait died, the number of hands that the planters owned had nearly doubled and they were working 2,100 acres; and by 1853 Tait, having supplemented his labor force through purchase from the interregional trade as well as natural increase, owned some three hundred slaves on top of the sixty or more he had given to his six children. It is clear that with work, careful planning, good investment of capital, and no doubt a touch of good fortune, migration to the Lower South was a venture that held great promise.

What proportion of slaves moving to the Lower South made the move as a result of planter migration rather than sale to a slave trader? The answer has been a matter of dispute. Until recently, many believed that by far the larger proportion of those transferred—two-thirds to three-fourths—moved as their owners relocated. Robert W. Fogel and Stanley L. Engerman in their widely criticized, quantitative study, *Time on the Cross: The Economics of American Negro Slavery* (1974), figured that 84 percent of the relocated slaves had migrated with their owners. But recently these figures have received

Slaves, 1790
Percent of Slaves in Total Population

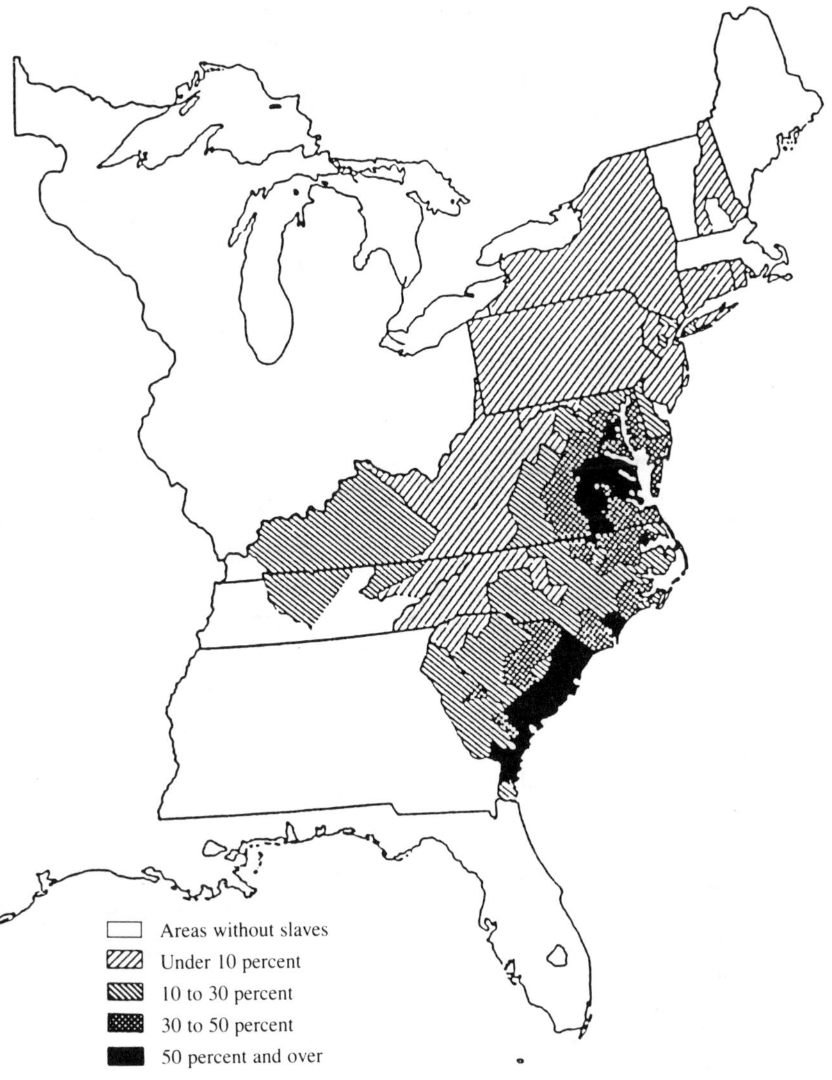

Reproduced from the *Atlas of Historical Geography of the United States* by Charles O. Paullin with permission from the Carnegie Institution of Washington.

a direct challenge. One of the multitude of valuable contributions of Michael Tadman's *Speculators and Slaves: Masters, Traders, and Slaves in the Old South* (1989) is his amassing of considerable statistical data and contemporary written evidence to show that previous ideas of planter migrations constituting the bulk of interregional slave movements are simply wrong. Planter migrants probably brought more slaves to the new lands of the United States than independent slave traders before 1808, and perhaps the two means of conveying black Americans to the Lower South were about equal for another decade. Tadman calculates, however, that by the 1820s, 70 percent of all slave migrants into the Lower South and West were the result of interregional slave trading, not planter migrations. Every year of the 1820s, on average, 15,000 African Americans were purchased by traders in the Upper South, then conveyed to and resold in the Lower South. By the 1830s the annual average would be 25,000—or a total of a quarter of a million persons transferred and sold over the decade.

The organized, interregional trafficking of African-American slaves began to occur in noticeable numbers almost immediately after the Revolution. Three days before Christmas in 1787, Moses Austin (whose son, Stephen F. Austin, would be the first Anglo-American to bring black slaves into Mexican Texas in the early 1820s) advertised in the Richmond *Virginia Gazette and Independent Chronicle* for "One hundred negroes, from 20 to 30 years old, for which a good price will be given. They are to be sent out of state, therefore we will not be particular respecting the character of any of them—Hearty and well made is all that is necessary."

The numbers of American-born blacks traded interregionally almost certainly picked up through the 1790s and 1800s. There is some evidence from contemporary sources. Betsey Madison, for example, a married slave living in Alexandria, told an interviewer some years later of how, around 1790 when she had been in her late twenties, she was sold to a planter from near Natchez, who took her (but not her husband) and eight other slaves to his Mississippi plantation. Newspaper accounts also hint at a growing internal slave traffic. But evidence is spotty and, in fact, pales considerably beside the detailed port statistics of the Atlantic trade through 1807. "Perhaps all we can

Slaves, 1830

Percent of Slaves in Total Population

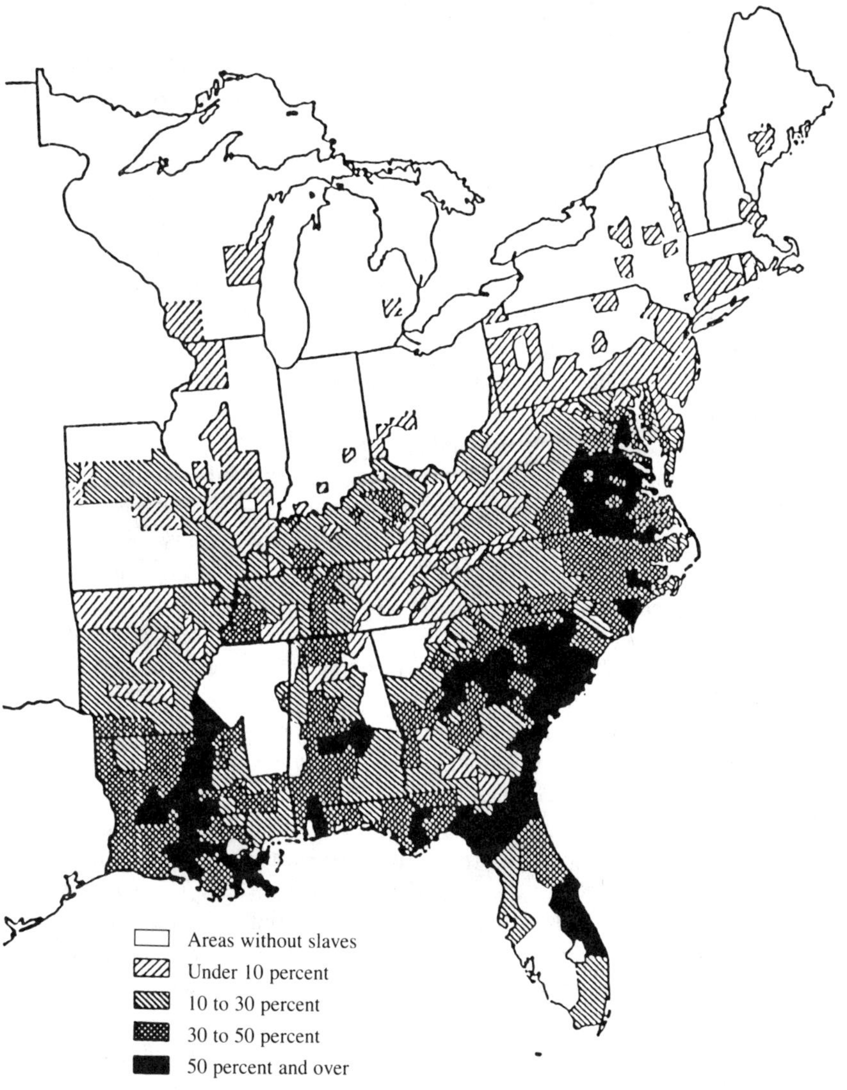

Reproduced from the *Atlas of Historical Geography of the United States* by Charles O. Paullin with permission from the Carnegie Institution of Washington.

do for the present," Tadman writes, "is to point to the possibility of a substantial pre–1808 domestic slave traffic."

By the time the supply of persons directly from Africa had halted, there is little doubt that the domestic trade had picked up. Virginians began to recognize slave dealers who were regularly in their midst, traders' advertisements in newspapers became more frequent, records became peppered with traders' contracts and lists of prices and fees, and observers from the District of Columbia to western Virginia encountered and sometimes fell in with "the negro traders." By about 1815 a widespread and efficient trading system was in place. Every year, "speculators," as they were euphemistically called, made the rounds of rural Virginia, seeking human laborers to buy to take South. The area of their quest for slaves grew rapidly. In 1816 a trader as far west as Kentucky was advertising, "CASH FOR NEGROES!" to be taken and sold in Mississippi. And as time passed, parts of the coastal lowcountry, then the Carolina and Georgia backcountry, and eventually even particular areas of Alabama and Mississippi themselves would become slave-exporting regions. Some of Tadman's estimates relating to the interregional trade are startling. Roughly one of every ten African-American slaves in their teenage years living in the Upper South would be sold and moved out of state during the 1820s, and the same was true for one of every eleven slaves between the ages of twenty and thirty. A slave residing in the Upper South after 1815 would have about a one-in-three chance of being traded out of state through the first forty years of his or her life.

The way the trade worked was simple, regular, effective, and, for planters and traders, profitable. Most of the buying, transporting, and selling was done by professional slave traders. A few planters from the Lower South ventured personally to the Upper South to buy slaves, and a handful of slave owners took their own slaves to the Lower South specifically to sell. The typical speculator in the Upper South was a semi-itinerant businessman. Based in a rural village, the slave trader would attend public auctions where he could bid on slaves, but much more commonly he would visit farms and plantations scattered over one or two counties—his "buying territory"—seeking human laborers.

Austin Woolfolk, the bogeyman in Frederick Douglass's Maryland youth, was one such businessman, though perhaps on a larger scale than many. In 1819 Woolfolk established himself as a slave trader in Baltimore. After a few years of steady success he had drawn five of his brothers into the operation, and the group of them extended their buying territory to several counties of Maryland's Eastern Shore. Woolfolk tended to remain around his headquarters on Pratt Street in Baltimore, where he had a secluded slave pen. He met there with sellers of groups of slaves who wished to do business privately. The other Woolfolk brothers scoured the Eastern Shore counties, setting up field headquarters when and where buying looked promising. In Talbot County the Woolfolk enterprise had a base in a tavern in Easton. Nearby was the site of the county's annual slave auction; nearer still were the offices of two county newspapers in which the Woolfolks advertised for slaves. Across the street was the courthouse, where they could record bills of sale, and the county jail, where they could board their purchased slaves for twenty-five cents a day until they could arrange for their transportation to Baltimore.

The Woolfolks tempted local planters with advertisements of top-dollar payments for slaves, and the Eastern Shore planters responded. Dickson Preston writes in *Young Frederick Douglass: The Maryland Years* (1980), "Old Eastern Shore families might claim—as many still do—that they never 'dealt with slave traders,' but the record proves otherwise. A roster of those who sold slaves to the Woolfolks and other buyers from the Deep South during the 1820s reads like a 'Who's Who' of Eastern Shore aristocracy." In one year, 1825, the Woolfolk business paid $22,702 for ninety-three African-American slaves in Talbot County alone.

Slave buyers had to know their business. Because the amount of work a person could perform was related directly to his or her physical development, traders paid particular attention to a slave's height and weight. It was common for them to offer prices for young slaves by the pound. One trader, Tyre Glen, who worked a rural area along the Virginia–North Carolina border, instructed his brother to buy "plough boys 5 or 6 dollars per pound. If the boy is very likely and weys 60 or 90 or 100—7 may be gone." Selling to the trader, right from the plantation, was the simplest and probably least noticeable way for a planter to dispose of slaves. It was a cash transaction on the spot.

Modern scholarship is fast eroding some of the long-held ideas about the domestic slave trade, particularly about planter benevolence and paternalism toward their slaves and about the purposeful "breeding" of slaves for sale. It was once thought, not such a long time ago, that planters were attached emotionally to the men and women they owned and thus sold individual slaves to traders only under the most extreme circumstances; nothing short of hard times bringing deep indebtedness, the need to rid the plantation of the most belligerent slaves, or judicial sales following the planter's death could force the sale of members of the "plantation family." Tadman shows this just was not so. The massive scale of the trade alone belies the benevolence-and-paternalism argument. By and large, planters sold their slaves because traders came around offering them good prices—in cash. "[T]empting speculative opportunities, not 'necessities' and 'emergencies,'" Tadman argues, "were the overwhelmingly important forces acting upon those who supplied the trader with his abundant stock."

Was "slave breeding" actually practiced on plantations in the exhausted agricultural lands of the Upper South, as abolitionists regularly charged? Were there the equivalent of "stud farms" where owners manipulated the sex lives of African-American men and women to guarantee for themselves the greatest profits? Did, as the American Antislavery Society argued, masters "regularly select 'breeders,' encourage licentiousness, reward amalgamation, punish sterility, coolly calculate the profits of fecundity, take vengeance for miscarriages and hold mothers accountable for the continued life and health of their offspring?" These questions have been argued since the 1830s, and they continue to be debated. In 1975 Richard Sutch in "The Breeding of Slaves for Sale and the Westward Expansion of Slavery, 1850–1860," in *Race and Slavery in the Western Hemisphere: Quantitative Studies*, edited by Stanley L. Engerman and Eugene D. Genovese, used abundant circumstantial evidence from quantitative data to draw conclusions on the subjects. In the late antebellum period, Sutch writes, many slave owners in the border states and along the Atlantic Coast systematically bred slaves for sale. . . . They held disproportionately large numbers of women in the child bearing age groups. They fostered polygyny and promiscuity among their slaves. . . . There is little possibility that the practice was innocent; it appears to have been the logical outcome of a system which treated slaves as assets, a system that stripped men of their humanity so that the market for their labor could operate efficiently and so that the profits of their exploiter could be maximized.

Some evidence hints at such activity. Various slave-exporting areas of the Upper South did have inordinately high slave fertility rates. Advertisements for sales of women slaves frequently touted "good breeders" (or, as a notice described one woman in a Charleston newspaper, "very prolific in her generating qualities"), and a number of former slaves, in interviews, recall living in circumstances that sound something like "stud farms." Still, a number of historians believe that while planters all across the South recognized the self-interest in having their slave women bear and rear large numbers of children (and many encouraged such with rewards and bonuses), relatively rare was the person who manipulated the sex lives of slaves, who earmarked certain slave infants for potential sale, or who even possessed the economic foresight to have tried to produce a group of humans that would be marketable perhaps a decade following their birth. Whatever slave breeding that occurred beyond what Tadman calls "an almost universal enthusiasm for natural increase from 'slave property'" seems to have been the exception rather than the rule.

Major cities along the southeastern coast—Richmond, Norfolk (Virginia), Washington, Alexandria, Charleston—were centers of "speculation," too. In these cities, trading firms acquired slaves from local traders and resold them, usually at auction to traders from the Lower South, or they purchased and held slaves until a ship was ready to embark for one of the major gulf or Mississippi River ports, New Orleans, Mobile (Alabama), or Natchez.

The trade was tied to the seasons. Buyers roamed the countryside of the Upper South in late summer and early fall, with the busiest buying season falling in October and November. Sales in the Lower South occurred between December and April. Hardly a slave was marketed in New Orleans, for instance, between July and October. Reasons for this rigid seasonality in slave trading had to do with crop cycles, terms of the trade, and epidemiology. In the Lower South, crops were marketed by December or January, so it was then that planters had cash in their hands. Slave traders all but insisted on cash transactions—they hardly had time to check credit references and, more important, they needed cash for quick repayment of the loans they had taken back in the Upper South in order to buy more slaves for the venture. They had to come selling at times during which buyers could meet their terms. But just as important a factor was the dangerous summer disease environment of the Lower South. Arriving in the winter and early spring months, when malaria- and yellow-fever-carrying mosquitos were not as prevalent, slaves from the Upper South could become acclimated to their new environment with less immediate threat of serious illness or death. Moreover, for similar concerns over health, the wealthiest planters, who were the biggest buyers of slaves, were simply not present in the summer months. Because of yellow-fever epidemics that swept through such cities as New Orleans and Mobile practically every summer in the early nineteenth century, persons with the means to do so left the region and did not return until healthier times, slaves on the market notwithstanding.

The African-American men, women, and children purchased in the Upper South were conveyed to the new locations in one of two ways: by a coastal shipping trade or overland on foot. In either case, speculators grouped their individual purchases and held (or "bulked," using the commercial term) them until it was time to move. Recent studies have determined that the mean duration from the time of purchase in the Upper South to the time of sale in the Lower South was 106 Days. The biggest variables were, of course, distance transported and means of travel.

Persons transported by water, the minority, were usually walked from point of purchase to a port on the Chesapeake Bay or southern Atlantic coast and held until a ship was ready. It was not a speedy process. Of ninety-six slaves shipped from Norfolk to New Orleans in 1830, on average they spent forty-seven days between the time of their purchase and their embarkation. Then once on board it was a "middle passage" all over again, only shorter and less rigorous than the notorious trip across the Atlantic that their ancestors had taken.

The coasting ships commonly carried between 100 and 200 African Americans; the normal voyage from a Chesapeake port to New Orleans lasted about three weeks. When it was possible, the slaves were allowed to be up and about on deck through daylight hours, though it was back below, on plank decks, come nightfall. When weather turned foul, all had to remain in the hold, and when crews feared uprisings, male slaves were chained and sometimes even bolted to the deck. Food was passable, water sufficient, and because they were coasting voyages there was not the dread of running out of either necessity, as had always existed on the Atlantic crossing. Arrival in a southern port did not mean an end to the ordeal. The same ninety-six slaves that had left Norfolk in 1830 had to spend another forty days after their arrival in New Orleans awaiting their sale. Thus, much of the 106-day ordeal had been spent waiting in pens.

A substantial number of black men, women, and children were transported to the Lower South by water, but many more made the trek over land. These, too, commonly spent a month or more waiting for a marchable gang, or "coffle," to be assembled. Typical coffles on the march contained thirty or forty slaves (though coffles of one hundred or more were fairly common). Full-grown boys and men were usually attached to one another, at least by twos, and sometimes all were connected to a long chain. Charles Ball, who was marched from Maryland to South Carolina in 1805, remembered, "The poor man to whom I was ironed, wept like an infant when the blacksmith, with his heavy hammer, fastened the ends of the bolts that kept the staples from slipping from his arms." Women were sometimes roped together, but they and younger children might be allowed to walk unattached. The procession was accompanied by one or more covered wagons holding food and cooking supplies and available to carry the lame or infirm. Several men, usually mounted, went along with the trader as "drivers" or guards. In good weather the coffle might make twenty-five miles in a day, and most hoped to average over twenty. At that rate, a coffle would march for nearly seven weeks to make the journey from Richmond, Virginia, for example, to Natchez, Mississippi.

The physical strain and discomfort of walking—almost always barefooted and often without warm clothing—over twenty miles a day for up to fifty days must have been considerable. Weather was variable, of course, but winter nights and most winter days were cold, even in the Deep South. Rains did not always deter the march, rivers had to be forded, roads could get soggy and rutted and then could freeze overnight. When spirits of individuals in the coffle flagged, the drivers might take action by distributing small quantities of rum or ordering the playing of music. They believed that music raised the spirits of the easily manipulated blacks, so many was the coffle that lit out with its own small band of musicians. Featherstonhaugh found the drivers he encountered in Tennessee using banjo accompaniment to get the marchers to sing "Old Virginia Never Tire."

Sleeping accommodations were crude at best. When coffles halted for the night, tents were sometimes erected, slaves might fashion lean-tos out of nearby wood and leaves, or the drivers could occasionally arrange some sort of covered accommodation on farms owned by acquaintances or in rough public houses. Featherstonhaugh found that at night children slept in tents, but males remained in chains, in groups of about a dozen, and slept on the ground. Meals were simple and lacking in variety by today's standards, but they were ample, consisting of the stuff of the country—cornmeal mush, hominy, cornbread. In addition to sore feet and stiff legs, especially for domestics who were not used to the extent of physical exertion that the march required, colds, influenzas, and intestinal disorders were the main physical ailments that afflicted the coffles. But through this host of maladies, they marched. Given the difficulties of the forced migration, it is surprising that the slaves' death rates in transit remained low. Tadman examined traders' accounts and calculated that only about 1.5 percent of all slaves purchased in the Upper South died or succeeded in escaping before being sold in the Lower South.

As they approached their destinations, traders began preparing for sales. *Caveat emptor* never applied more thoroughly. Typically, persons being readied for sale were washed, men were shaved, and gray hairs were either plucked out or covered with a "blacking brush." Any individual who had not fared well on the journey was "fed up"—that is, taken aside and given larger quantities of food over several days or weeks to improve his or her marketability. Slaves usually brought higher prices—or at least the traders believed that they did—when they "looked spry and talked up." How to convince a person who had been uprooted from his home and likely his family and then forcibly marched perhaps a thousand miles over seven weeks to appear happy and to speak well to the very people responsible for his or her circumstances must have been a common problem for slave merchants. Sometimes the carrot was offered—promises given, presents made—but more often the stick remained close at hand. Persons who failed to "speak up and look bright and smart" when being examined by potential buyers could expect a flogging. Traders did this with a broad, short, leather piece attached to a wooden handle. On administration, the pain was intense but no marks remained on the merchandise.

Most traders disposed of slaves in the same way they had acquired them, working rural areas of a particular region. Some set up in small villages, others based their operations on the plantations of friends. In either case, they ventured regularly into the countryside, taking their coffles to plantations and selling slaves individually or in groups of three or four. Sale through direct, individual negotiation was standard. Domestic slaves sometimes were left for short trial periods; field hands often came with a guarantee of good health. Not until March or April, the end of the "selling season," would traders take persons remaining in their coffles to public auctions in villages.

Although traders sold far more slaves through this itinerant method in the rural South, there were significant markets in urban areas to which planters ventured in search of new laborers. The biggest urban markets for slaves by 1830 were in New Orleans, Natchez, Mobile, and Montgomery, Alabama. New Orleans's market was the biggest. At the start of the 1834 trading season there were over 1,200 blacks for sale there and, as one observer put it, "small lots constantly coming in." The Natchez market was big too. By December 1832, when the trade season was just beginning in some southern areas, one thousand slaves had already been sold in Natchez.

One of the many racism-based myths surrounding the domestic slave trade was that this great uprooting and movement to a new region of the country and a new home among strangers had only an insignificant and temporary effect on the persons most directly involved—the African-American slaves. White southerners whose present and future financial well-being relied on slavery and the interregional trade of human beings wanted to think this way. It eased their consciences to carry such assumptions on the slaves' reaction to it all. Persons of African descent, southern whites argued, lacked the same kind of close affection for home and kin that whites held. Whatever grief the blacks felt over their uprooting lasted only for short periods. "Sometimes they don't mind it a great while," answered Alexandria slave dealer John Armfield when asked of blacks' reaction to being separated by sale from a spouse, "but at other times they take on *right smart*, for a long time." Blacks were basically a happy-go-lucky group, the convenient belief went, and the grief that they felt was nothing that a dram of spirits, some lively music, and a fast-stepping dance could not snap them out of.

"The Iron Entered Into My Soul"

The greatest difficulty slaves met in their sale and movement was neither the long march nor the ride above or below decks on a tossing ship. Most were accustomed to regular, strenuous physical exertion and hardship. The greatest pain was emotional, caused by the separation, usually upon short notice, almost always permanent, from family, friends, and comfortable surroundings. The interregional movement of African Americans was a harsh and complete physical and emotional uprooting.

Students of American history have not always believed that such separation happened with regularity through the years of the domestic slave trade. An important element in the defense of slavery that emanated from the antebellum South was an argument that the interregional traffic of slaves did not separate families. A few states had laws that regulated slave family separation, but such laws were unnecessary, apologists argued, because of the paternalistic relationship between master and slave. Masters cared deeply for those they held in bondage. They encouraged slaves to marry and have children, they respected the slave family, and they bore this respect in mind as they sold (when necessary) and bought (when likely profitable) human laborers. Good masters (as most were) were reluctant to break up marriages and even more reluctant to separate children from their parents.

Was this so? Now and then, historians have supported the argument. Phillips in *American Negro Slavery* emphasizes "the good nature of the competing bidders," who tended to purchase the mate when they purchased a married slave. "Young children," Phillips writes, "were hardly ever sold separately," and "the great majority of women were bought in family groups." Fogel and Engerman, relying on statistical analysis of New Orleans sales records, reinforce many of Phillips's arguments. The New Orleans data, the authors state, "sharply contradict the popular view that the destruction of slave marriages was at least a frequent, if not a universal, consequence of the slave trade." Not quite 13 percent of the interregional sales in New Orleans resulted in the breakup of marriages, they argue, and rare was the sale of a child under thirteen years old without a parent—except for orphans. From their "hard data" Fogel and Engerman assert that, indeed, "slaveowners were averse to breaking up black families," largely because of "the extremely important role that the master class assigned to the family institution."

Quite a number of historians have taken issue with these arguments, however, and Tadman's recent study of the interregional trade refutes many of these arguments, hard data notwithstanding. Frederick Bancroft marked the trail. Bancroft was a diligent collector of documents and a practitioner of oral history. Early in the twentieth century he traveled across the South, interviewing scores of southerners—planters, traders, former slaves—and collecting a mass of manuscripts and newspapers. Using these materials, he eventually wrote *Slave Trading in the Old South* (1931), long the most scholarly and authoritative treatment of the interregional traffic and long the standard critique of family separation in the trade. Bancroft scoffed at the idea of planter paternalism as an overriding factor in planter dealings with slaves. "Virtually everybody preferred to be humane when it was not financially disadvantageous or inconvenient to be so . . . ," he writes. "Slavery maintained as a profitable and convenient institution was essentially ruthless in general and inhumane in some of its main features." He calls the sale of children separated from their parents "hardly less than a staple in the trade," and he labels separation of spouses by sale "the rule . . . when a positive advantage was expected."

Other supportive studies appeared now and then, including references to extensive family separation in Herbert G. Gutman's *The Black Family in Slavery and Freedom, 1750–1925* (1976), but a full half century after Bancroft's book first appeared Tadman completed the doctoral thesis (eventually published in revised form as *Speculators and Slaves*) that would bear out Bancroft's conclusions on family separation. Based on statistical analyses, from broader samples of data than Fogel and Engerman's, and documentary evidence, Tadman's work is exhaustive and detailed. He states his conclusions bluntly. "[The slaves'] dread of separation was unending." And why so? Because "over half of all slaves who fell into the hands of traders would either have been forcibly separated from a spouse or have been children who were forcibly separated from one or both of their parents."

The extent of family separation was even greater than Bancroft had imagined, because he did not figure in planter migrations and local sales. The migration of planters split families, Tadman notes, because African Americans often were married to slaves on neighboring plantations. Furthermore, planters separated spouses, and children from parents, when they bought slaves locally to take with them on migrations. And local and regional sales added to the family separations. Through most of the first half of the nineteenth century, certainly from 1820 on, the black family remained in jeopardy. Tadman concludes, "Over a lifetime . . . in the exporting states it would have been quite rare [for an African-American slave] to have survived into middle age without being sold locally or interregionally." Forcible separation probably destroyed one of three first marriages of slaves in the Upper South, and one of three Upper-South slave children fourteen years of age and under probably was separated from one or both parents because of the slave trade.

Why was family separation so frequent in the interregional trade? Simply because it was considerably more profitable to sell family members separately than together. The market was the master in the domestic slave trade. For example, the more strenuous work requirements on sugar plantations made sugar planters prefer male to female slaves. Thus, over 70 percent of the slaves sold in Louisiana sugar parishes were men, and thus husbands and wives had little chance of being sold together.

Generally, low prices for slaves or high costs of transportation increased the incidence of family separation. Both of these factors reduced the slave traders' profits, so only those slaves who would command the best prices—"prime-age" persons between the ages of eleven and thirty—were sought, and most of the prime-age slaves that were purchased in the Upper South were children without their parents, or parents without their children.

Ironically, even "humanitarian" legislation designed to regulate the slave trade on either end could effect more family separation. When a Louisiana Act of 1829 prohibited the introduction into the state of children under ten without their mothers, the result was that slave traders buying a slave mother for transport to and resale in that state simply did not purchase any of her young in the first place.

Donald L. Sweig studied ship manifests for 3,750 slaves shipped from Alexandria, Virginia, to New Orleans between 1828 and 1836. In "Reassessing the Human Dimension of the Slave Trade," *Prologue*, 12 (1980), he labels profit the villain. "The ready market for prime-age, single men and women in the Deep South," Sweig writes, "and the high percentage of such individuals on the Alexandria manifests testify to the disastrous effect of the marketplace on slave marriages and the black family." Focusing on Armfield, the same slave dealer that Andrews visited in Alexandria in 1835, Sweig writes,

> Armfield was neither iniquitous barbarian nor enlightened humanitarian but a good businessman. When it was good business to divide families and sell young children he did so. When it was better business to maintain the slaves in family units he did that. . . . He and Isaac Franklin [his partner, with whom he was reputed to have made over half a million dollars in the interregional trade] were clearly on good terms with the selling farmers and planters of Virginia and Maryland and with those buying in Louisiana and Mississippi. Armfield's success indicates that he operated according to *their* standards of morality and ethical propriety in the buying, selling, and treatment of slaves. Other traders would have been subject to the same standards in

order to stay in business. To do less might have jeopardized the willingness of owners to sell their slaves; to do more would have increased costs, decreased profits, and given the edge to competitors.

Thus, by the 1830s the experience of separation from immediate family was a common one for African Americans through the decades of the interregional trade. The fear of sale and separation and the pain endured upon its occurrence must have been powerful forces in slaves' lives across the South for half a century: the records they left confirm it.

The terror of being sold "down South" or to the "Georgia Men," away from home and kin, was always present for slaves in the Upper South. Planters played on that fear, using threats of sale as a means of social control and of extracting more work from their slaves. Douglass knew that being "sold to Woldfolk [*sic*]" was the worst thing that could happen to an Eastern Shore slave in the 1820s: recalcitrant slaves could be brought around quickly by the mere mention of Woolfolk's name.

But the fear of possible sale and separation did not always correspond to the pain of the event once realized. Tales of bitterness over separations abound in slave interviews and narratives; some are particularly revealing of human emotions and belie the old racist argument that "sometimes they don't mind it a great deal." Josiah Henson's remembrances are among the most moving. Early in the nineteenth century, when Henson was a small child, he stood on an auction block in Montgomery County, Maryland, with his mother, brothers, and sisters. In *Father Henson's Story of His Own Life*, edited by Walter Fisher (1962), he writes,

> Common as are slave-auctions in the southern states, . . . still the full misery of the event . . . is never understood till the actual experience comes. The first sad announcement that the sale is to be; the knowledge that all ties of the past are to be sundered; the frantic terror at the idea of being sent "down south"; the almost certainty that one member of a family will be torn from another; the anxious scanning of purchasers' faces; the agony of parting, often forever, with husband, wife, child—these must be seen and felt to be understood. Young as I was then, the iron entered into my soul. The remembrance of the breaking up of McPherson's estate is photographed in its minutest features in my mind. The crowd collected round the stand, the

huddling group of negroes, the examination of muscle, teeth, the exhibition of agility, the look of the auctioneer, the agony of my mother—I can shut my eyes and see them all.

Henson watched as his brothers and sisters were sold away; then his mother. As the bidding for him was underway, Henson's mother begged the man who purchased her to buy her remaining son, but her new owner swung at her and drove her away. Henson remembers his mother crawling away from the man, sobbing, "'Oh, Lord Jesus, how long, how long shall I suffer this way!'"

"I must have been then between five and six years old," Henson continues:

I seem to see and hear my poor weeping mother now. This was one of my earliest observations of [white] men; an experience which I only shared with thousands of my race, the bitterness of which to any individual who suffers it cannot be diminished by the frequency of its recurrence, while it is dark enough to overshadow the whole after-life with something blacker than a funeral pall.

Henson's was a pain shared by many persons of African descent in America, before and after his experiences. A long thread of migration—a good part of it forced—is woven through the fabric of African-American history that began in Africa nearly four centuries ago. If the Atlantic slave trade was the first wave of forced migration, the second was the movement of a million or more African-American men, women, and children that began with the end of the American Revolution and continued through the first half of the nineteenth century, bringing persons of African descent to the Deep South.

This second forced migration, nearly always overshadowed by the first, affected much that came after it for African Americans and for American race relations. After all, it was this migration that made the states of Georgia, Alabama, and Mississippi the center of America's black population as well as the heart of African-American culture for about a century. It was the resulting mixture of Africans and creoles, of Chesapeake house servants and lowcountry field hands, of persons of varied ethnic backgrounds and levels of acculturation in the emerging cotton states of southern America that reshaped and helped make unique the southern black culture that came into being well before the start of the twentieth century. It was the movement further south of America's peculiar institution that strengthened slavery and made it all the more clearly a sectional matter, thus beginning the disagreement that ultimately would lead to the Civil War and the ending of slavery in the United States. And it was the fear of being sold away from family and friends and the hatred of masters who would not only abide such activity but threaten with and participate in it, that etched in the minds of African Americans a picture of the insensitivity and brutality of white people. This made living together, not just for whites but for blacks as well, difficult in the years following emancipation.

CHAPTER TWO

The Varying Nature of Life in Slavery

A person wanting to know what it was like to be a slave during America's early decades could hardly do better than to read *Slavery in the United States: A Narrative of the Life and Adventures of Charles Ball*, edited by Isaac Fisher (1837). Like a number of others, Ball was a fugitive from slavery, who eventually felt secure enough in his existence in freedom to tell of his experiences and to allow the narrative to be published. Ball's story of his years in slavery through the time of the early republic is specific and detailed.

Ball was born into slavery around 1780 in southern Maryland, on the west side of the Chesapeake Bay. His grandfather had been purchased off a slaver from West Africa, but Ball, two generations removed from that experience, was an acculturated African American. Over his half century in slavery, Ball had eleven different masters (if one counts two under lease arrangements); he worked on plantations or farms in Maryland, South Carolina, and Georgia, growing tobacco, corn, cotton, rice, and indigo (as well as garden vegetables); he worked for two years on a frigate in the Washington, D.C., Navy Yard; and he managed seasonal fishing operations. He was forcibly separated from family or community on four different occasions, for the first time when he was four years old. He escaped from slavery in Georgia in 1806 through a long and treacherous overland journey to Maryland, which included months of hiding in the woods by day and hiking by night, fording and swimming across rivers, ambling boldly through Richmond at midday, and escaping from a Virginia jail. After finding his family in Maryland, Ball lived for eighteen years as a farmer and, ultimately, a landowner, only to be recaptured and returned to Georgia. His second escape not long afterward was for good.

Were Ball's experiences typical of an African American's life in slavery through the early decades of the American republic? Antebellum slave owners did not want to think so. This narrative was one that white southerners tried hardest to discredit. But John W. Blassingame in *Slave Testimony: Two Centuries of Letters, Speeches, Interviews, and Autobiographies* (1978) cites antebellum gazetteers, travel accounts, and plantation records to verify much of Ball's narrative. On the whole, aside from the editor's sometimes flowery prose, long dialogues that represent only approximations of what was said, and what is probably an embellishment of some details for dramatic effect, Ball's narrative allows one to read about the kinds of things that African-American men and women in slavery were likely to have experienced if they came of age over the half century following the American Revolution. Above all else, it shows how much slavery differed according to time and place and particular circumstances. It is clear from reading Ball's account that slaves led different sorts of lives even on adjacent farms or plantations, depending on the nature of the owners and persons in authority, but depending, too, on such things as the size of the labor force, the work required of individual slaves, and the prosperity of the operation. More generally, Ball's life shows how much systems of slavery varied in different regions of the country, with larger or smaller farms or plantations, different crops, and different systems of labor management. And it shows, through Ball's experiences over several decades, how the nature of slavery wherever it existed in the United States changed over time according to altered economic or social conditions. Such seemingly insignificant factors as the growing of new varieties of a crop, the use of new kinds of tools or crop-growing methods, change of ownership, a region's or the nation's economic upturns or downturns, the threat of sale—even the coming to the area of a wave of religious revivalism—could all modify the way slaves lived in any location in the country. Slavery was an institution that not only was different from one property to the next and from one region to the next but also was a dynamic institution that changed in one place over time.

Slave Systems, Work Systems

At the time of the American Revolution, three systems of African-American slavery existed in the United States. One, in the states north of Maryland, was not plantation slavery at all. African Americans were a small portion of the total population; they worked on small farms or were craftsmen, seamen, valets, or domestics. A second slave system existed in the Chesapeake region, where African Americans had long produced tobacco on small plantations. A third system, that of the Carolina and Georgia lowcountry, involved large plantations with the heaviest concentrations of African Americans working primarily to produce rice.

By early in the nineteenth century two more slave systems had appeared. In southern Louisiana, large plantations specializing almost exclusively in sugar production came into existence and grew fairly rapidly into the 1830s. And finally, the continually advancing frontier of cotton production brought about a fifth slave system, a combination of large plantations and small farms that spread from upland South Carolina across central Georgia, Alabama, Mississippi, Tennessee, eastern Arkansas, and western Louisiana. African Americans lived differently in each of the slave systems, and the type of crops grown, the methods of production, the nature of the individual master, and the ability of the African Americans to affect decisions combined to dictate much about slaves' regimen of work.

Slavery was on its way out in most of the northern states as the new country was beginning. The rhetoric of the Revolution had brought this on. The inconsistency of claiming the equality of all men while holding some in bondage seemed to bother northerners more than southerners—no doubt because slavery was less vital to the northern economy. Massachusetts's Supreme Judicial Court struck down the constitutionality of the institution for that state in 1783, and soon other northern states began passing laws that called for abolition to be effected gradually. New York and New Jersey were the last states north of Maryland to pass such laws, in 1799 and 1804 respectively, and thus slavery lingered in those states into the 1820s.

Yet northern slavery did not go quietly into the night. Of nearly 25,000 African Americans in New York State in 1800, three-quarters remained enslaved. Between 1790 and 1800 the number and proportion of slaves in New York's Rockland County (along the west bank of the Hudson River, just north of the New Jersey border) actually increased. In 1800 one of every eleven persons in the county was a slave, and in one turn-of-the-century Rockland community, 42 percent of the households possessed slaves. Twenty years later, however, the number of slaves in Rockland County had shrunk to 124, not quite 1.5 percent of the population. Most black youngsters born of slave parents since July 4, 1799, had been placed under indenture agreements to work as servants in white homes, as the state's Gradual Manumission Act allowed.

New York City did not give up slavery's ghost lightly, either. In 1790 New York was second only to Charleston, South Carolina, in the number of slaves in an urban setting—there were 2,056 African Americans in slavery in New York, 6.6 percent of the city's population. Through the 1780s, New York whites who were skilled artisans, petty retailers, or ship's captains used slave labor in their businesses. In the 1790s and 1800s, slave ownership increasingly became a thing of the city's white economic elite. Wealthier merchants and professionals used persons in bondage as servants and symbols of status. Thus did slavery in New York City linger into the nineteenth century. In 1800 there were 2,534 African Americans in bondage there, making up 4.4 percent of the urban population; in 1810 there were 1,446 (1.6 percent), and New York City still had 518 persons in slavery in 1820. On top of these were the young African Americans serving in white homes under indentures.

On the whole, life for slaves residing north of the Mason-Dixon line was better than life for slaves on the tobacco farms and rice plantations of Virginia and South Carolina, but not appreciably so. There exists a "myth of the mild nature of the northern slave regime," argues Shane White in *Somewhat More Independent: The End of Slavery in New York City, 1770–1810* (1991), probably because northern slaves were held in small numbers and lived in close proximity to white families rather than on larger plantations, somewhat removed from the lives of their owners. But White shows how northern masters extracted considerable work from the men and women whom they held in bondage and how they could be just as brutal as the cruelest southern overseer. He contends, too, that it was every bit as difficult for slaves living in the North to establish and maintain family ties and a distinctive African-American culture as it was for slaves living in other parts of the country.

Life must have been especially unpleasant and difficult for northern black people who remained in slavery as the majority of African Americans in the region were gaining their freedom. Making their situations particularly precarious and making them constantly fearful was the real possibility of being "sold South." Masters knew of the rising value of their human property in the early part of the nineteenth century, as abolition was creeping up with the years. Nothing could prevent them from selling their slaves to traders headed for the region of the country where the institution remained legal. No doubt, certain bonds existed between some masters and their lifelong, family slaves that would have made sale out of the question. But a good portion of the final group of northern slaves must have lived with fairly constant trepidation over being sold away from parents, spouses, loved ones, and community. For them, family life was about as tenuous as it was for slaves anywhere. Add to this the torturous feelings involved in living in bondage amidst increasing numbers of African Americans existing in freedom and one can easily imagine that the last years of slavery in the northern states were hardly the best of times for those who remained enslaved.

For slaves living in northern cities in the early decades of the nineteenth century, working and living conditions remained largely as they had been before. Most bondsmen lived by themselves or with one other slave in their owner's home; nevertheless, African-American slaves in northern cities seem to have formed families and reared children. Most of the urban slaves were domestics, with women primarily working in homes throughout Boston, New York City, and Philadelphia. Men worked at a variety of tasks—skilled trades, maritime work, as personal servants, or around the home. And in whatever the task, nearly all of them hoped that their freedom would come soon.

In the Chesapeake region, slaves had traditionally produced tobacco and some grains and livestock. Tobacco production required considerable labor. It was eighteen months between the planting of a crop and its marketing, meaning African-American slaves were working on the cultivation of a new crop while still processing the last one. And the labor-intensive stages of producing tobacco were many: clearing, "grubbing," hilling, sowing, replanting, cultivating, topping, suckering, cutting, pegging, curing, packing, and shipping. The land and the people suffered. Thomas Jefferson spoke from his experience as a tobacco grower when he said,

> It [tobacco] is a culture productive of infinite wretchedness. Those employed in it are in a continual state of exertion beyond the powers of nature to support. Little food of any kind is raised by them: so men and animals on the farms are ill fed, and the earth is readily impoverished.

It was tobacco growing's declining fortunes following the Revolution, coupled with the lingering egalitarian spirit of the age in the northern parts of the region, that brought changes to the lives and work of African Americans in the Chesapeake. A significant drop in tobacco prices that began in 1792 forced many tobacco planters to turn for good to mixed grain and livestock farming and to expand and diversify the production of their households (as they had done temporarily when exports were blocked during the Revolutionary War). Raising corn, wheat, and livestock required less labor than did growing tobacco, so planters had men and women slaves on their hands whom they no longer needed in the fields. A number of these they moved to household work. African-American men took up craft work—carpentry, smithing, boating—or functioned as waitingmen, coachmen, hostlers, or gardeners. Black women in increasing numbers did domestic work, especially cooking and laundry tasks, but also served as nurses, personal servants, and household drudges (carrying water, emptying chamber pots, making beds, and such). Also, slave women were more important than men in expanding household production through their increasing performance of tasks lumped together as housewifery: dairying, tending poultry and hogs, candle and soap making, vegetable gardening, and cloth and clothing manufacture. Occurring at the same time, and as part of the same process, was a steady leaking of Chesapeake whites and blacks to the West—a continuation of a movement that had begun in Revolutionary times. African-American populations grew in counties as far west as the Blue Ridge and Cumberland mountains in Virginia and Maryland.

But a slow wave of manumissions in Maryland, perhaps triggered as much by the fact that tobacco no longer was such a moneymaker as by growing egalitarianism in the country, would have a deeper meaning, for over the long run this led to a broad splitting of the traditional circumstances of African-American life in the Chesapeake. According to Richard S. Dunn in "Black Society in the Chesapeake, 1776–1810," in *Slavery and Freedom in the Age of the American Revolution*,

> Blacks acquired considerably greater independence, mobility, and opportunity—freedom—in the Upper Chesapeake than in Tidewater and Piedmont Virginia. But in those Chesapeake districts where most blacks lived, slavery was more deeply rooted when Jefferson stepped down from the presidency than when he composed the Declaration of Independence.

Roughly speaking, the dividing line for the split of the Chesapeake region was around the District of Columbia. In Maryland from the 1780s to the Civil War, the proportion of the African-American population that was enslaved would decline. It was 96 percent in 1776, 80 percent in 1810, and 50 percent in 1860. The actual number of Maryland blacks in slavery began to decrease after 1810. But in Virginia the situation was different, for there slavery remained entrenched in society. In 1810, 93 percent of the state's African Americans were enslaved, and fifty years later nine out of ten blacks in Virginia were still enslaved.

The size and distribution of slave living and working units in the

Chesapeake affected slaves' lives considerably, and these arrangements changed according to region. What had been predominantly African-American slaves living in moderately sized groups dispersed across the landscape and working in gangs turned slowly into a complex variety of living and working arrangements. In some of the northern-most counties of Maryland the size of slave living and working units diminished—in Harford County, on the Pennsylvania border, the average size of slave living units shrunk to under five persons by 1810. While few African Americans in the Upper Chesapeake lived alone, few, too, lived and worked within large slave communities and many performed a variety of tasks independently. However in many of the region's other areas the size of the living and working units had remained stable, in the middling to large size, so gang labor and extensive communal living were still the norm. Where large units still existed (and there remained a number of "grandees" of Old Virginia, those families that owned one hundred or more slaves), planters continued to divide their slaves into several crews that lived apart from one another and worked as separate gangs on plantation plots.

The result of all this by the 1820s was the existence of three loosely defined areas of the Chesapeake in which slavery was instituted in different forms, from the Pennsylvania-Maryland border on the north—the actual Mason-Dixon line—on down into North Carolina on the south. In the top area, on the northern extreme of the region, the trend clearly was to emancipate slaves and to allow them to rent property and, as it turned out, scrape along as best they could. The men and women who remained in bondage in this area lived on small units and did a variety of tasks. The emancipation trend was spreading in Maryland; the state was moving toward becoming by 1860 what Dunn would call "a semislave state."

Farther down, in some counties bordering the Chesapeake Bay, slavery remained intact, but in a different form. Owners tended to hire out their slaves to small farmers who were trying to make it on the tired and eroded land. Slavery persisted in the region's cities, too, but as noted below, the institution was not nearly as confining in urban as it was in rural areas, and in some cities, Baltimore especially, the number of free African Americans grew dramatically from the 1820s.

Farther down still, in much of Virginia, the commitment to slave labor remained and even grew more solid. Slave agriculture there long had been the basis of the region's prosperity, and it would continue to be, even with the falling tobacco prices. After 1806 Virginia's assembly restricted manumission and required freed blacks to leave the state. Slaves continued to live in fair-sized groups and to work in gangs on tobacco and grain crops. And when commodity prices did not sustain the institution, owners either picked up and moved or paid closer attention to the prices speculators offered for their human property. Nowhere did the threat of sale permeate the slave community more than it did in the Chesapeake region between 1815 and 1835.

In the Carolina and Georgia lowcountry, there was an ironic turn for life in slavery through the years of the early republic. In the colonial period, the steamy lowcountry had been where the extremes of slavery existed. Blacks outnumbered whites in the lowcountry counties, perhaps four to one generally and as much as nine to one in some, and the minority white population kept enslaved persons in close check with careful patrols and firm punishments. When egalitarians raised questions about the morality of slavery, lowcountry planters turned deaf ears. They continued to have the lowest rate of manumissions in the country. But the successful rebuilding of the lowcountry plantation economy after the Revolution and the continuing growth of the slave population there ironically brought a degree of improvement to slaves' lives.

Over the country's beginning years, slavery became even more entrenched along the Carolina and Georgia coasts. Rice production was slow in coming back after the Revolution, but by the mid–1790s lowcountry plantations had reached prewar levels of rice production and had begun to grow the new sea-island cotton as well. Furthermore, by this time, the reopened Atlantic trade was providing laborers for the expanding backcountry (and thus precluding any real drain on lowcountry slaves), and the lowcountry slave population had recovered in numbers and was growing rapidly. Once again some of the largest holdings with the greatest number of slaves in the country were lowcountry plantations.

But all this did not necessarily bode ill for the African Americans living there. The increased concentration of African Americans in the lowcountry meant that slaves there had the broadest social and communal contacts with other blacks. Also, changes in the methods of producing rice that had been creeping onto the plantations since the middle of the eighteenth century and changes in working systems, that gave black "drivers" greater authority and allowed individual slaves more autonomy, tended to improve the lives of many African Americans in the lowcountry. The task system of slave-labor management had always worked well on rice plantations. Under this system, individual slaves were given particular tasks to accomplish as a day's work; once their daily allotments of work were completed, they then had time to themselves. The transition to tidewater cultivation of rice required more work on dikes and ditches in the winter months, but less work cultivating in the hot and humid summers. It was still year-round work, but on balance it probably made slaves' working lives easier. Also, the switch from indigo to cotton as a second crop in the 1790s meant that less sustained, rigorous work was required of slaves.

Management of the lowcountry plantations fell more and more into the hands of African Americans. They had brought rice-growing technology and expertise to the colonies from West Africa long before, and during the Revolution, slaves had stayed on and run affairs—to their liking—on many a plantation, as owners and their families had made for safer territory. As the country settled down and production returned to prewar levels, planters seemed content to give their capable blacks greater authority. (This allowed the owners to absent themselves from the unhealthy lowcountry, too, which was one of their cherished goals.) More African-American drivers were put in charge of operations, setting out tasks and insuring their completion; more individual slaves were granted autonomy within the broadly restrictive slave system. In spite of laws against it, some slaves acquired property of their own and participated in the brisk, waterborne trade of the coastal region.

There is evidence that slave-family security grew with these changes. With slave imports once again meeting demand in the back-country, fear of sale in the lowcountry was diminished. Masters may even have acquired greater respect for slave families. When slaves were sold, more of them seem to have been sold—purposefully—in family groups. Lowcountry family ties grew to be so broad and deep that, by early in the nineteenth century, runaway slaves were harder to find because they had kin all over the region with which to find shelter. Philip D. Morgan in "Black Society in the Lowcountry, 1760–1810," in *Slavery and Freedom in the Age of the American Revolution*, cites one advertisement for a runaway in 1803 which noted that a forty-five-year-old woman

> had a husband at the plantation of Hugh Willson, esq., James Island, has relatives at the plantation of the Rev. Dr. Frost, Goosecreek and has a son at the plantation of Dr. Jones, in the same parish; she is well known in the city, probably she may make for Georgetown, being well acquainted there.

"So commonplace had the legitimacy and stability of slave marriages become," writes Morgan of the Lowcountry in America's early years, "that planters could specially note illegitimate births."

If African Americans in the Lowcountry were not so content as to stop running away, their owners still believed they were satisfied enough to eschew insurrection. Through the first two decades of the nineteenth century, insurrectionary scares in the Lowcountry were attributed to imported slaves. Therefore, whites did not seem to be as threatened by slave uprisings as they once were.

The result of all this, by about 1800, was what Morgan calls "a distinctive lowcountry social world—one in which planters were more deeply committed to slavery and slaves enjoyed a larger degree of autonomy than anywhere else on mainland North America." It was an autonomy that would enable the lowcountry slaves to maintain more African cultural elements, including language (the unique patois called "gullah"), folklore, religious and medical practices, works of art, burial practices, and more.

Probably the most demanding crop to produce, at least in terms of seasonal, hard work under severe conditions, was sugarcane. It was about the only southern crop that African-American men worked on in considerably higher numbers than women. Work in the cane fields was especially difficult and unpleasant partly because of the environment in Louisiana, where about 95 percent of the country's sugarcane was grown. The cane thrived best in the state's rock-free bayous and river bottoms, where slaves had to do heavy ditching and draining in order to prepare and maintain the fields. Also, slaves had to cultivate the cane fairly constantly through the hottest and wettest months, when mosquitoes, the vectors of malaria, were everywhere.

The Louisiana climate was the best in the country for sugar production, but it was still not ideal. This meant that the crop required more work there than it did under more favorable conditions in the West Indies—more frequent and larger plantings with smaller yields. As with most crops, the harvest and preparation for market of sugarcane was the most physically demanding time of the cycle. Slaves had to cut the cane—they hacked it down with heavy knives—in a hurry. The harvest could not begin too early, for the laborers would be taking in unripe cane that would not produce sweet juice; nor could it begin too late because frost would damage the standing stalks and render the juice sour. And the cut cane had to be boiled in several processes (which demanded large quantities of cut wood to fuel the fires), clarified, and crystallized, all fairly rapidly. Thus, when harvest began in mid-October, able African Americans on sugar plantations worked all day, sixteen to eighteen hours at a stretch, and about every third night without a day's break for a ten-week span until about Christmas. The introduction of earlier-ripening "ribbon" cane in 1817 and regular improvements in production techniques might have lessened the amount of work as similar changes did with other crops, but when better methods at any stage brought the possibility of reduced work, planters simply raised the acreage of cane that each slave had to produce. In 1802 one good "hand" was expected to tend and harvest about two acres of sugarcane. By 1830 one hand was required to take care of about twice that amount. For these reasons, in the first half of the nineteenth century, many slaves believed that being "sold down the river"—down the

Mississippi to the sugar plantations around New Orleans—was a fate just slightly better than death.

In spite of the nature of the work and the preponderance of males on the sugar plantations, at least some African-American families developed early in Louisiana and persisted. Herbert Gutman studied the Stirling Plantation in West Feliciana Parish, Louisiana, from 1807 to the Civil War (in *The Black Family in Slavery and Freedom*) and found black society there moving rapidly by the 1810s toward stable families and primary kinship identity. Women were especially important in this family development. The cane fields were about the only work sites across the South on which slave women were relieved of some of the heavy toil (except during the harvest). Thus, they generally remained healthier, had healthier children, and had more time and inclination to pass along family and cultural values than slaves in other regions. The Stirling Plantation probably was atypical of the sugar plantations generally. More often men outnumbered women three or four to one, women of childbearing age (and thus small children) were few, and death rates for all were high, all of which added to the real difficulty in creating and maintaining families. But that such a situation as in the slave quarters of the Stirling Plantation existed in the Louisiana sugar parishes is evidence of the importance African Americans accorded to kinship and family relations.

Finally, and most noticeably, throughout the southern states the continually advancing frontier of cotton production kept the working and living conditions of American slaves in a long process of regular change through the first third of the nineteenth century. John Hebron Moore in *The Emergence of the Cotton Kingdom in the Old Southwest: Mississippi, 1770–1860* (1988) recognizes different stages of development of cotton plantations and suggests the effects the changing stages had on the African-American laborers. Moore identifies a *pioneer phase* that lasted from five to ten years on a new plantation, during which slaves carved fields out of forests and began growing cotton and corn; a *mature phase*, realized when the plantation reached full production, with new land cleared and brought under production about as fast as the old fields eroded beyond usefulness or lost their fertility; and a *declining phase* during which there were no more plantation woodlands left to clear for cultivation and the fields still planted in cotton were no longer productive. Often during this last phase, a planter purchased fresh land in another county or state and then, over a few years, moved his slaves to a new plantation and began the cycle anew. Until the 1840s, when land became more dear and planters began to realize the importance of taking better care of the soil and renewing its fertility, cotton agriculture with slave labor moved across the Lower South in this leap-frog fashion.

For many African-American men and women living in upcountry South Carolina, Georgia, Alabama, or Mississippi through the 1820s, the pioneer phase of the cotton plantation brought especially hard work and primitive living conditions. Getting land cleared and cotton growing was the focus of their work—food, shelter, clothing, or anything approaching an amenity were secondary. Cutting forests and clearing land to precede plowing and planting was particularly rigorous and heavy work. Those doing the cutting and clearing were crowded into crude dwellings that they had constructed with haste upon arrival. Their diets consisted of dried corn and salt pork, supplemented with what they could hunt or gather in their limited spare time. Until the plantation was producing cotton, there was little opportunity to build families or participate in anything beyond the most basic community activities.

The mature phase of southern cotton agriculture tended to bring better conditions for the slaves—more varied diets, more and better clothing, and, in time, improved dwellings. In most instances slaves continued to live in log cabins that had dirt floors and stick-and-mud chimneys. Contrary to the popular image, work on a mature cotton farm or plantation was not the most onerous of the slave regime. It was no match for the toil required on sugar or rice plantations or on tobacco farms. This is not to say that the plowing and planting between February and April, the mid-summer chopping, or the fall picking were not hard tasks, nor is it to suggest that there was not plenty of work on cotton-growing units throughout the year. But cotton did not have to be transplanted, pruned, topped, or cured as did tobacco; it did not require elaborate ditching for draining or flooding of fields as did sugar and rice; and it had a long "lay-by" season through hot times in late summer and early fall.

From the time cotton agriculture took hold in the Lower South, most planters worked their slaves in the gang system that had served tobacco planters so well. On small farms, gangs might consist of nothing more than a master and a few slaves, doing whatever work had to be done under the master's watch. On large plantations, slave forces were divided into gangs of manageable size, maybe twenty or thirty, and they worked in their group under the direction of a slave designated the "driver." Gangs of slaves on cotton plantations did whatever needed to be done out-of-doors. Moore writes, "There were plow gangs, hoe gangs, cotton-picking gangs, corn-pulling gangs, fence-building gangs, land-clearing gangs, ginning gangs, cotton-pressing gangs, and still other gangs." Men and women worked alongside one another unless the work was especially heavy—felling trees, digging ditches, and the like.

Of course, no matter where slavery existed and no matter which slave system was employed, a full day's work was almost universally the slave's lot. Charles Ball knew this as a slave in the early decades of the country's existence. Whether he was hauling tobacco to market in Maryland, picking cotton in South Carolina, clearing trees and building cabins in Georgia, or running fish traps on rivers in any of these places, Ball was up and ready for work with the sun, six days a week, and worked until a time approaching dark. But the pace of work was not always the same, depending on crop, season, weather, inclination of master or overseer, and mood of the slaves.

Generally speaking, the slave's working pace had been established back in colonial times. It required compromise, for masters naturally wanted their slaves to do more work and slaves sought less. The master's normal method of getting more work was to punish the slave not meeting expectations and to rely on the threat of punishment to keep up the pace; the slave's way to deal with masters or overseers who required too much was to break tools, ruin crops, feign illness, or run away. The more one learns about southern plantation slavery from both sides of the situation, the more one recognizes that the slaves were far from powerless in determining the pace of their work. Masters or overseers could whip a slave, but that usually meant losing the individual's labor through a period of convalescence (for severe whippings were incapacitating). They could imprison laggards, but this lost them labor as well, and masters soon found many a slave who preferred confinement indoors to the rigors of cutting cane or chopping cotton. In the end, both parties generally settled on a relatively slow pace of work, provided that the work was done reasonably well. And there were seasonal variations. During the busy times of planting or harvest, slaves had to work faster than at other times. In recognition of this, masters threw feasts for their workers and gave them days off after the tobacco was hung, the rice milled, the cotton ginned, or the sugar refined.

Sometimes masters working slaves in gangs incorporated ideas from the task system and set out incentives to encourage hard work. When Ball picked cotton in South Carolina, he (and each of the other pickers) was given a quota for the day. All the cotton he picked above his quota earned him a reward, in this case, money. Such incentives seemed to quicken the pace of work more than threat of the lash.

There were differences in slaves' work patterns and requirements that depended on the farm or plantation's major crop. Even common field hands came to be specialists of a kind, for they learned to work a specific crop as they were growing up. Ball grew to manhood in a tobacco-producing area of Maryland. When he had to begin work in a part of South Carolina where cotton was the primary crop, he had difficulty. Ball was strong and willing—he had brought top dollar when he was sold at auction in Columbia—but it took a while for the trained tobacco hand to get the knack of picking cotton. It was a skill "reckoned among the arts," he believed. "A man who has arrived at the age of twenty-five before he sees a cotton field, will never, in the language of the overseer, become *a crack picker*."

There were also differences in levels of specialization that depended on the size of the farm or plantation and its number of slaves. Early in the nineteenth century, more slaves lived on smaller holdings—the enormous plantations with army-like labor forces existed, but they were much more a fact of later antebellum slavery—and when their numbers in a single unit were small, slaves did a little bit of everything, from clearing to plowing and hoeing to fencing and tending livestock. On plantations with larger numbers of slaves, forty or fifty or more, some individual workers would specialize. There might be several cooks and domestics, persons to care for horses and vehicles, perhaps a blacksmith or two, carpenters, coopers, and more. Some specializations were seasonal—Ball managed the plantation's fishing after the cotton was ginned. As the size of plantations grew, slave specialization became more common, but, on most plantations, come harvest time specialization meant nothing. When it was time to pick cotton or cut cane, every able slave, including children nine-years old and women seven-months pregnant, might spend long days in the field.

By standards of today, slaves' living and working conditions were difficult—cramped and crudely fashioned log homes, cotton or straw pallets for sleeping, basic and often substandard diets, heavy clothing in the hot weather and often not enough warm clothing for the cold, and long hours of daily work throughout the year. With such a proportion of the slave population migrating toward the western and southern frontiers of the country in the early nineteenth century, and with plantations and farms starting from scratch in the new areas, it is likely that most blacks living in slavery through this time saw their lives get worse rather than better.

Urban and Industrial Slavery

If the early republic was the time of the beginning and rapid spread of America's best-known form of slavery, that of the southern cotton plantation, it also was the period when the rise of a long-overlooked variant, urban slavery, took place. America hardly had urban areas to speak of in 1790. Only 5.1 percent of its population lived in an area containing more than 2,500 people. There were twenty-four such "cities" when Washington took office. But over the first four decades of the country's existence, cities grew with a regular if not startling pace, so that by 1830, 8.8 percent of Americans lived in ninety different cities, and eighteen of them were in states south of Pennsylvania and the Ohio River. Growing along with the cities was urban slavery. By 1830 the ten largest southern cities contained about 50,000 African-American slaves.

Urban slavery was not a new phenomenon in nineteenth-century America. Through the middle of the previous century the few cities that existed along the eastern seaboard, where labor was usually in short supply, came to have sizable slave populations. Boston held around 1,500 slaves at midcentury; Philadelphia had nearly that many in the mid–1760s; and Charleston, where slave ships docked more frequently than anywhere else, had a whopping 11,000 slaves—outnumbering its white population—in 1770. But with the increasing numbers of manumissions that followed the Revolution in the North, urban dwellers in that region turned to free labor whenever they had the opportunity. The number of slaves in northern cities dwindled at different rates. Between 1790 and 1810 Philadelphia's slave population declined by 99 percent, Providence's by 88 percent, and New York's, more slowly, by 29 percent. Only in the southern states, where the "peculiar institution" was stronger than ever, was urban slavery on the rise.

Richard C. Wade, whose *Slavery in the Cities, 1820–1860* (1964) awakened historians to the extent and importance of urban slavery, recognized that by 1820 the South had an "urban perimeter"—ten cities around the edge of the southern states that held about 90 percent of the region's urban white population and most of its urban slaves. The cities were Baltimore, Washington, Richmond, Norfolk, Charleston, Savannah, Mobile, and New Orleans on or near the coast, and St. Louis and Louisville (Kentucky) on the region's northern extreme. Slaves made up 22 percent of these cities' populations in the 1820s—more in such cities as Charleston and New Orleans, less in Baltimore and Washington. In each city, Wade found that slavery was different than it was on the southern farms and plantations. The urban milieu was much freer for slaves—they were able to conduct a variety of activities "beyond the master's eye."

"A city slave is almost a freeman, compared with a slave on the plantation," wrote Frederick Douglass, who spent a good portion of his youth after 1826 as a slave in Baltimore. "He is much better fed and clothed, and enjoys privileges altogether unknown to the slave on the plantation." Douglass's privileges in Baltimore included learning to read, working outside his master's home, eventually finding his own work and living away from his master, and coming and going with slaves and free blacks in a fashion that would have been impossible back on the eastern Maryland plantation of Douglass's birth. Although Douglass was especially able and perhaps more privileged than many, his urban experience was not altogether atypical of slaves living in cities in the 1820s and 1830s. According to Wade, urban slaves were "more advanced, engaged in higher tasks, more literate, more independent, and less servile than those on plantations."

Slaves had many occupations in the urban setting. The one that occupied the largest number was the broad category of house servant—cook, maid, driver, butler, gardener, and the like. More women filled these sorts of jobs than men, and for this reason slave women usually outnumbered their male counterparts in the urban setting. Men tended to work more outside the home, in skilled trades, as common laborers, and on public works projects. Skilled slaves had an advantage in competition with white tradesmen because masters often leased slaves for less than the going rate or "hired them out" to break strikes or boycotts: episodes of tension and violence were common under such circumstances. Douglass experienced white animosity when he was an apprentice calker in the Baltimore shipyards. After months of being cursed and degraded by the white apprentices, Douglass was set upon by four young white men. As fifty white adults watched, the four youths beat and kicked Douglass until one of his eyeballs "seemed to have burst." When he took after his assailants, the adults seized him long enough for them to escape.

Urban masters could "hire out" their slaves by the day, week, month, or even year. So long as a slave lived in the master's home, all of his (or more rarely her) wages came to the master. Fortunate was the slave whose master allowed him to live outside the home and "hire his own time." When it was done, the slave had to turn over to the master a weekly amount of money from wages. Whatever the slave earned above that amount paid for room and board and provided extras.

Freedom was at the heart of the rural-urban difference in bondage—not freedom as opposed to slavery, but freedom of movement and association, freedom to have human contacts and a life outside the normal bounds of the slave system. Not that stringent laws were not on the books. State laws that made slaves property and demanded their submission to authority applied equally to urban and rural areas. Mindful of the possibility of insurrection and the potential to undercut white authority that freedom of movement for slaves held, city governments even set out their own restrictive codes for blacks in bondage: curfews and requirements for possession of identification papers, the wearing of badges, and the registration of skilled tradesmen were common. Some locales even passed ordinances prohibiting self-hire. But the openness and bustle of the city made it difficult to enforce all of the restrictions on the books. Thus, under normal circumstances, slaves could come and go in the urban environment without much interference, so long as they showed proper respect and demeanor, looked as if they were about their business, and did not appear to be "up to something."

Ball's account of his first escape from slavery shows how clearly this was the case. Through Georgia, South Carolina, North Carolina, and southern Virginia, all in rural areas, he had to hide by day in the deep woods and travel only by night. He feared everyone, white or black. But when, after several months of walking, foraging, and sleeping in the wilds, he reached Richmond, Ball sensed that the best way to get through the city of 10,000 residents (one-third of whom were slaves) was to act as if he belonged there. Ball laid low until midday; then, carrying his stolen food supply as if it were a parcel he was delivering, he emerged unseen from a thicket, entered the city, and walked through its main streets. As he expected, by keeping to his business he received scant attention. Only when Ball got a mile or two outside of town did he wait until the coast was clear and then dash for the woods to wait out the remaining daylight.

As southern cities grew in size and population through the 1820s, the lives slaves led there must have improved. Such cities as Louisville, St. Louis, Richmond, and Mobile experienced dramatic growth in their resident African-American slave populations. The increasing size of the cities' populations in general heightened slaves' anonymity, and greater numbers of slaves and free blacks gave individual African Americans more persons with whom to associate. Thus, although most slaves living in cities continued to reside on their master's property, often in buildings adjoining the master's house that were only a cut above slave quarters on the plantation, and although the master's and society's restraints on blacks' activities remained a part of slaves' lives, their freedoms were relatively great. They worked with other blacks (and often with whites), worshipped together, met socially, and enjoyed family and kinship relationships, all within the loose restraints of the urban variant of the South's truly peculiar institution.

The early decades of the nineteenth century were years, too, when slaves began to prove their worth in southern industry. The South was no industrial match for many of the northern states, but neither was it void of industry. From the 1790s, southerners began industrial operations to process agricultural products, mine ores, manufacture turpentine, and mill lumber. By the 1820s the southern iron and textile industries were developing as well, and not long afterward, slaves worked in the budding transportation industry. Helping the southern industries compete was a heavy reliance on slave labor. Belying the myth that African Americans could not master the skills necessary for industrial work, southern owners of industry employed slaves in large numbers and in a variety of ways.

Industries could purchase their own slaves, and many larger industries tried to do so over the long run. They also could hire slaves by the month or year. Slave labor was generally profitable for the owners, according to Robert S. Starobin, whose *Industrial Slavery in the Old South* (1970) remains a standard work on the subject. Slave rental rates rose by 50 percent between 1800 and 1833, and prices for slaves increased proportionately, suggesting that productivity and demand for slaves in industry was growing as fast as it was in agricultural work. For the African-American laborers involved, industrial slavery seems to have been a mixed bag. Starobin stresses the difficulties of the situation—"long hours, hazardous work, subsistence living levels, sickness, and inadequate medical care." But other historians disagree, suggesting that once southern industries began to rely heavily on slave labor, the slaves were able to use this reliance to their advantage and to insist on improved working and living conditions. In several articles on slavery in the early-nineteenth-century iron industry, Charles B. Dew shows that "a subtle process of mutual compromise and accommodation" rather than "excessive use of physical force and coercion" characterized the relationship between master and slave, that a good number of slaves were able to obtain compensation for extra work, and that at least some masters recognized and respected the slave family for its role in training, motivating, and disciplining the African-American laborers. In at least certain instances, writes Dew, "industrial slavery did not totally degrade and brutalize the black workers; in fact, it seems in some ways to have done something quite different, to have provided these men with an environment in which they could develop some sense of personal dignity and individual initiative in spite of the psychological and physical confines of their bondage."

Neither urban nor industrial slavery was a particularly big issue through the first decades of the nineteenth century. Like the southern cotton plantation, through the 1820s slavery in cities and in industries was passing through formative stages toward maturity. African Americans were finding more to do, in larger numbers, in southern cities; they were proving themselves efficient and often more valuable than free laborers in industry. The future of the two forms of the institution seemed bright at the start of the 1830s.

Living and Dying in Slavery

History is more than the study of the past actions of the healthy and long-lived, but for many years historians did not act as if that were so. Only recently have some historians begun to recognize that human illness, debilitation, and premature mortality had considerable effect on the way whole societies functioned. In few instances is this more true than for African Americans in slavery. Several recent examinations of disease environments, related aspects of nutrition, and patterns of wellness, sickness, and death among American slaves have provided a deeper understanding of the unhealthy conditions in which the slaves existed and of the harsh environment into which they migrated. For most African-American slaves through the first part of the nineteenth century, life was hard, illness was frequent, and death was always close at hand; for women in slavery, pregnancy was an especially dangerous ordeal; and for newly born children of

African Americans in bondage, just reaching the age of five was a struggle that over half did not win.

Studying African Americans' illnesses and mortality in slavery and trying to understand why blacks suffered more and died earlier than contemporary whites have been formidable tasks. Investigation of death and disease for any population from a time beginning two centuries ago is neither easy nor exact. Evidence is lacking—the census of 1850 was the first to include a question concerning causes of death—and such records that exist are subject to the inaccuracies of lay diagnosis. Moreover, even members of the medical profession did not know about many of the diseases endemic or epidemic in the population. Thus, one is forced to make judgments on such vaguely noted causes of death as "fevers," "dropsy," "nervous system diseases," or simply "old age." That we know as much as we do about the broad subject is a tribute to several historians who have brought to their study of African Americans in slavery broad knowledge of medicine and pathology.

The American South of the early nineteenth century was a particularly unhealthy place. This was so partly because of its climate. The South had hot and often wet summers followed by mild winters, a combination that allowed disease-carrying mosquitoes, insect larvae, protozoa, bacteria, and viruses to thrive. But the South was even less healthy than many other, similar subtropical regions because of its epidemiological heritage. By 1800 the southern part of the United States was a real mixing ground of substantial human populations from different disease environments. Europeans were the first unwitting carriers of diseases to the region—they brought smallpox, measles, dysenteries, gonorrhea, and a somewhat milder strain of malaria called vivax. Then, the several hundred thousand Africans who were brought to the British North American mainland between 1619 and 1808 arrived with their own baggage of microbes, bringing three diseases in particular that would come to set off the South as a distinct disease environment. These diseases were falciparum malaria, which was more deadly than the vivax strain; hookworm, which invaded the bodies of children and adults, stifling physical development and mental activity; and yellow fever, a real killer if only in epidemics in populated areas. Although falciparum malaria struck the young and the weak and was especially hazardous for pregnant women and infants, it and hookworm were more important as secondary causes of death. They sapped the strength of slaves and made them much more likely to acquire other diseases. Yellow fever originated in Africa and was transported to the United States on ships from the Caribbean; there were regular, serious yellow-fever epidemics in the coastal cities, but little problem with the disease in rural areas.

Persons of African descent were more or less susceptible than whites to these and other diseases. To some diseases Africans had certain levels of immunity. Because of properties in the blood of many West Africans and their descendants, including the sickle-cell trait and an enzyme deficiency, most African Americans were immune to vivax malaria, and one in three was immune to falciparum malaria. Blacks possessed some genetic resistance to yellow fever, too. But selective immunities were only a part of the slave's epidemiological story. Specific physiological characteristics of people descended from Africans, combined with the effects of diet, dress, and shelter on their resistance to diseases, led African Americans in the South to suffer more from a number of maladies and in general to live shorter lives than whites.

The same genetic blood conditions that provided blacks a handful of immunities caused them no end of serious physical problems. Those who acquired the sickle-cell trait from both parents developed sickle-cell disease, and many with this disease died in their youth. Also, a number of the once-unexplainable maladies peculiar to American slaves, from a high rate of miscarriage to aching joints, respiratory infections, and leg sores, are now recognized as being related to blacks' unique hemoglobin traits.

In addition, African Americans had special physiological, nutritional, and dietary problems that, when combined, caused them serious physical difficulties and rendered them highly vulnerable to a number of diseases. For reasons related to centuries of adaptation to living conditions in tropical West Africa, blacks could not tolerate lactose (and thus could not digest most calcium-rich dairy products) and could not effectively synthesize vitamin D from sunlight. Because of their unique blood characteristics, blacks tended toward anemia and they required more folic acid and protein than others; because of the hard labor they performed in hot weather, they lost calcium rapidly through perspiration. The typical slave diet of corn and pork, even as African-American men and women supplemented it through fishing and hunting, gathering and gardening, was probably sufficient in quantity but was nowhere near the nutritional quality needed by persons of West African descent. It did not provide enough niacin to enable proper metabolization of fats, proteins, and carbohydrates; it was always deficient in calcium, vitamin C, riboflavin, protein, and iron; and it was seasonally deficient in vitamin A and thiamine. These deficiencies led slaves to experience an abnormally high incidence of noticeable health problems: blindness or inflamed and watery eyes; lameness or crooked limbs; loose, missing, or rotten teeth; and skin sores. Also, they made African Americans much more apt to suffer from a number of serious and often fatal diseases—tetanus, intestinal worms, diphtheria, whooping cough, pica (or dirt eating), pneumonia, tuberculosis, and dysentery.

What served as clothing and shelter for slaves did not add to their ability to fight disease. Again, because of their inherited, long-developed physiological adjustment to West Africa's tropical conditions, blacks lacked tolerance for the cold. In addition to being fair game for respiratory diseases, they got frostbite much more readily than whites. Slaves were always interested in having enough clothing in the colder months—much more interested than their masters were in providing it. Two pairs of pants, two shirts, and a pair of shoes were a standard, annual dress issue for a slave on a southern plantation. Some masters provided more, a coat and hat, perhaps socks, and a blanket. But all across the South, African Americans used means both fair and foul to acquire extra coats, shawls, blankets, and wraps to repel the cold. Warm clothing was especially important because slave dwellings were almost uniformly cold and drafty in the winter; they were miserably hot in the summer, too, and they provided no barriers to flies and mosquitoes. Slaves on larger units often lived in crowded and cramped quarters, so germs and diseases contracted by one became problems for all. "What might have been considered a personal illness in the isolated white rural family dwelling," writes Todd L. Savitt in "Slave Health and Social Distinctiveness" in

Disease and Distinctiveness in the American South, edited by Todd L. Savitt and James Harvey Young (1988), "became in a three- or ten- or thirty-home slave community a matter of public health and group concern."

Hygiene was another matter. Rare was the privy in slave quarters; most relieved themselves behind shrubs or bushes, a short walk from the dwelling. John B. Boles in *Black Southerners, 1619–1869* (1983) describes the result:

> With dogs, chickens, and children underfoot, human and animal feces and urine contaminated the yard, were washed into the sources of drinking water, and contaminated food and clothing by hand contact. Flies swarmed from decayed food and table scraps to excrement to the table. Food prepared under less than hygienic conditions and with no refrigeration made spoiling a constant problem. Dysentery, typhus, food poisoning, diarrhea, hepatitis, typhoid fever, salmonella, and intestinal worms often resulted from crowded living in squalid conditions.

Poor southern whites lived in these conditions, too, but they did not have blacks' genetic, nutritional, and physiological problems with which to contend.

Two groups of black people probably suffered more from the effects of diet and disease than the rest: women who were mothers, and children under ten years of age. Their situations were, naturally, related.

Nineteenth-century American slave women experienced an extremely high fertility rate, substantially higher than white women of the same time. The average nineteenth-century African-American slave mother had seven children. All women who give birth to several children are prone to calcium deficiency and anemia. Given their diets, slave mothers must have been particularly deficient in calcium and iron, as well as the other important nutrients noted, through much of their adult lives. Compounding these nutritional deficiencies was a difficult work regimen throughout pregnancy. It was typical for slave women to receive no reduction in work load before the fifth month of pregnancy, and if it was a labor-intensive time on the plantation—planting or harvesting—the pregnant women worked to the very time of delivery. If this was difficult, dangerously unhealthy, and sometimes life-threatening for the woman involved, it was all this and more for the fetus and infant.

The infant mortality rate—that is, deaths before the first year of age—for the entire African-American slave population to the middle of the nineteenth century remained at about 350 per thousand, and over half of all slave children died before they reached five years of age. This last figure is twice the proportion for the entire United States population at the same time. The difference was not at all the result of parental ignorance (for black and white parents were similarly ignorant about most aspects of nutrition, medicine, and child care), nor of parental neglect or infanticide, as is sometimes suggested. The major factor leading to the high rate of infant mortality was low birth weight. The great majority of African Americans born into slavery in the nineteenth century weighed less than five and one-half pounds at birth. Poor maternal nutrition was part of the reason, but so was the amount of hard work expected of pregnant women until late in their pregnancies. On rice plantations, where African-American women did more continual hard work on their feet than anywhere else in America, infant mortality was at its highest. Conversely, on sugar plantations, where work was more seasonal and where much of the toil was so heavy that women were exempted from it, infant mortality was significantly lower. Richard H. Steckel in "A Dreadful Childhood: The Excess Mortality of American Slaves," *Social Science History*, 10 (1986), suggests that on cotton plantations, periods of peak infant mortality corresponded with periods of most intensive fieldwork by women through their pregnancies.

Breastfeeding was an important factor in the health of young slave children. As we know now, breast milk is the ideal nourishment for infants. In addition to being clean and excellent nutritionally, it provides infants with some immunity to diseases. But because of planters' desires for women to return to full-time work in the fields soon after delivery, nineteenth-century slave women were not able to breastfeed as long as were most white women. Many slave mothers began weaning their children within a few months of birth, substituting different varieties of pap or gruel (a combination of bread, cow's milk, water, and brown sugar was common). Such supplements were nutritionally poor and often contaminated. Infants weaned early became more susceptible to disease; African-American infant mortality rates climbed after weaning.

One further reason for the high rate of infant mortality among slave children was sudden infant death syndrome (SIDS). African-American slave children experienced SIDS an astonishing fifty-three times more frequently than white children of the time. Observers spoke of "smothering" or "overlaying," assuming that the deaths occurred when mothers, sleeping with their infants, simply rolled over onto them, thus suffocating their infants. Today we know that low birth weight, magnesium and calcium deficiency, and anemia all predispose infants to SIDS, so it seems evident that the nutritional problems of pregnant slave mothers and the low birth weight and mineral deficiencies of slave infants were largely responsible for the sudden deaths.

But practically all of our knowledge about why stillbirths occurred, why newborns were small, and why infants and children died in such large numbers was far beyond the ken of blacks and whites through the middle of the nineteenth century and beyond. All slave parents knew was that half of the children they bore never reached the fifth year of life and that those who lived beyond five years were often thin and weak and susceptible to a host of illnesses into early adulthood. What the adults did to overcome their grief was to mourn openly, to receive the comfort of the slave community, and to draw even closer to the remaining family. But what they did to offset the heavy losses was to conceive more children and simply hope against hope that at least some of them would survive what Steckel calls "a dreadful childhood."

Some periods in American history were particularly unhealthy ones for African-American slaves, and one of those periods seems to have been the time of the early republic. Steckel, in several statistical studies involving slave childhood mortality and data on slave heights, suggests that slaves' overall health declined from the beginning of the nineteenth century to about the mid-1830s before beginning a trend toward improvement. One must look to a variety of reasons for declining slave health during these years, but some of the factors most likely involved were the fast and furious importation of Africans between 1788 and 1808, the forced migration of African Americans from one regional disease environment to another, and the primitive living conditions through the first several years following migration.

"Raw" Africans probably had the worst of it. Those captive persons who were imported into Savannah, Charleston, Mobile, or New Orleans in the 1790s and 1800s had little time to become adjusted to their New-World surroundings before being hiked toward the interior. In the backcountry of Georgia or South Carolina, or down along the lower Mississippi River, they were quickly forced to participate in some of the most strenuous work slaves had to do—beginning agricultural production on uncleared land. Records of mortality rates for newly arrived Africans in America are particularly poor, but from what is known of the experiences of first-generation slaves—of the high death rates among those awaiting sale and of the difficulties experienced by Africans becoming "seasoned" in America—the number of deaths among the newly arrived African population must have been startling.

The movement of acculturated African Americans from one disease environment to another, occasioned by the spread of cotton production and the interregional trade of slaves, created problems with illnesses of varying seriousness. K. David Patterson in "Disease Environments in the Antebellum South," in *Science and Medicine in the Old South*, edited by Ronald L. Numbers and Todd L. Savitt (1989), shows how if one had traveled from the Chesapeake's tidewater region to the Gulf Coast during the early republic, he or she would have passed through regions with strikingly different epidemiological characteristics. Therefore an African American forced to make a long-distance move from coastal Maryland to backcountry South Carolina, as was Charles Ball, faced special hazards. Ball came from a cooler environment where respiratory diseases were frequent but where persons were almost never exposed to many diarrheal diseases, hookworm, yellow fever, or the more deadly falciparum form of malaria. He was taken to a region six hundred miles south, where summers were hotter and winters shorter and cooler. There, respiratory diseases were not such a problem, but a person was almost certain to be exposed to falciparum malaria, a variety of serious diarrheal diseases, and hookworm. Yellow fever was even a sporadic problem of epidemic proportions in Savannah, where Ball visited in his labors. Epidemiologists estimate that it takes two years to become physiologically accustomed to a new disease environment—that is, to contract the new diseases, live through them, and build up enough immunities to make it likely that subsequent contractions of the diseases will not be life threatening. So until African Americans like Ball became "seasoned," the amount of debilitating and life-threatening disease among America's population of black slaves remained high.

As noted, living conditions in the early settlements on the cotton frontier were especially primitive and difficult. The foremost goal of the plantation owner was to clear land and get crops under production. Slave housing was thrown together quickly; lean-tos often sufficed through the first year. Clearing land was some of the most strenuous work slaves had to do, and because they worked fairly constantly in wooded lands or swampy grounds that needed ditching and draining, these exhausted people were continually bitten by mosquitoes and flies. Diets must have varied from the standard as well, for corn had to be parched in order to be brought along, there were no domestic animals to slaughter, it would take an entire season to bring a vegetable garden under production, and slaves were allowed little time in the busy initial years in which to hunt and gather for themselves in order to supplement their diets. It is little wonder that malnutrition, disease, and higher rates of mortality among the human laborers moved south and west with the advancing line of slave-based agriculture.

What finally caused slaves' health conditions to improve steadily, and consequently their mortality rates to begin to drop slowly, almost immediately following the last years of the early republic is a matter open to conjecture. Neither blacks' genetic hemoglobin traits nor their special nutritional needs changed; slaves' diets did not improve significantly, for masters remained pitifully ignorant of proper nutrition; the interregional migration of African Americans did not end; and the disease environment of the South did not change significantly—though there is a possibility that by the mid–1830s the cumulative white and black migration was great enough to render the entire southern disease environment more homogenous and thus less threatening to humans moving from one part of the region to another. The improvement of slaves' health may therefore be tied closely to their growing value to their owners. By the 1830s, with the southern cotton kingdom firmly established and still growing, with the spread of the more easily picked cotton (like the "Rodney" variety) making individual slaves annual producers of half a bale of cotton apiece, and with replacement slaves costing hundreds of dollars, there is reason to believe that masters began to take greater steps to insure the health of their slaves. This included more than improving shelter or handing out more clothes. It certainly included more than employing physicians to care for slaves, for although owners did this increasingly, with some even maintaining infirmaries and nursehouses on the plantations for their slaves who were ill, receiving attention from a physician, with their contemporary weapons of surgery and their propensity to let blood and purge the alimentary tract, was likely to be more detrimental to slaves than receiving treatment from blacks who practiced folk medicine. It seems that masters slowly came to the realization that one could indeed work a person to death, or into serious illness, and that strenuous work over long hours at certain times of the year made slaves more susceptible to sickness and thus unable to work. In some of the unhealthiest seasons and areas, planters even began hiring free labor to perform tasks they regarded as dangerous for their slaves. It was simply a way for the capitalist to protect his investment. Thus, it was not so much anyone's high personal regard for the persons involved as it was their status as valuable pieces of property that began to make African Americans' lives in slavery a little more comfortable, a little healthier, and a little longer—soon after the time of the early republic.

The Cycles of Family and Community

Herbert G. Gutman wrote *The Black Family in Slavery and Freedom* in reaction to an academic controversy. Sociologist (and later politician) Daniel P. Moynihan wrote *The Negro Family in America: The Case for National Action* in 1965, in which he blamed many contemporary problems of urban blacks on "the deterioration of the Negro

Family." Moynihan followed conventional historical wisdom of the time in tracing that deterioration to the time that African Americans spent in slavery. "It was by destroying the Negro family [beginning in slavery] that white America broke the will of the Negro people," Moynihan argued. Gutman disagreed. The black family survived through all the adversity heaped upon it by slavery, Gutman believed, and with its strength provided the glue that held together the slave community. He conceded that slave marriage, family structure, and family life were not the same as those of whites of the time. By necessity, slave husbands and wives often lived on neighboring plantations. Fathers might be with their families only on weekends, and slave families were fragile, inasmuch as they existed at the sufferance of a master who could disrupt them in a moment through sale of a family member. Still, in its unique form, the African-American family in slavery was the premier institution that helped create and pass along the African-American culture.

One of the points Gutman makes that tells the most about the lives African Americans led in bondage is his statement on the cyclical nature of the slave family and community. These cycles were tied to the economic turns and natural occurrences of the slaves' owners and their families. They were operant, perhaps in even more dramatic fashion than Gutman states, in the years during which the sale and forced movement of slaves was growing to a peak—that is, through the first third of the nineteenth century.

According to Gutman, one cycle consisted of three general phases—destruction, construction, and dispersal. In the destruction phase, a farmer or planter on the economic rise would purchase individual laborers needed to begin or enhance his enterprise. He would do so without regard to the slaves' family situation. "Breeding" women, "likely" children, prime hands—all were the human stuff that appealed to the owner of a growing agricultural concern. Men and women, children, adolescents, and young adults would have to leave their families or communities forever and take up residence elsewhere with African Americans they had never seen.

The construction phase would begin in the new location, where, to serve his interests, the master would encourage family ties among his slaves. Over time adults would find spouses, on or off the plantation, and would begin new families. If the master prospered, the family might remain together for a number of years. On large plantations or in the neighborhood of smaller ones, a group of slaves might even experience "kinship imbeddedness"—family relationships extending broadly enough to link most members of the group, while the marriage framework would remain exogamous. Barring the unforseen, which could include a severe economic downturn experienced by an owner, an especially good price offered for a slave by a speculator, or the untimely death of a master, slave families and communities could achieve a high level of permanence and stability.

The stability would be shattered eventually, however, when the planter's situation changed. Masters might decide to make gifts of slaves to sons or daughters heading off to begin adult life on their own. And when masters died, the result often was division of the estate and separate sale of the human property. The dispersal would again destroy the slave family and community. In a number of different locations the slaves then would begin again the construction phase of a new cycle. Sometimes, of course, because of a sequence of early deaths of masters or unexpected sales of family members, the cycles were compacted, resulting in much briefer periods of family stability. And even the most stable slave families were forever on edge over the possibility of family disruption.

The experiences of Charles Ball show how the cycles of family and community operated. When he was born in the early 1780s, Ball's mother lived on a plantation near Leonardtown in St. Mary's County, Maryland. His father lived on a neighboring plantation and visited his wife and several children on Saturday nights and Sundays, bringing them small gifts and extra provisions. But when Ball was four, his master died. To settle the estate, all the slaves were sold at auction. Ball's mother was sold to a "Georgia trader"; every one of his siblings was sold separately and taken out of state, but Ball, who was purchased by a local tobacco planter, remained in Maryland. His father, once "of a gay, social temper," turned gloomy and morose over the loss of nearly all of his family. When he learned that his master was readying to sell him because of his noticeable change of temperament, Ball's father ran away. Still a young child, Ball found himself with only one relative, his eighty-year-old grandfather, in the same state.

The first construction phase of Ball's life thus began earlier than it did for many slaves. He narrates little about these years, and one gets the idea that he worked hard, was obedient, and was punished infrequently. He had difficulty mainly in getting enough food to sate his adolescent appetite. He was taken from his community for two years in his late teens when he was "hired out" to work on a frigate in the Washington, D.C., Navy Yard, but he found a community there and seemed to enjoy the ambience and relative freedom of the city. Then, abruptly, he returned to southern Maryland and was sold to a Mr. Gibson on a nearby Calvert County farm. Some time after arriving at his new home, Ball began a family of his own by marrying a slave woman who served as chambermaid on a neighboring plantation. Like his father, Ball visited his wife and, before long, his children as frequently as his circumstances would allow, providing such things as he could for their livelihood and pleasure. Even his transferral to another farmer in the neighborhood did not disrupt his close family ties, for his new owner lived still closer to Ball's wife and children. Over less than two decades, then, it seems that Ball had overcome the devastating family separation of his youth. By his early twenties he was living with his African-American family and participating in a larger slave community, within a few miles of his birthplace.

But Ball's enjoyment of his family and community in Maryland came to an abrupt end in 1805 when his master, for reasons that are not clear in the narrative, took him to the bank of the Patuxent River and sold him to a slave trader. Despite his pleas, Ball was not allowed to return home for a last time or to see his wife and children. "[I] was told that I would be able to get another wife in Georgia," he relates. Instead, he was taken across the river in a scow, joined by iron collar and chain to thirty-two other black men in a group that included nineteen women, and marched southward. For four weeks and five days the coffle hiked. Interestingly, persons in the coffle developed close community ties during the march—to the point that when two women were sold away from the gang, Ball's "heart bled" for them and the women "wept aloud" in parting. Not until he crossed the

South Carolina border did Ball see cotton growing for the first time in his life. He would see more. Following the five-hundred-mile trek, Ball was given twenty days of rest and better food than he had been given while on the march to improve his appearance for sale. He was sold in Columbia on the Fourth of July to General Wade Hampton, one of South Carolina's wealthiest planters, owner of over one thousand acres and producer in 1810 of six hundred bales of cotton.

Remarkably resilient, Ball again began to construct ties to a slave community—Hampton owned several hundred slaves—among people he did not know. He moved in with a plantation slave family of seven that lived in one cabin and soon began contributing his rations to the family food supply. He worked with a gang in the fields of cotton, rice, indigo, corn, and potatoes; he added to "family provisions" through gardening, gathering, and trapping; he secretly (but unsuccessfully) assisted a not-yet-fully assimilated African in divesting himself of an iron collar received for running away. Through the narrative one gets an impression that, without much fanfare or waiting, Ball's construction phase within the slave community on Hampton's plantation was short and smooth. Within months he was an accepted and functioning member. Full family construction would take longer, longer than Ball had.

Another dispersal phase in the cycle came to Ball after some months of relative comfort with the African Americans on the large South Carolina plantation. One of Hampton's daughters married a man of small means who did not own land in the state. The man decided to move to the newly opened, inexpensive land to the west, in Georgia, and begin his own cotton farm. To assist the couple, Hampton gave his daughter a dozen slaves, one of whom was Ball. For the next two years Ball lived and worked among a much smaller number of African Americans in a younger and less-stable community on the cotton frontier in Georgia.

Ball's narrative here takes a turn that deviates from the stories of most, but one that further adds to the cycle of destruction, construction, and dispersal. Ball escaped from slavery in Georgia over the fall and winter of 1806–07, leaving one slave community and returning to another, his former family in Maryland. Ball lived as a free person (albeit a fugitive from slavery) in Maryland. He remarried after the death of his first wife and became a successful farmer and small landowner near Baltimore. But after eighteen years of living with his new family, he was finally captured and returned to Georgia. Ball escaped again, only to find upon his return to Maryland that his wife and children had been captured and sold to slave traders in his absence. He ceased the narrative after he had moved to Pennsylvania, where he was to live out his life with yet another family in another African-American community.

Ball's life in slavery did consist of a series of cycles like those Gutman describes, some longer and more complete and some shorter. That the family structure survived and remained a cohesive force in African-American culture through the time of the early republic is as remarkable as is the story of Ball's regular separation and movement and his never-ending ability to reconstruct personal ties to different communities throughout his nearly half century in slavery.

Christianity Among Slaves

Given the situation in which Africans came to America—the harsh uprooting and transplanting, under difficult conditions, in an alien culture—and the subordinate relationship they were forced into with white Americans, many of whom were Christian, it is not surprising that African Americans adopted a form of Christianity. What is surprising is that it took so long for them to do so. The conversion of slaves to Christianity was a gradual, and thus not always particularly noticeable, process. "From the moment they arrived in America and began to toil as slaves," writes Eugene D. Genovese in *Roll, Jordan, Roll: The World the Slaves Made* (1972),

> they could not help absorbing the religion of the master class. But, the conditions of their new social life forced them to combine their African inheritance with the dominant power they confronted and to shape a religion of their own.

This shaping of a distinct religion and the ultimate conversion to and practice of an African-American form of Christianity took place over a long time. By the late eighteenth century, a good portion of the American slave population was practicing some form of the

Christian religion. But Christianity spread widely and deeply among African-American men and women in bondage in the years immediately following the turn of the nineteenth century.

When Africans first arrived in the British colonies of the North American mainland, their white masters regarded them as "outlandish"—so culturally and linguistically different as to be unsuited for most European ways, including Christianity. The longer slaves retained African customs (and the longer the Atlantic trade introduced more unacculturated Africans to perpetuate these customs), the less apt masters were to urge slaves to convert. Through the late seventeenth and early eighteenth centuries this had a ring of convenience, for to control the "outlandish" population, outlandish punishments were often necessary—punishments that were more severe than one ought to mete out to a "fellow Christian" of whatever physical appearance.

By the middle of the eighteenth century, however, two phenomena were underway that worked to accelerate the process of converting slaves to Christianity. On one hand, the number of American-born slaves was growing rapidly, evening sex ratios, increasing the number of blacks living with their families, and making it possible to identify, at least in hindsight, an early form of a separate, distinct African-American culture. Living in slightly more stable groups, adult slaves became increasingly desirous of having a more formal religious foundation for their families in order to regularize rites of passage such as birth, marriage, and death and to pass along to the young the important elements of their culture. On the other hand, the Great Awakening, an evangelical movement that was sweeping through the middle colonies of mainland North America, began exposing blacks and whites alike to Christianity in its most vivid and (for some) most alluring form. Many aspects of the evangelical religion—the exhorting, shouting, singing, physical movement, and group participation—were amenable to African Americans, for religious practices across a broad expanse of their West African homelands contained these elements. Thus, by the time of the American Revolution, a good portion of the mainland slave population was beginning to accept Christianity and to practice the religion in its own, distinct way.

Setting the stage for the much wider conversion of slaves was a second evangelical movement, the Great Revival, or Second Great Awakening, of the first decade of the nineteenth century. Beginning in the Cumberland region of Kentucky in 1800, this wave of camp meetings and revivalist religion captured the attention of persons across the rural South and spread with unprecedented speed. It moved quickly into the same regions in which plantation slavery was growing—backcountry South Carolina, the interior of Georgia, and settled portions of Mississippi Territory. For whites and blacks alike, in the areas of disruptive population movement and spreading cotton agriculture, revival meetings lit the night and awakened the populations to the prospects of conversion and salvation. Eventually the evangelical fervor became institutionalized in hundreds of new churches of the relatively new Baptist, Methodist, and Presbyterian denominations. African-American slaves fell to their knees alongside whites and converted at camp meetings, met in services with whites, and even signed documents inaugurating new churches. Conversion to Christianity, which had been an idea in the wind through the southern states at the close of the Revolution, came on like a gale in the nineteenth century's first decades.

It is not possible to determine the proportion of African Americans who became Christians during the first three decades of the nineteenth century. Conversion was widespread, especially among blacks living in or close to towns or cities. Slaves living nearest their masters—domestics and skilled slaves—were the most likely to convert first and to attend church with their masters. For every black who joined a church (and left a record of it), it seems that many more attended Christian services and considered themselves to be Christians. Records of African-American preachers, slave as well as free, in black and mixed congregations, are commonplace from the early nineteenth century, and there were many slave preachers on plantations whose activities never received mention in the record books.

Rural slaves were more apt than their urban counterparts to remain outside the organized church, for there seem to have been lingering obstacles to their conversion. One such obstacles was the simple reluctance of a good number of masters to have their slaves become Christians. Two fears fostered this attitude. One was the fear of rebellion. Rightly or wrongly, masters thought that slave rebellions often had a grounding in religion. Gabriel's rebellion, which Virginia slaves had planned to carry off in late August of 1800 (just two months after the camp meeting on the Gasper River in Kentucky that served as the catalyst for the Great Revival), was planned after religious meetings; a majority of the slaves executed following Denmark Vesey's conspiracy in Charleston in 1822 were members of the city's African Methodist Episcopal Church; and Nat Turner, who led the nation's most famous slave rebellion, in southern Virginia in 1831, was himself a preacher who saw omens and signs connected with his religion that urged him to lead a rebellion. Since it was possible in many planters' minds to link slaves' conversion to Christianity to their aptness to become more rebellious, many masters felt that their slaves could do without the Gospel.

The other fear was of abolition. A sense of egalitarianism pervaded the minds of the early evangelicals and brought many of them to condemn slavery. Baptists, Methodists, and Presbyterians with the greatest religious fervor had difficulty giving up their antislavery sentiments, and until they did, southern masters remained intransigent about slave conversions. Through the first two decades of the nineteenth century, though, most evangelicals gradually backed away from their strident antislavery attitudes. Eventually they argued that it was better to get access to slaves and convert them (and thus improve blacks' lives in slavery) than to continue to denounce slavery and never reach the slaves at all. In time, the evangelicals not only accepted slavery, but argued to masters that conversion made the slaves more docile by their subjection to the discipline of the church.

Another obstacle to slave conversion, one that is probably the most important, yet the most easily overlooked—especially with so much focus placed on the master's will rather than the slave's—was the latter's perception of Christians. The early republic was a time of growing slave sales, of the splitting of African-American families, of cold business calculations that often had painful effects for the slaves. And masters condoned and practiced harsh punishment of slaves. Many of the persons doing these things to the slaves were persons who professed to be Christians, and the slaves seem to have nurtured long memories. More than a few African Americans who witnessed the conversion or the regular religious practice of their masters must have questioned the appropriateness of the new evangelical religions for themselves. Some had even stronger views of Christianity because of whites' cruelty. Frederick Douglass never made bones about his thoughts of Christianity and what religion did to slave owners. "I assert most unhesitatingly," wrote Douglass in his famous *Narrative of the Life of Frederick Douglass, An American Slave* (1845),

> that the religion of the south is a mere covering for the most horrid crimes,—a justifier of the most appalling barbarity,—a sanctifier of the most hateful frauds,—and a dark shelter under which the darkest, foulest, grossest, and most infernal deeds of slaveholders find the strongest protection. Were I to be again reduced to the chains of slavery, next to that enslavement, I should regard being the slave of a religious master the greatest calamity that could befall me. For of all slaveholders with whom I have ever met, religious slaveholders are the worst. I have ever found them the meanest and basest, the most cruel and cowardly, of all others. It was my unhappy lot not only to belong to a religious slaveholder, but to live in a community of such religionists.

Thus, while the Great Revival no doubt led to more widespread slave conversions, what it did that turned out to be of greater importance over the long run of African-American history was to spread the evangelical churches throughout the southern population. These Baptist, Methodist, and Presbyterian churches, established by blacks and whites throughout the South early in the nineteenth century, would be the major vehicles for converting the biggest group of plantation slaves after 1830. Through the three decades before the Civil War, more slave owners themselves converted and more of them desired conversion of those they held in bondage. They came to believe all the more strongly that a proper form of Christianity, which set out duties of master and duties of slave, would bring about a sense of mutual obligation that would result in an orderly society. The spread of churches in the first part of the century led to the much broader spread of Christianity among slaves in the years before the Civil War.

It is difficult to tell how much of an underground black church existed across the slave states early in nineteenth-century America. Slaves, of course, did not confine their thoughts and feelings about religion to church services, and they may well have congregated by themselves in order to listen exclusively to their own preachers and sing in their style. But if there was a substantial "invisible institution" (as Albert J. Raboteau calls the slaves' underground church in *Slave Religion: The "Invisible Institution" in the Antebellum South* (1978)) across the South, it was largely a phenomenon of later times, when more rural slaves who were Christians lived together in larger numbers and thus found separate congregation possible as well as spiritually and psychologically rewarding.

Thus, what Boles writes in *Black Southerners* seems particularly pertinent to the early decades of the nineteenth century: "Historians have sufficiently recognized neither the role of the slave in the so-called white churches nor the role of those churches in the lives of slaves." If slave participation in organized church activities began in the middle of the eighteenth century, it was in the time of the early republic that this shared experience became common. Black slaves made up sizable proportions of many southern Baptist and Methodist churches. These biracial congregations sang together, listened to the same sermons, took communion together, watched one another be baptized and confirmed, and even shared burial grounds in ways that would have shocked white southerners a century later. All was not equal, of course. Segregated seating prevailed, and sometimes blacks were allowed, or encouraged, to have separate buildings for their own autonomous worship services. But slaves assumed positions of leadership in certain churches and blacks and whites alike were held to the moral standards of the congregation.

There was latitude in religious practice, and it was within broad bounds provided by the church that African Americans framed their own form of Christianity and thus had a unique, Afro-Christian religious experience. Mechal Sobel in *Trabelin' On: The Slave Journey to an Afro-Baptist Faith* (1979) explains how over scores of years in slavery African Americans preserved basic concepts of a West-African world view and melded them with the views of American Christianity, in this case Baptism, to create an "Afro-Christian Sacred Cosmos." According to Sobel, enslaved blacks held onto an African concept of there being part of a supreme spirit in each person. Once the melding of African and Christian views had taken place, the spirit in the African American "could go home to Jesus and find him sitting in a green field surrounded by lambs 'mourning' a neo-African dirge and shouting and dancing in a neo-African religious drama."

Some expressions of African-American Christianity were more "African" than others. Special variants of slave religious practices that tended to catch the eyes of historians and others existed on the Sea Islands of South Carolina and Georgia and in the sugar-producing areas of Louisiana, where there were fewer whites to participate with blacks in services. Noted Africanisms in religious practices in these areas included conjuring, witchcraft, and, around New Orleans, magic, which many referred to as voodoo or hoodoo, and a mix of dancing and shouting during worship.

But generally worship services in these early, mixed southern churches were more standard, if not less emotional. Worship was almost always fervent, preaching was emotional, singing was participatory and joyful. This is not because such was the style of the white evangelists. The cultural borrowing that went on passed in both directions. The image one holds of white southern Christianity—of emotional exhortation; of congregations standing, moving, shouting, and singing; of spiritual possession and encounters with God or the devil; even of spiritual death and rebirth to bring about heightened religious feeling, may have a heritage that rests as much upon what African Americans brought to influence the white evangelicals as what Euro-Americans began with several centuries ago.

CHAPTER THREE

An Age of Slave Unrest

Neither the British colonies on mainland North America nor the United States thereafter was the scene of regular, large-scale slave insurrections or rebellions. This is different from the experience in much of the rest of the Americas, where slave uprisings were more frequent and on a grander scale. Reasons for this difference are many. Unlike in Latin America and the Caribbean, blacks almost everywhere in the United States were outnumbered by whites, they worked under the direct supervision of whites in a white milieu, and they were separated from groups of African Americans on other farms or plantations by longer distances across which travel and communication were difficult. The physical geography of the United States did not provide as many unsettled, mountainous, or swampy havens nearby where runaways could gather, organize, and defend themselves, or from where they could launch marauding expeditions. Furthermore, working conditions in the United States, however unpleasant, were not so harsh as on Caribbean islands and lands southward; the influx of young, male, rebellious Africans with little to lose was not nearly so heavy or concentrated in the United States; and by the middle of the eighteenth century, many slaves in the United States were living with and caring for families that would suffer mightily as the result of any failed insurrection. The upshot of it all was that, north of the Caribbean, organized slave rebellions were relatively infrequent and seldom got beyond the planning stages before they were detected. Then, repression was swift.

But it would be incorrect to think necessarily of African-American slaves in English-speaking North America as abnormally docile. They resisted their bondage in a variety of ways over the two centuries and more of the institution's existence, and in certain periods their resistance had important effects on the country's history. The time of the early republic was one of particularly widespread and significant slave unrest. It was unrest manifested in more than the usual number of conspiracies and rebellions among the African-American slaves, on scales greater than ever before or after. In the third of a century following the massive slave rebellion on the French island of Saint Domingue in the Caribbean, the United States experienced its largest, most thoroughly planned, and most violent slave conspiracies and uprisings—Gabriel's plot around Richmond, Charles Deslondes's uprising northwest of New Orleans, Denmark Vesey's plot in Charleston, and Nat Turner's fierce rebellion in Southampton County, Virginia. It was unrest manifested also in a number of lesser-known but almost equally significant insurrections, what many whites considered to be the widespread growth of "insolence" among the African-American population, and increasing incidence of slaves running away. By the 1830s, when antebellum slavery was coming into full flower, African Americans constituted for white southerners what Kenneth Stampp in *The Peculiar Institution: Slavery in the Antebellum South* (1956) calls "a troublesome property."

Like so much that happened afterwards, the heightened slave unrest during the period of the early republic had causes lying in the American Revolution. Before the 1770s, slave society in the British mainland colonies was maturing nicely in the eyes of British colonials. There were enough slaves to make the tobacco and rice plantations productive from Maryland south to Georgia, with more slaves to come from Africa if needed, and slave society was about as stable as a society in which some humans hold others in bondage could be. Planters realized that newly arrived Africans commonly went through a fractious period during which they were apt to run off short distances and spend several days as "outliers." Sharp punishment made them aware of the futility of such actions. Many of them still would acculturate more slowly than their masters would have wished. But by the time white colonists were working up a strong animosity toward the mother country, many African Americans were already one or more generations removed from their African heritage, had acquired English, were practicing a culture that was a useful blending of African and English ways, and were living with families and surrounded by members of larger kinship groups. In the main, such resistance to slavery that occurred was institutional—it appeared in the form of shoddy work, feigned illnesses, broken tools, or simple malingering.

The Revolutionary era brought considerable change to America's slave society. The ideology supporting the struggle was an important factor. American colonists justified severing ties with Great Britain by purporting the Enlightenment idea that all men are created equal and have rights to the blessings of liberty merely by the fact of their creation. Did "all men" include Americans of African descent? Many northerners thought so and thus began the long process of ending slavery in their section of the country. Some southerners did, too, so from the 1770s on there appeared growing numbers of free blacks—slaves who had been manumitted—amidst the large slave population, especially in the Upper South. But a larger number of southern planters and farmers did not believe African Americans were a part of the body of all men. Slavery was at the heart of their economic prosperity and social status. They would not emancipate away their well-being. The British Governor of Virginia, Lord Dunmore, played on the slaves' desire for liberty during the Revolutionary War by offering them immediate freedom for joining the British ranks and fighting against the rebellious colonists. Hundreds of them did, and many more joined the British at later stages of the Revolution. Though the colonists won and slavery remained a part of American life in most of the states of the new country, African Americans were never the same after encountering the natural-rights philosophy. For many African Americans, freedom had become more than something good to obtain: it was something one had a right to expect.

Heightening black people's growing contempt for living in bondage in the United States were revolutionary activities of the Third Estate in France and of African-American slaves in the Caribbean. Rising expectations generated by the French Revolution were affecting blacks across the Atlantic. The National Assembly in Paris was not thinking of French slaves when it declared in August 1789, "All men are born and remain free and equal in rights," but persons of African descent on French islands in the Caribbean got wind of the *Declaration of Rights of Man and Citizen* and believed it should apply to them. When French colonial, slave-trading, and planter interests blocked any extension of rights, even to the free people of color on the French island of Saint Domingue, black slaves on the island rose in revolt. Eventually under the leadership of François Domingue Toussaint L'Ouverture, a literate and skilled bondsman, slave forces attacked and slaughtered whites on the island, then fought against troops from various French governments, a British expeditionary force, and the island's free blacks through the 1790s. In 1800 Napoleon Bonaparte, with his eyes on a slave-based New-World French empire that included the recently acquired mainland territory of Louisiana, sent thousands of French soldiers to subdue the Saint Domingue rebels, but the blacks' guerrilla tactics and the yellow fever of the tropical island destroyed the emperor's army and with it his imperial plans. Napoleon sold Louisiana to the United States in the spring of 1803 for a song—fifteen million dollars. In the fall of the same year, the few remaining French soldiers on Saint Domingue sailed back to France in defeat, and the former French slaves, now successful revolutionaries themselves, proclaimed the Republic of Haiti on January 1, 1804.

Refugees from both sides of the war on Saint Domingue trickled into the United States through the decade of the 1790s. A French fleet brought a large group of their supporters from the island to southern coastal cities following the slave forces' sacking of Cap François in June 1793, and the numbers of refugees increased steadily thereafter. Their stories of the horribly bloody uprising not so far to the south of the new country's primary slave states brought fear to many a slave owner. South Carolina Governor Charles Pinckney recognized "that a day may arrive when [the southern states] may be exposed to the same insurrection." With the heaviest concentration of slaves in the country, South Carolinians had more reason than others to fear the "cancer of revolution." The state kept its ports closed to blacks "from Africa, the West India Islands, or other places beyond the sea" until the Haitian Revolution had ended. Southern congressmen pressed President John Adams to commit himself to using the federal army in case of any slave uprising.

But news of the slave rebellion on Saint Domingue had more telling effects on African-American slaves in the United States than on their owners. Philip S. Foner in the first volume of his *History of Black Americans* (1975) brings together evidence of growing pride, self-reliance, and restiveness in the country's slave population that suggests word of the rebellion reached and moved many an American slave. One Virginian noted that the growing insolence of slaves was "common talk on the court Green, particularly since the arrival of the French from C F [Cap François, Saint Domingue]." Virginian John Randolph overheard two of his slaves plotting among themselves, one saying to the other, "You heard how the blacks has killed the whites on the French Island and took it a little while ago." Thomas Jefferson summed up the situation when he wrote, "The course of things in the neighboring islands of the West Indies appeared to have given considerable impulse to the minds of slaves in different parts of the United States. A great disposition to insurgency has manifested itself among them. . . ."

Collective insolence turned into insurgency on a number of occasions. The 1790s experienced two and one-half times as many slave revolts as the previous decade. African-American blacksmiths were caught making spears; slaves were discovered harboring guns, lead, and powder; urban blacks were tried for arson; and throughout the country there was a general feeling of unrest among the slaves and disquiet over the possible effects of the mutually contradictory issues of natural rights and human bondage.

Underlying the growing insurgent spirit of American blacks were important economic and social developments. The Revolution drew the American colonies into an economic crisis. With imports and exports reduced for nearly a decade, the economy of English-speaking North America shifted at least temporarily from its overriding export focus to one concentrating more on small-scale manufacturing, artisanship, and commerce. Towns grew, there were welcome opportunities in these towns for tradesmen, local markets lured persons in from the surrounding countryside—in short, there were opportunities in urban areas that simply had not existed before the 1770s.

This economic upheaval affected slave owners. Geared for export crop production but suddenly sapped of an export market, southern planters had to put their slaves to other tasks. Some changed crops—from tobacco to comestible wheat in the Chesapeake, for instance—or engaged slaves in trades or home industries. When masters no longer needed so many slaves on their plantations, they "hired out" the surplus laborers or let them hire themselves in the new markets for artisanal skills. More slaves with better and broader skills began to appear, especially in and around the urban areas. As they existed away from their owner's farm or plantation, interacting with larger numbers of people, these African Americans further developed social and cultural skills that enabled them to function more effectively in the broader society. One might encounter black boatmen guiding vessels up and down rivers and canals, African-American blacksmiths manning forges beside heavily traveled roads, or slave carpenters working on ships or buildings along the waterfront. In spite of white fears and increasingly stringent state laws regulating slave behavior, practicality prevailed. Thus, for some, the bonds of slavery were loosened.

Some African Americans flourished in the more open, urban milieu. Their associations with other slaves, with free blacks, and with white tradesmen broadened considerably; a number became literate and increasingly aware of what was going on in the town, the city, the state, and the budding nation. As they came to understand their position in relation to other slaves, they recognized that they were of the privileged few in bondage. But as they grew to understand their position in relation to other humans, they saw more clearly than ever the rigid boundaries of slave life. And as they read and listened to the libertarian ideas that remained popular in post-Revolutionary America, they became less enchanted with their lives as privileged slaves and more inclined to want the freedom that was theirs by right, but that, as they judged, was not likely to come with anything approaching speed. As the end of the eighteenth century approached, the relatively new class of urban, acculturated, skilled, capable, and informed African Americans made up a restless group, some of whom might be inspired to begin or to expedite the process of ending the institution that separated them from their white counterparts and denied them the fundamental "rights of man."

Such was the case around Richmond, Virginia. It was there that in 1800 a group of skilled African Americans, aware of the freedoms implied by the American Revolution and of the freedom slaves had gained by force in the West Indies, disgusted by their situation in bondage—however much better it might have been than others—and no longer satisfied with merely using their abilities and guile to live in a quasi-free environment, conceived what Virginia Governor James Monroe described in a letter to Jefferson as "unquestionably the most serious and formidable conspiracy, we have ever known of the kind."

Gabriel's Plot

In several counties bordering Virginia's capital city of Richmond, and in the city of six thousand residents itself at the beginning of the nineteenth century, a group of slave artisans (blacksmiths, coopers, weavers, carpenters, shoemakers, and tanners) moved about with minimal restriction. Many hired their own time and worked on contracts of various lengths in the city, often side-by-side with white craftsmen. The slaves saw one another in their shops and on the streets, congregated at festivals, met at boat landings, and drank spirits together and talked in grog shops. Some of them were literate, and a growing number of them were aware of the important social and political issues of the day. They knew of the coming presidential election in the fall of 1800, hotly contested in Richmond, Petersburg, and Norfolk, all small Federalist islands in the Republican sea of Virginia. They probably spoke with some anger of the merchants in Richmond, who doled out work sparingly to the city's artisans as they tried to keep skilled wages low and prices of raw materials high, often taking advantage of the hired-out slave craftsmen who had little recourse of action when cheated. They almost certainly talked about their discontent in bondage and their hostility toward those who kept them there. Although they were about as free to come and go as persons in bondage could be, they remained slaves.

Over a period of several months, beginning perhaps as early as April of 1800, some of these relatively privileged slaves began to talk of organizing an uprising. Who first hatched the idea is unclear—it may not have been a single person so much as loose talk that took root in the fertile minds of several people—but slaves on the plantation of William Young, six miles northeast of Richmond, were involved in the earliest stages. Ben Woolfolk, a slave hired out to Young that summer, learned of the plot while he was chopping wood. A slave who was "recruiting" for the conspiracy, George Smith, emerged from the woods and asked Woolfolk if he wished to join "a society to fight the white people for [our] freedom." Once Woolfolk agreed, he was introduced to other conspirators over subsequent weeks. These included Jack Ditcher (sometimes called Jack Bowler), an imposing hired-out bondsman, six-feet-five-inches tall with long hair; several men like Smith, who were actively traveling about and recruiting; and three brothers who ran a blacksmith's shop on Thomas Prosser's Brookfield plantation in Henrico County—Solomon, Martin, and Gabriel.*

Gabriel was not around Prosser's plantation all that much. He did not care for his master nor, it seems, did he care for one of the plantation's neighbors. In 1799 Gabriel and his brother Solomon got into a spat over a stolen hog with neighbor Absalom Johnson, and Gabriel ended up "biting off a considerable portion of [Johnson's] left ear." For this he spent a month in jail and was branded with a "T" at the base of his left thumb. If Gabriel was hard to manage, his master may have been happy to permit him to hire out a portion of his own time, most of which Gabriel spent doing blacksmith work in Rich-

* There is no evidence that Gabriel used the surname Prosser. Records from the time refer to him as "Prosser's Gabriel." I refer to him here only as Gabriel to avoid giving him a last name that he likely did not want.

mond. It was there, Douglas R. Egerton suggests in "Gabriel's Conspiracy and the Election of 1800," *Journal of Southern History*, 56 (1990), that Gabriel grew dissatisfied with the merchants of the city, began to feel a sense of solidarity with the city's other artisans, white and black, and probably began to consider the chances of waging a successful strike for freedom and equality in the workplace in the disorganized, poorly prepared, and politically divided capital.

If the rebellion was not Gabriel's brainchild from the beginning—he told his brother that he had first heard of the conspiracy from Ditcher—he nevertheless became its leader, its tactician and strategist. Gerald F. Mullin in *Flight and Rebellion: Slave Resistance in Eighteenth-Century Virginia* (1972) argues that Gabriel won the position at the head of the rebellion because of good leadership and managerial skills. "Because he was able to make decisions, delegate responsibilities, and pursue routine tasks to their completion in order to avert the strong possibility of disaster," Mullin writes, "the rebellion came to be his." But Egerton believes that Gabriel became the leader also because he, as a man aware of his class and its position in the political and economic milieu of Virginia in 1800, had the clear idea of how urban slaves might get rural slaves to rise up, how the leadership of Virginia might be forced to concede the slaves' freedom, and how the conspirators might be able to use the contemporary Federalist-Republican split to their advantage. If all this was so, Gabriel was astute indeed.

But whatever the plot's origin, for several months in the spring of 1800, across half a dozen counties and into the several cities in the region, recruiters sidled up to urban and artisan slaves whom they believed they could trust and invited them to learn more about their plans. Slave boatmen became effective recruiters; black post riders carried the message up and down the roads; slaves working on canal projects and in Virginia's coal pits were induced to join. Lists of names the leaders could count on grew through July and August.

The plan that Gabriel finally settled upon was more of a coup than a revolution, though with success of the coup Gabriel believed the revolution would be at hand. At midnight a force of some two hundred slaves, armed with clubs, knives, and a handful of guns, would meet at a bridge six miles outside of Richmond. Because few of the insurgents knew even the slightest bit about military operations, Gabriel hoped that a Frenchman who lived in Caroline County would join them and serve as "commander and manager" through the first day. The force would storm Richmond under a banner reading "Death or Liberty," setting fire to the city's sprawling tobacco warehouses, killing whites they encountered (except for Quakers, Methodists, and French people, whom they considered "friends of liberty," and poor women who owned no slaves), capturing the capitol where they hoped to obtain firearms and take Governor Monroe hostage. Once this occurred, Gabriel hoped one of two things would happen. Either the white leadership would be so stunned as to accede to the conspirators' demands for freedom or, failing that, hundreds or thousands of slaves in the surrounding countryside, once aware of the sensational actions of the few, would join and become the many. Then the revolution might indeed become unstoppable.

What we know of these plans comes largely from the records of the trials of the conspirators, for the simple reason that no part of the plan was put into action. The insurgents who were to assemble on Saturday night, August 30, found it impossible to do so. It had begun raining heavily Saturday noon and the downpour continued into the night. Streams ran over their banks, bridges washed away, roads became impassible and communications were cut. Gabriel postponed the attack until the following night. In the meantime, a few slaves broke their silence on the conspiracy, and word soon reached the governor in Richmond. Once he realized the potential of the plan (and perhaps became aware of his own fate in the operation at the same time), Monroe directed a sweeping, systematic roundup of the conspirators. Within a few days the state had arrested several score of suspects among the slave population in and around Richmond and a few more in neighboring cities. Following trials, twenty-seven African Americans were executed by hanging, twelve were acquitted, and seven were pardoned. Gabriel was among those hanged, but not before coming close to escaping. A white ship master on the James River carried the conspiracy's leader down toward Norfolk, but two slave crewmen recognized Gabriel from earlier contacts and brought authorities on board to seize him. He went quietly, said little at his trial, and faced his execution before the month of September was out.

Was it truly "the most serious and formidable conspiracy" the country had yet known? This is difficult to answer, given that commitments to the leaders were oral and probably vague, that the conspirators did not keep careful records, that numbers were often exaggerated to aid recruitment, and that no insurgents ever assembled as was planned. Trial testimony does suggest that word of the conspiracy reached selected slaves a long distance from Richmond. Apparently there were some African Americans who had been ready to act in some fashion once word of Gabriel's initial assault on Richmond arrived in Norfolk and Petersburg. One recruiter made a foray to Charlottesville, sixty-five miles away from Richmond, and claimed to find slaves there "very willing to join." Three weeks before the rebellion was to commence, at a recruitment gathering, Gabriel announced that he had ten thousand men at the ready. Ten days later his brother Solomon estimated their potential force at three thousand, and the night before the fateful rendezvous was to take place Gabriel's wife, Nanny, said "that 1000 Men were to meet her husband near Prosser's Tavern the ensuing Night." The number of committed conspirators, at least for the first night's action, was probably fewer still.

Mullin, whose 1972 book remains one of the most important works on slave resistance, believes Gabriel understood and accepted that he had a small number of followers and limited resources. Those committed to the conspiracy and sustained by the idea of it were the skilled slaves like Gabriel who, no longer content merely with their relatively advantaged position in bondage, wanted to end slavery altogether. The larger number of African Americans around Richmond, men with fewer skills and less freedom to come and go, were more cautious than their more assimilated brethren. For them, the ideology of revolution and the real possibility of dying for freedom did not hold the same glamour. If they had volunteered to join the insurrection at a mass meeting, or even when pressed individually, their words were empty of commitment. Gabriel knew, argues Mullin, "that unless he struck suddenly, sensationally, and decisively—

presenting slaves as well as free men with a *fait accompli*—there would be no mass uprising." He believed that his core of committed slaves, familiar with the urban scene if not with military tactics, could pull off the bold, initial strike and in that way capture the interest of the rural slaves.

But why did Gabriel believe that fewer than two hundred men could so thoroughly terrorize Richmond in such a short time? A good part of the reason, Egerton believes, is that he was tuned into what was going on in the state capital at the time. He knew that most artisans were as bothered as he by the merchants exploiting them and by the inability of good skilled craftsmen to make decent money with their work. He thus believed that even those urban people of his class, white or black, who would not take up with the rebellion from the start would at least be supportive by refusing to join in fighting to squelch the movement. Moreover, he could not help but to be aware of the fierce and divisive Federalist-Republican debate that was taking place at the time. There were fears that the presidential election of 1800 would result in civil war. Gabriel naturally sided with the Republicans. He saw his struggle for liberty and economic rights as fitting perfectly into Republican ideology, and thus probably expected the Republicans with whom he was familiar—the white artisans, primarily—to appreciate his cause. A major mistake was never recognizing that there were Republican planters outside the narrow confines of Richmond and its environs, who held property in general and slavery in particular more dear than they did liberty. "[Gabriel] simply failed to recognize," writes Egerton, "that the Jeffersonian cry for liberty and equality was meant to apply to whites only."

Governor Monroe and other white officials in Virginia and outside the state were careful not to make sensational statements about the plot. They hoped to avoid widespread panic among the larger white population. But their efforts to instill calm and reassurance to Virginia's whites were in vain. Merton L. Dillon in *Slavery Attacked: Southern Slaves and Their Allies, 1619–1865* (1990) writes, "The mood in parts of Virginia from 1800 to 1802 strikingly resembled the Great Fear that swept rural France only a dozen years earlier, terrorizing the populace with the delusion that 'the brigands' were coming." No doubt fueled by the bloodletting on Saint Domingue, slave owners began to believe that their ordinary bondsmen, long a peaceable group in their eyes, could wax ruthless and ferocious without much provocation. When they did, there would not be much military force around the state to meet them. Thus, the state and its cities took action. Within months of the execution of the conspirators, Virginia enacted a law restricting the movement of slaves and free blacks. Richmond quickly established a sixty-eight-man Public Guard with an officer corps and its own band. Some Virginia whites wanted to attack what they saw as the roots of the problem—libertarians (including at various times Jeffersonians, Jacobins, evangelicals, Quakers, and abolitionists), whom they wished to silence, and free blacks, whom they wished to colonize somewhere across the seas.

But some of those not jumping to arms thought about the issue more deeply. More important than the new laws (which, as ever, might soon fall victim to a lack of enforcement) or the uniformed guards were the refined outlooks of at least some white slave owners on the men and women whom they kept in bondage. Gabriel's conspiracy had highlighted for them the inconsistencies in their position and pointed toward problems of the future with a clarity sharpened by fear. Virginian St. George Tucker wrote during the trials of the conspirators,

> These, our hewers of wood and drawers of water, possess the power of doing us mischief, and are prompted to it by motives which self-love dictates, which reason justifies. Our solid security, then, consists in their ignorance of this power, and their means of using it—a security which we have lately found is not to be relied on, and which, small as it is, every day diminishes. Every year adds to the number of those who can read and write; and the increase of knowledge is the principal agent in evolving the spirit we have to fear. . . .

It turned out that there was indeed reason to fear. The spirit of revolt lingered in Virginia long after the deaths of the conspirators in Richmond. Unruly gatherings of blacks occurred in towns across the state, and evidence of other conspiracies appeared regularly. Between February and April of 1802, whites unearthed a slave conspiracy that stretched across eight counties of southeastern Virginia and northeastern North Carolina. A reprise of Gabriel's plot, the 1802 conspiracy seems to have been the brainchild of a slave named Sancho, who was likely one of the Petersburg group that had been ready to rise with Gabriel in 1800. African-American rivermen spread the idea of an 1802 Easter rebellion, and in some locales skilled and literate slaves developed their own plans that grew independently of the main plot. Once authorities got wind of the conspiracy (or conspiracies), as was almost inevitable with an idea in so many minds and on so many tongues, they dealt swiftly with the conspirators. By June 27, twenty-five African Americans from Virginia and North Carolina had been hanged for their involvement, and others were sold and transported out of state.

Reports of conspiracies continued to roll in from states south of Virginia. Herbert Aptheker, the best-known chronicler of such deeds in *American Negro Slave Revolts* (1943), found plots and conspiracies taking place with regularity for a decade after Gabriel's plan had come to naught in Virginia, and then between 1810 and 1816, Aptheker writes, "Rebellious activity amongst the slaves entered a more intensive phase. . . ." Aptheker cites evidence of unruly black people being apprehended, communications being intercepted, conspiracies being foiled, and persons being punished. "A dangerous conspiracy among the negroes" was discovered in Lexington, Kentucky, in 1810; justices of the peace in North Carolina reported, "a spirit of rebellion is very obvious in this country" in 1812; and Governor David Holmes of Mississippi Territory reported in the same year that "Scarcely a day passes without my receiving some information relative to the design of those people to insurrect."

But the largest slave uprising in the history of the United States—one oddly underplayed by most historians, probably because it took place in what was then a frontier (and partly French-speaking) area—may well have been the slave rebellion that occurred thirty-six miles northwest of New Orleans just a year before Louisiana achieved statehood in 1812. This episode showed Americans that the threat of rebellion entered the union with each new slave state.

Since the 1790s, fear of slave rebellion had been part of white planters' lives along the Mississippi River in the neighborhood of New Orleans. An abortive revolt at Point Coupée in 1795 brought the execution of some two dozen African Americans and sentences of ten years of hard labor for nearly as many others. Rumored plots in 1796, 1804, and 1805 sent new waves of alarm through the planter class along the lower Mississippi.

Then, on January 8, 1811, slaves in the heart of Louisiana's sugar-producing region rose against their masters and brought to Louisiana, in the words of a person living in New Orleans at the time, "a miniature representation of the horrors of St. Domingo." A mulatto slave named Charles Deslondes, who had probably been brought to Louisiana from Saint Domingue following the revolution there, began the rebellion in St. John the Baptist Parish, northwest of New Orleans, on the plantation of Colonel Manuel André. Deslondes attacked André and his son, wounding the former and killing the latter; then he made a prearranged rendezvous with slaves from neighboring plantations and a number of fugitives who had been living in the woods. By various estimates, Deslondes pulled together an army of between 150 and 500. The leaders were mounted, the troops were armed mainly with cane knives and axes, and they marched, according to one report, with their "colors displayed and full of arrogance." The army swarmed over plantations in a fifteen-mile path along the River Road that headed toward New Orleans, plundering each and setting fire to two houses. Whites in their path lit out for New Orleans, and for a day, Deslondes and his troops held the field. On the tenth, however, two hastily mustered Louisiana militia companies, backed by thirty federal regulars, marched against the slave army in the woods and fields along the Mississippi's west bank. According to James H. Dormon in "The Persistent Specter: Slave Rebellion in Territorial Louisiana," *Louisiana History*, 18 (1977), "What followed was hardly a battle at all; it was more in the form of a mass execution, an open season on blacks in the vicinity." The leaders of the rebellion were killed in the fighting along with a number of others, sixty-six persons in all. Patrols continued to come upon "*beaucoup de cadavres*" for some days after the engagement. Of the remaining slave forces that were captured, twenty-one were convicted of "rebellion, assassination, arson, and pillage." Each was executed—shot first and then decapitated; their heads were then placed on poles to warn others of the fate of rebels.

But the unrest continued. Virginia was again "threatened with an insurrection of our Negroes" in 1813; in 1816 six slaves were executed in Spotsylvania, Virginia, for being members of a conspiracy to free the slaves; and a few months later a letter from Camden, South Carolina, reported, "Our gaol is filled with negroes" after the uncovering of a slave conspiracy that convinced one Camden resident, "it is time for us to leave a country where we cannot go to bed in safety." Gabriel's conspiracy might have been the most thoroughly planned and might have had the greatest potential for destructive change at the time, but it seems clear that ideas of rebellion were bubbling through the African-American population of the slave states through the first two decades of the nineteenth century.

Denmark Vesey's Conspiracy

Charleston was not like any other American city in the early 1820s, for blacks outnumbered whites in that South Carolina seaport: there were just over 10,000 white persons and some 16,000 African Americans, one-fifth of whom were free. Some of the free blacks had acquired property and wealth, had organized their own fraternal societies, and had formed their own African Methodist Episcopal Church. When slaves happened to worship with free blacks in the church, Charleston whites looked on with a mixture of fear and contempt. Several years of white harassment of the AME churchgoers, with a number of arrests of members for educating slaves, culminated in a series of state laws designed to restrict the ability of free African Americans to come and go as they pleased, to compete successfully at their trades, and to communicate with other free blacks, particularly AME church officials, in other states.

One member of the AME branch in Hampstead, a section of Charleston, was a fifty-odd-year-old free black carpenter named Denmark Vesey. He was a product of the Caribbean slave system, having spent his youth in slavery on the Danish island of St. Thomas. In 1781 Captain Joseph Vesey, a Caribbean slave trader, carried the adolescent slave Denmark along with 389 others to Saint Domingue, where he sold him to one of the island's French sugar planters. But after three months on the plantation his new owner returned Denmark to Captain Vesey, having found the slave "unsound and subject to epileptic fits." Honoring a kind of warranty, Vesey reclaimed the bright thirteen-year old and made him his personal servant. For two years, "Vesey's Denmark," as he was then called, sailed throughout the Caribbean and at least once to Africa on his master's slaving vessel. Then, in 1783, Captain Vesey sold his ships, took up residence in Charleston, and began a business as a ship chandler. For the next seventeen years Denmark served his master in the growing bustle of the South Carolina seaport. Along with seven other slaves, Denmark carried ship supplies and tended to the Vesey family. He must have watched and listened intently in the 1790s as ships unloaded refugees from the rebellion on Saint Domingue.

Late in 1799 the good fortune so many today hope for smiled on Vesey's slave Denmark—he won the lottery. With the $1,500 prize from the East Bay Street Lottery, now with the surname Vesey, Denmark purchased his freedom for $600 and used part of the remainder to set up shop as a carpenter. Over the next two decades he apparently succeeded at his trade—in 1822 he owned $8,000 worth of personal property—and he had acquired a family of some size—several wives and a good many children, all, however, still in slavery. He could read and write; he spoke several languages, he knew much about the Atlantic commercial world and New-World slavery, he was well versed in the Bible and Christian doctrine, and his was generally a respected presence among Charleston's African-American community.

As he approached middle age, the artisan Vesey seems to have grown increasingly discontented with his life and the lives of his family and associates. Perhaps affecting him more than his family's remaining in bondage or his awareness of the successful slave rebellion in the Caribbean was simply his having lived his life surrounded by slavery. He seemed particularly aware of and displeased with the fundamental wrong of slavery in the libertarian age. Over time he came to be known by blacks in Charleston as a forceful critic of slavery and of blacks' acquiescence to their position. He berated African

Americans for kowtowing to whites. Those who quietly accepted their subservience deserved to remain slaves, he believed. Increasingly, he used religious teaching in his arguments against slavery. At Vesey's conspiracy trial, fifteen-year-old Benjamin Ford remembered,

> Denmark Vesey frequently came into our shop which is near his house, and always complained of the hardships of blacks . . . *his general conversation was about religion which he would apply to slavery*, as for instance, he would speak of the creation of the world, in which he would say that all men had equal rights, blacks as well as whites, &c. *all his religious remarks were mingled with slavery.*

Vesey was particularly fond of biblical verses having to do with the deliverance of the children of Israel out of bondage in Egypt.

The "Missouri Debate" of 1819–21 seems to have served as another catalyst for Vesey's malcontent. He was in touch with and enlivened by the heated argument over whether to end slavery in Missouri as it applied for statehood, thus setting a precedent for Congress's limitation of the institution in new states. Congressional speeches like those of New York Senator Rufus King, which southerners feared would "sound the tocsin of freedom to every Negro in the South," had just that effect on Vesey. Coming at the time of the harassment of Charleston's AME church members and the new restrictions on free blacks in South Carolina, the debate over slavery that preceded the Missouri Compromise further riled the already angry Vesey.

By the end of 1821 Vesey was moving away from the mere voicing of his disgust of slavery and closer toward enticing Charleston blacks to take action against it. He began enlisting close friends and trusted acquaintances—Ned and Rolla, slaves of South Carolina Governor Thomas Bennett, who lived near Vesey; Peter Poyas, a ship carpenter; Gullah Jack, a slave originally from Angola, known among blacks as a "conjurer"; and Monday Gell, a skilled harness maker and member of a society of Americans of Ibo descent. Vesey then proceeded, in the spring of 1822, to hold inspirational meetings at his house on Bull Street in Charleston. Some of Vesey's lieutenants went off into the rice-producing plantations outside of Charleston to recruit for the conspirac [illegible] at the conspirators' trial suggests that they [illegible] had two decades earlier, they pro [illegible] rt. Gullah Jack may have be [illegible] the less-assimilated slaves on [illegible] g figure, wizard-like, with a bu [illegible] on a very large trunk. Slaves be [illegible] ction from whites. Back in Ch [illegible] on of such weapons as pikes, bay [illegible] bly figured that most of the weapons that his ban [illegible] ld be stolen from local arsenals and shops once the insurrection was underway.

Vesey's plans were specific to a point. When the attack was to begin, just after the sentinel at St. Michael's church sounded midnight, the rebels were to move out in six coordinated units, divided on the basis of their African ethnic identity, striking the city's guardhouse, arsenals, and stores that carried guns, and gaining control of major roads leading into Charleston. A cavalry force was to ride through the city's streets to prevent whites from organizing a counterattack, and individual slaves were to be lurking at their owners' gates, ready to slay them before leaving to join the fray. William W. Freehling, in what may be the most careful assessment of the Vesey plot in *Prelude to Civil War: The Nullification Controversy in South Carolina, 1816–1836* (1965), believes that, as in Gabriel's conspiracy, the key to success of Vesey's band rested on complete initial victory. "If the six attacking bands captured the arsenal and roads," Freehling writes, "the impoverished, poorly armed insurgents would control almost all the weapons in Charleston and could hope to hold their own against the tidewater aristocracy." What success was to bring over the long term is not clear, however. One of the conspirators wanted to fortify Charleston and hold out there, but Vesey talked of leading the victorious rebels by sea to Haiti.

Vesey set July 14 as the date for the rebellion, but on May 30 a house servant, whom one of Vesey's group had tried to recruit, informed his master of the conspirators' activities. Over the next two weeks, several of the plot's leaders used their aplomb at dealing with whites to allay suspicions. Vesey was alarmed nevertheless, enough so to move the date of the rebellion forward to June 16. But two days before the date arrived, on June 14, another house servant disclosed what he knew of the group's plans and Charleston authorities reacted quickly and vigorously. The mayor and governor activated five military companies, and the streets of Charleston were soon filled with soldiers. Vesey wisely called off the rebellion, but word of the plan spread rapidly through Charleston's white population and none of the rebels was safe. Roundup of the conspirators was swift, made swifter still by a small number of the plotters who had provided names of others in exchange for leniency. Within two months the state had tried and found guilty seventy-two African Americans. Thirty-five were hanged, thirty-seven were banished from the state.

Like Gabriel's, Vesey's conspiracy was stopped short. Unlike historians' treatment of Gabriel's plot, however, there is disagreement over the very existence of Vesey's, as well as over its extent. Governor Bennett doubted at the time that Vesey's plot involved more than eighty blacks and suggested that it never approached consummation. More recently, Richard C. Wade has taken the idea one step further. Basing his argument largely on the absence of evidence—no arms caches nor lists of participants were ever found, no unusual activity occurred on the designated date in Charleston's environs—and on discrepancies in the testimonies of those apprehended, Wade concludes in "The Vesey Plot: A Reconsideration," *Journal of Southern History*, 30 (1964), "The 'Plot' was probably never more than loose talk by aggrieved and embittered men." Wade's was not a particularly popular argument in its time, when African Americans and their supporters were seeking roots for the protest and resistance of the Civil Rights Movement, and it has not gained in popularity since. Freehling's assessment, in agreement with Bennett's conservative estimate on the plot's extent, is probably closer to being accurate. Placing the number of serious conspirators at fewer than one hundred, Freehling writes, "While the terrorized community exaggerated the extent of the danger, there was, in fact, a conspiracy worth getting excited about."

Whites living in lowcountry South Carolina over that summer and fall in 1822 would have agreed whole-heartedly with Freehling's conclusion—it was something worthy of their excitement, and they rose to the occasion. "A more painful degree of anxiety has never been experienced here," wrote Charlestonian George Logan several months after the trials and executions. Edwin C. Holland spoke for the lowcountry gentry when he wrote in *A Refutation of the Calumnies Circulated Against the Southern . . . States . . .* (1822),

> Let it never be forgotten, that "our NEGROES are truly the *Jacobins* of the country; that they are the *anarchists* and the *domestic enemy*; the *common enemy of civilized society*, and the barbarians who would, IF THEY COULD, become the DESTROYERS *of our race*.

Vigilance committees rode or marched nightly throughout South Carolina's tidelands, and whites at home kept their arms at the ready. All of this was for protection. What to do to keep their inscrutable blacks from beginning to conspire in the first place was another matter. Those who searched for scapegoats for the unrest scattered blame widely. The example of Saint Domingue and encouragement from unidentified Haitians were obvious targets. Most whites agreed, too, that the large number of free blacks in their midst and the freedom of movement and the relative independence of skilled slaves had helped to bring on the problem. But growing numbers blamed primarily what Charleston's General Thomas Pinckney called the "indiscrete zeal in favor of universal liberty," the incipient antislavery movement that was gaining momentum in the North and Upper South. Under particular suspicion were Yankee peddlers, who South Carolina planters believed traded liquor to their slaves for stolen plantation goods. While the slaves imbibed, or so the planters fantasized, the peddlers filled their heads with libertarian propaganda. White southerners already knew that the security of their peculiar institution relied on "a conspiracy of silence" on the part of the ruling class. Many feared that the whites' conspiracy was breaking down and the result was conspiracy of another kind on the part of the African Americans.

To prevent more plotting and acts of insurgency, the South Carolina legislature took swift action. It passed one law that called for the imprisonment of black sailors coming to South Carolina on British ships, under the assumption that such sailors had been to Haiti and thus had the potential to bring seditious ideas to the state's slaves. It also passed laws: barring free African Americans who ventured outside the state from returning; taxing all free blacks between the ages of fifteen and fifty who had not lived in the state for five years; requiring every free black over fifteen to have a guardian; prohibiting slaves from hiring their own time; and defining any person aiding insurrectionary activity as a felon and thus being subject to execution.

Strict measures these were, but they did not stifle black rebelliousness. African Americans continued to give white lowcountry residents good reason to sleep lightly. On Christmas Eve in 1825 a massive fire burned part of King Street, one of Charleston's main thoroughfares. Then, almost nightly for the next half year, unknown persons set fires across the city. The conviction of three blacks on arson charges did not bank the inferno—in mid-June a larger fire than the first consumed more of King Street. And the unrest spread outside of Charleston just as the fires were spreading in its downtown. South Carolina officials tried to hush news of a planned insurrection in Georgetown in 1829, but it was hard to conceal the fact that the town's jails were full of African Americans. (Knowing the harvest season was approaching and noting how many Georgetown blacks were incarcerated, one Charleston resident warned, ". . . you must take care and save Negroes enough for the rice crop.") Georgetown authorities hanged half a dozen or more African Americans whom they convicted of conspiracy.

Outside of South Carolina, whites faced the same kinds of problems. Suspicious fires swept through Alabama and Georgia cities in the first half of 1829, prompting Georgia Governor John Forsyth to appeal to the Secretary of War "for arms to protect the people of the state in case of slave revolt." The white leadership of Augusta did not take lightly the conviction of an African-American woman for setting that city's massive fire in April. Following her execution, they "dissected and exposed" her. Fires continued to rage in southern cities through 1830—one causing $300,000 worth of damage in New Orleans broke out almost simultaneously on all sides of a city square, prompting one observer to note, "The evils of the infernal system are beginning to re-act upon the Christians. . . ."—and conspiracies leading to a number of arrests and executions were reported in New

Orleans; Wilmington, North Carolina; Nashville, Tennessee; and Plaquemines Parish, Louisiana.

Through the latter part of the 1820s, state and national issues heightened Americans' awareness of slavery and focused it on the section of the country where the institution existed and was growing. In 1828 Congress passed a protective tariff that southern cotton planters called an "abomination" and South Carolinians, led by John C. Calhoun, believed they could and should nullify the law. Implied in Calhoun's nullification doctrine was the idea that a state could reject any federal law that threatened its basic institutions—such as slavery. In 1829 Virginia lawmakers argued openly about slavery in a convention to draft a new constitution for the state. At the time the arguments were going on, an African American living in Boston, David Walker, published *Appeal to the Colored Citizens of the World*, which used religious reasoning and revolutionary rhetoric to urge slaves to rise up and slay "our cruel oppressors and murderers." And on January 1, 1831, William Lloyd Garrison and Isaac Knapp began publication of the *Liberator* newspaper, demanding immediate, uncompensated abolition of slavery and warning southerners, "Woe if [abolition] comes with storm, and blood, and fire."

Yet in spite of the libertarian philosophy of the American and French revolutions, in spite of the heritage of the slave rebellion on Saint Domingue, in spite of the slave conspiracies and rebellions so barely nipped in the bud in their own country, and in spite of the fires, the threats, and the warnings, most southerners in early 1831—certainly those outside the cities that were the relative hotbeds of African-American unrest—were confident in the loyalty of their slaves and in their own security. As much as anywhere, this was the case in Southampton County, Virginia, on the state's southern border with North Carolina. Southampton County was removed by several days ride from any of the major disturbances, and its white population believed that slaves there were well treated and content. Southampton masters could afford to let their African-American slaves come and go freely on Sundays to visit relatives and friends and to attend religious gatherings as they chose. They had no reason to expect trouble, and their guard was down in the months before August

1831, when a Southampton slave brought the rage that slavery could produce down onto the farms and fields and white people of the county.

Nat Turner's Rebellion

In the early hours of Monday morning, August 22, 1831, a slave preacher and religious visionary named Nat Turner led a band of African Americans on a rampage of killing through Southampton County's rural heartland. The number of rebels that began with a group of seven had swelled to sixty or seventy by midafternoon as they traveled from house to house, systematically slaying the whites they encountered. Well-armed volunteer armies of whites were able to quell the rebellion the following day, but by the time it was over, Turner's band had invaded some fifteen white dwellings and had killed sixty white men, women, and children. "It turned out to be the bloodiest slave revolt in Southern history," writes Stephen B. Oates in the most thorough study of the event, *The Fires of Jubilee: Nat Turner's Fierce Rebellion* (1975), "one that was to have a profound and irrevocable impact on the destinies of Southern whites and blacks alike."

It is not easy to determine just who Nat Turner was. The major source for information on his life is the long statement he made to his court-appointed attorney, Thomas Gray, over a three-day period before his trial. Gray wrote down what Turner told him and published it, practically verbatim, he claimed, in *The Confessions of Nat Turner* (1831). Some have considered the document tainted because Gray was a white slaveholder, because he accurately saw profit in his sale of Turner's "confessions," and because he regarded Turner as "a gloomy fanatic," deranged by religious zeal. Most, however, accept the general authenticity of Gray's document.

But hindering the task of recreating the historical Turner is author William Styron's 1967 novel, *The Confessions of Nat Turner*, which rode the very top of the best-seller lists and won a Pulitzer Prize for fiction. Styron affected the popular image of Turner when, in spite of evidence to the contrary, he portrayed the African-American rebel as a celibate bachelor, addicted to masturbating as he thought of white women. Sexual angst was a major motivation for Styron's Turner. Styron's is a work of fiction, of course, however much the author claims it reflects a broad reality from Turner's place and time, and the massive, sometimes venomous body of criticism that the book elicited from historians merely demonstrates the differences between history and literature.

So who was Nat Turner? Deranged religious fanatic or candidate for Freudian analysis? Oates comes as close as we have gotten to answering the question.

Turner was born a slave on the Southampton County farm of Benjamin Turner on October 2, 1800—ironically, just months after Denmark Vesey purchased his freedom in Charleston and only five days before Gabriel and fifteen others were hanged for conspiracy seventy miles to the north, in Richmond. Southampton County was heavily wooded, dotted by farms and small plantations. By 1830, following several decades of economic decline that prompted some whites to hie for better prospects in the Lower South, 9,500 of Southampton's 16,000 people were of African descent, and a surprisingly large number of the African Americans, 1,700, were free. Turner knew some of the county's free blacks, and in his upbringing he may have gotten an idea that he, too, might in time join their ranks. But in his thirty-one years, he knew only slavery.

Because of a normal pattern of death and inheritance, Turner had four masters in his thirty-one years. Each lived within a few miles of Turner's birthplace, and each came to know him as an especially bright person. He learned to read and write in his youth—his parents and others praised his brilliance and probably planted in his mind the idea that he was too smart to remain a slave. Turner admitted, "Having discovered [myself] to be great, I must appear to be so, and therefore studiously avoided mixing in society, and wrapped myself in mystery, devoting my time to fasting and praying."

By the time he reached manhood, Turner seemed to be obsessed with religion. Reading, memorizing the Bible, and preaching to neighborhood slaves were his pastimes. He traveled fairly widely in the county giving moving sermons to slaves, free blacks, and even some whites. It seems that his peers respected him for his learning, his abilities, and his pious manner. Some must have been bewildered when, in 1821, Turner escaped and was missing for an entire month—patrols with dogs could not find a trace of him—only to return on his own volition, because "the Spirit" had directed him. Thereafter, Turner saw signs and had visions—drops of blood on corn growing in the fields, mysterious writings and drawings on leaves in the woods, and even visits from the Holy Ghost. For Turner, the signs portended the Judgment Day. He told blacks assembled for praise meetings to ready themselves. His strong voice and high energy raised their interest. For some of the African-American men and women in Southampton County, Turner became "The Prophet."

That Turner was not happy with his lot in slavery was evident in his escape, perhaps in the visions he saw, and in the increasingly militant tone of his daily discourse and Sunday sermons. In his eyes, he had more to be unhappy about than the typical African American in bondage. Basic to this unhappiness was his well-founded and regularly reinforced belief that he was a brilliant, gifted, and special person. Why did he not receive better treatment? It was not so much that he got an occasional whipping as it was that he remained a common field hand, forced to toil with his hands in the sun as others, less gifted and talented, achieved the loftier status of being house servants. And intermixed with the Southampton slaves were blacks who were free, yet even they did not rival Turner's abilities.

Then, too, not long after he returned from his escape, Turner married an African-American slave named Cherry, who lived on the same farm. She seemed special to him, but within a year of their marriage their master died, and the two were sold to different owners living a few miles apart. After 1822, Turner could see his wife, and eventually their two or three children, only after a long day of work or on his busy Sundays. None of this was any way to treat a gifted person. It was because of slavery that he received such treatment, he reasoned, and his religion gave strength to his reasoning. The signs he had seen had meaning in them. He believed he had been called to act.

Early in 1831 Turner began having new visions that channeled his feelings toward action. An eclipse of the sun in February prompted him to tell four trusted slaves of plans he had to lead an uprising. He wanted to begin on July 4, but a brief illness forced him to put it off. Then, an odd atmospheric condition that discolored the sun along the entire eastern seaboard of the United States convinced him that the time was nigh. "As the black spot passed over the sun," he announced, "so shall the blacks pass over the earth." He told his four compatriots plus two others to meet him at Cabin Pond, deep in the woods on his master's farm, on Sunday, August 21. From there they would strike.

The events of August 22nd and 23rd show how vulnerable unsuspecting whites were to slave uprisings, particularly in rural areas, and how vulnerable groups of slaves in rebellion were once the marshaled forces of white society set after them. The seven African Americans, with Turner at the lead, left their meeting place just after two o'clock in the morning and went directly to the home of Turner's master. Turner climbed a ladder to a second floor window to gain entry; then he let the others in the front door. They went to the house's bedrooms, located each resident, and with axes quickly killed every member of the household. Mercy was not on their minds. When finished there, they moved on, proceeding from farm to farm, surprising and slaughtering the occupants. With the exception of the family of Giles Reese, on whose farm Turner's wife and children resided, the family of John Clark Turner, the Prophet's childhood playmate, and a poor white family who, Turner believed, "thought no better of themselves than they did of Negroes," the rebels did not discriminate in their attacks on whites. A newspaper reporter on the scene soon afterward described what lay in the rebels' wake: "whole families, fathers, mothers, daughters, sons, sucking babes, and school children, butchered, thrown into heaps, and left to be devoured by hogs and dogs or to putrify on the spot." Although Turner was clearly the leader of the insurgents, he held back when the time came for killing. Throughout the day, his hands were responsible for but one of the sixty deaths.

As the rebels traveled, they took horses, weapons, and jugs of the tasty and potent apple brandy produced on every farm in the region. They recruited slaves from the farms they overran, welcoming some and forcing others to join their ranks. Some who had refused to join they took as "prisoners." By daybreak the group numbered fifteen, by noon perhaps sixty or seventy, divided into infantry and cavalry. It was a disorganized bunch that The Prophet had difficulty keeping focused. Out of his sight, individuals tended to head for the brandy stills. Some got good and drunk. But once on the scene of a white farm, the force regrouped, and when it did, its strike was lethal.

After daybreak on the 22nd, as the rebels stalked on, word began to spread of the murder and mayhem. Turner's men began coming upon deserted houses. By midmorning the alarm had reached the county seat of Jerusalem (which is Courtland on modern maps), armed groups of whites were forming, and a local judge had dispatched an express rider toward Petersburg and Richmond. Around noon, as Turner was leading his men toward Jerusalem (where church bells were clanging and there was alarm in the streets), the rebels came upon their first organized opposition, eighteen volunteers looking to engage them. Following a brief, standup fight, Turner led his men away from the better-armed whites and in the opposite direction of Jerusalem. They spent the rest of the day eluding the growing number of patrols, which eventually included a mustered militia that crisscrossed the region looking for them, and trying to recruit more slaves from those remaining on the local farms and plantations. By nightfall, desertions had taken a toll, but Turner's force still numbered about forty. Turner looked for a place to rest the night, hoping to recruit more blacks for his army in the morning and then head again toward Jerusalem.

But it was not to be. About half of the group fled when they mistakenly thought the militia was attacking in the dark of night. Then in the morning, when Turner led his remaining men on a recruiting mission to a local farm, they encountered withering gunfire and a rush upon them by blacks loyal to (and perhaps frightened of recriminations from) their master. Several of the rebels were wounded or killed. With the dozen or so followers who remained, Turner headed back toward where the rebellion had begun, only to encounter militia, more gunfire, and armed whites swarming like bees across every farm and open field. More members of his group fell away. By nightfall, having sent his two remaining troops off to look for stragglers, it seemed that his only friend was the woods near home. Thus, under cover of darkness, Turner returned and spent

Tuesday night at Cabin Pond, the spot where he and the six others had launched their rebellion forty-odd hours earlier.

What followed was a massive manhunt for the remaining rebels and a cruel and frightening vendetta against African Americans in general in Southampton County and beyond. For the next five days, white vigilantes went on a rampage, torturing or killing whatever luckless blacks they came upon. They arrived from as far away as Richmond and northern North Carolina, as one rider put it, "to kill somebody else's niggers." Frequently, African Americans were shot and their heads mounted on poles "as a warning to all who should undertake a similar plot." Oates estimates that at least 120 innocent blacks died in this "reign of terror," which ran through the remainder of August.

By the end of the month, Turner and five or six others were the only insurgents still alive and not in jail. Turner had moved about for two days; then he had dug a hole underneath some fence rails on the farm where he lived and settled in. For the next two months he hid out, venturing away from cover only at night to get water or to steal food. It was inevitable that he would be spotted and he was, finally, on October 30, by an armed white man tramping through the woods on his way to a neighboring farm. The surprised traveler marched his captive off, eventually to jail in Jerusalem, and received about a thousand dollars in reward money.

The trials of the other captured rebels were completed by the time Turner had been taken to the county seat. Most of those convicted had been hanged; some had been transported out of the country. It was in the Jerusalem jail that Turner spent three days "confessing" to his defense attorney. Although he pleaded not guilty—because he did not feel guilty—there was no case to be made for the rebel leader. His conviction and sentence were preordained. Just after noon on Sunday, November 11, a crowd looked on in a field just outside of Jerusalem as the sheriff of Southampton County hanged Nat Turner. He was one of twenty-one found guilty and executed for "conspiring to rebel and insurrection." According to Oates, if one counts the twenty or thirty executions of blacks in other counties in Virginia and North Carolina for complicity in the insurrection, and adds the slaves and free blacks killed indiscriminately in the days immediately following the uprising, more than two hundred African Americans and sixty whites died as a result of Nat Turner's rebellion.

Unlike with Gabriel and Denmark Vesey, there is no need to discuss what Turner might have done had the rebellion been put into action—it had been. Turner's long-range goals are not clear, however. No doubt he expected his band's initial success to prompt large numbers of Southampton's black population, slave and free, to join, and once his force was large enough he intended to take Jerusalem and thus control Southampton County. He may have believed that once in control of the county he could consolidate his position and hold out against whatever forces were sent against him, thereby making Southampton County a kind of maroon enclave in southern slave society. But it is more likely that he had no specific plans beyond the taking of Jerusalem. Oates suggests that Turner expected God to guide him, perhaps in additional signs, once his forces had been fully assembled. Just as Ezekiel, at The Lord's direction, brought down holy wrath upon the wicked of Jerusalem, so did Turner lead his followers off to "Slay utterly old and young, both maids, and little children, and women." Turner may have preferred to leave the aftermath in Jehovah's hands.

The major slave rebellions that occurred during America's early republic did not have as much in common as some have suggested. Two of them, Gabriel's and Denmark Vesey's, were urban based and led by skilled artisans, the latter by a free black; the third, Nat Turner's, had no urban dimension (for even Jerusalem, the county seat that Turner had hoped to take once his force had grown large enough, had only 175 residents) and was led by a field hand. Two of the insurrections, Vesey's and Turner's, had strong religious elements and rational groundings in Christian teachings; Gabriel's was largely devoid of a religious component—other than using the frequent religious gatherings of blacks of that era as fertile ground for recruitment. The African heritage of the potential participants played a role in Vesey's plot, as did what were likely African-based magical practices for the protection of the insurgents, but such was not the case of the others. In *From Rebellion to Revolution: Afro-American Slave Revolts in the Making of the New World* (1979), Eugene D. Genovese suggests that all three rebellions had similar ends—overthrowing slavery as a social system rather than more simply securing the freedom of the individuals involved—but it is difficult to agree given the little that is known of the stated ends of the rebel leaders. Vesey seems to have had in mind taking his successful insurgents, and perhaps others who wished to go, to join the black republic of Haiti, and one can only guess at Turner's grand strategy. It may have been only Gabriel, whose planning was done as the French and Haitian revolutions were being played out, who had an end to slavery in sight. He hoped to strike such a strong initial blow and to gain such a formidable following of armed African Americans that state authorities would have no alternative but to negotiate, possibly for the dissolution of slavery.

One factor that the major rebellions did share was contact with free African Americans. Vesey himself was a free black (as was Charles Deslondes, who had led the large Louisiana uprising in 1811), Gabriel worked and associated regularly with free black artisans, and Turner probably had much more association with African Americans who were not slaves than heretofore acknowledged (since almost one of every five blacks in Southampton County was free). This leads one to believe that white southerners were correct when they said that the very presence of free African Americans in the slave states undermined the institution of slavery and made those enslaved long so much more for free status that some would risk their lives to gain it.

But the major element that all of the plots and risings of the early republic had in common was their futility. Genovese writes that by the end of the eighteenth century, "The slaves of the United States faced a highly unfavorable relationship of forces . . . ; in general their position steadily deteriorated over time until revolt became virtually suicidal." Those who led or participated in slave revolts must have known that their chances of succeeding, of making their lives better in any way, or even of surviving were slim. For this reason, Genovese wonders not that the United States had fewer and less significant revolts than other slave countries to its south, but that it had any at all. One must conclude that Gabriel, Deslondes, Vesey, Turner, and others who led or participated in slave revolts were exceptional people, ready to die for a cause that perhaps was as futile as it was noble.

The certainty of failure and the likelihood of death in slave rebellions meant that African Americans intent on acting against their situation in slavery, but wanting as a result of their action something besides martyrdom, had to seek other ways to resist. The modes of resistance they found were far less dramatic and less frightening to whites than out-and-out rebellion. But they were effective within certain broad bounds, and they provided African Americans with the psychological lift necessary to maintain a sense of their own humanity and, for individuals, a concept of self that must have been vital to coping with the difficult conditions of life in bondage.

Resisting and Running Away

If the largest slave rebellions known in the country occurred between 1800 and 1831 and thus showed the early republic to be an age of extraordinary slave unrest, so did the increased level of slaves' daily resistance. Most slaves resisted their existence in bondage in subtle ways. Learned over the years and passed along to children in the family's rearing process, certain ways of speaking, tones of voice, facial expressions, such behaviors as feigning incomprehension or illness, or merely moving slowly were among the slaves' weapons in their psychological war with their masters. Black Americans found they could practice these less-direct and less-threatening forms of resistance without bringing down the most dangerous manifestations of their masters' wrath. If whites mistakenly considered some of these behaviors to be aspects of the Africans' nature, they just as certainly recognized others as expressions of resistance that were beyond their ability to control.

African-American slaves could increase or decrease their general level of resistance when there was cause to do so. Life in slavery required a degree of accommodation on the part of everyone involved. Masters wanted slaves to work steadily, with the interests of the farm or plantation in mind, and to be easily managed. African Americans had scant incentive to do any of this. Although nearly all slaves eventually accepted certain basics—that their work went to the profit of another and that seriously disruptive behavior brought punishment—they had something to say about a number of aspects of their lives in bondage.

By late in the eighteenth century, certain norms of behavior of both slaves and masters prevailed in English-speaking North America's slave society. These norms necessarily differed between urban and rural settings, they differed regionally, and they changed gradually over time. But masters understood them and spoke and wrote of them as they advised others how the system worked. Slaves, too, understood the norms, talked of and compared them as widely as they could, and made sure that their children learned them as they were growing up. Masters punished slaves who did not meet the common expectations of work or behavior, but African Americans devised ways to resist when masters pushed them beyond acceptable limits of work or attempted to cut into what the norms dictated were their minimal rights and privileges. A master who worked his slaves too hard might find his field hands making mistakes resulting in broken tools or uprooted plants. One who failed to provide accepted amounts of food or clothing might find hogs missing from the pen or field hands working more slowly than ever before. More serious breaches by masters of these tacit agreements might bring about mysterious fires. And when circumstances for the African American reached a critical point, when something beyond the norm of resistance was required, running away was widely preferred to the almost certainly suicidal option of organizing a rebellion.

From long experience, masters had learned that a certain amount of running off was to be expected. Persons straight from Africa in their first year or two of slavery were among the most apt to flee. They seldom went far and did not stay away for long. Some masters considered several episodes of running away to be a part of the learning process of "outlandish" Africans. Eighteenth-century Virginia planter Robert "King" Carter put it in simple terms when he told his overseer, "Now that my new Negro woman has tested the hardships of the woods, she'll stay nearer to home where she can have her belly full."

Even for more acculturated slaves, short forays away from the plantation, often made in response to a perceived injustice, were common expressions of displeasure. The slave Jacob, who fled from

John Ellis in Virginia in 1793, is a single example. Ellis wrote in a letter to his brother Charles that Jacob ran away "for no other provocation than a small correction" applied to him "for neglecting his business." Ellis's "small correction" was Jacob's injustice, and the latter ran off. Most of such runaways stayed close, even sneaking into the slave quarters at night for food, and returned after a few days in the woods. For the slaves, it was cathartic. They got temporary relief from the daily work routine and they "got even" with their masters or overseers by depriving them of their labor for a short time. Masters may have come to look upon these episodes as necessary for the release of slaves' anger, and preferable to the more damaging expressions of that emotion that could have taken place. Whippings that masters or overseers meted out in response to these occurrences were no doubt painful and humiliating, as ever, but they did not seem to reduce the frequency of short flights from home.

Some African Americans ran away to be with their family members or loved ones. Persons separated by only a few miles could usually see one another frequently by merely heading off at night and returning before it was time to work in the morning. Indeed, there was a fairly active nocturnal coming and going of slaves among neighborhood farms and plantations—something else that most masters realized they could not, and for their own good probably should not, put an end to. But when distances between loved ones were longer than a good evening's walk, more long-term escape was in the offing. This kind of escape was prevalent enough that wise masters learned where their slaves' closest kin lived, so they would know where to seek and fetch them when they escaped.

As far as individual masters and the general well-being of the institution of slavery were concerned, the most serious and costly form of resistance occurred when African Americans who rejected slavery completely attempted to escape to a place where they could live the rest of their lives as free persons. Male slaves between the ages of sixteen and thirty-five and persons more acculturated were the ones most apt to try to escape slavery for good. Through the colonial period such flight could take the form of heading for the Atlantic coast, signing on as a ship mate and hoping to arrive in a distant port where freedom might be secured. Alternatives included escape toward frontier areas, where whites who were trying to scratch out an existence needed labor to clear land and might hire fugitives without asking questions, or where, farther out still, Native Americans might offer a welcome reception. Slaves in Georgia sometimes headed for Spanish lands on the colony's southern border. On top of this, a few black Americans escaped to the woods and swamps of the colonies themselves and lived in small "maroon" communities, raiding farms and plantations and holding off whatever weak attempts colonial authorities made to stifle their marauding and bring them to justice. The existence of harsh colonial laws aimed at curbing these bands of lawless ex-slaves suggests that there was more maroon activity, which colonials euphemistically called "outlying," than most slave owners wished to admit. But this hardly meant that in each year of the colonial period there was an exodus of slaves from the plantations. With slavery existing in all thirteen colonies and in most parts of the western hemisphere, there were simply few promising places to which slaves could escape and expect to remain comfortably unfettered.

The forces of the American Revolution, played out over the years of the early republic, altered the circumstances surrounding slave escape. Some of the same factors that brought increased rebelliousness among African Americans, in combination with other changes of the age, led persons in slavery to take flight in greater numbers than ever before. Events of the Revolutionary War provided blacks who desired to escape from slavery a place to go to do so—British lines. As noted, British officers tried to lure slaves away, and thousands of African Americans heeded the call (though most who went with the British found that their lives were not much better and often were worse than they had been in colonial slavery).

Once the war was over, the movement of planters with their slaves into the newly opening backcountries of several southern states, followed by the beginning of the massive movement of African Americans into the cotton-producing lands of Mississippi Territory, broadened slaves' motives for escape, but, for some, made the act more difficult. Slaves naturally dreaded being sold away from family and community. One suspects that more slaves in the Upper South struck for freedom once they suspected their sale was pending than at any other specific time. (This brought about ironic circumstances on many a plantation—masters deciding to sell slaves they believed were planning to escape; slaves deciding to escape when they believed their masters were planning their sale.)

But the sale and extended movement of African Americans farther south and west in the early decades of the nineteenth century cut into African Americans' ability to run away in order to be with loved ones or to escape in any direction for their permanent freedom. Gradually, the Native-American groups that had provided some sanctuary for runaway slaves were overcome by the United States military. The frontier that once had offered at least a glimmer of hope for a life outside of bondage soon became a place to which white planters moved with their slaves to carve out new plantations. And the distance and rugged terrain that separated African Americans who were traded to the Lower South from their families in the Upper South or from the states where slavery no longer existed were daunting. Charles Ball traveled for several months, through the cold of winter, sleeping in the woods by day and walking the roads and ridges by night, living on parched corn and what he could trap, to get from backcountry Georgia to Maryland in 1806. Most slaves who gave in to the same longing to see loved ones were either not as strong of will or as fortunate as Ball. Escaping from a developing part of the country and traveling hundreds of miles overland without being apprehended, and with virtually no one to trust or lend help, was close to impossible. Between 1790 and 1830—that is, before there were real railroads, let alone any semblance of an "Underground Railroad"—it was African Americans residing in the Upper South, not so far from their loved ones or a reasonably secure haven from slavery, who would have by far the best prospects for a flight to freedom.

Also affecting African Americans' inclination to escape following the Revolution was what Willie Lee Rose calls "the vigorous circulation of the idea of freedom" in *Slavery and Freedom*, expanded edition, edited by William W. Freehling, (1982). Rumors of out-and-out abolition in some northern states and of selective emancipation in the South, news of the blow to freedom struck by blacks on Saint Domingue in the 1790s, and the message of equality preached by evangelicals scouring the South inspired more southern slaves than ever before to strike out for their freedom. On top of this, the dramatic social and economic changes of the period—the growth of a sizable community of free blacks across the Upper South, the appearance of more towns and larger cities that had a demand for skilled artisans, the increasing number of white tenant farmers in need of laborers in the Upper South, and the eventual ending of slavery in the North—altered the circumstances of slavery considerably, placed freedom in a whole new light, and made flight to secure that freedom still more appealing and easier for some to accomplish.

What Rose identifies as the most significant consequence of the American Revolution for blacks, the rapid formation of a large free black community, probably had the greatest effect on slaves' desire and ability to run from the plantation and seek their freedom. Slave owners long sensed what the existence of free blacks in the midst of slave society would do to those still in bondage. It showed more clearly than anything could have the possibility of their own freedom. Those in bondage did not have to consort regularly with free blacks to be affected. The mere existence of so many fellow humans of African descent who were not in slavery made many African Americans want the same status enough to attempt escape to get it.

At the same time, the existence of so many more free blacks also made it easier for fugitive slaves to avoid detection. Before the 1770s the community of free blacks was tiny and members of that community were easy to identify, for nearly all were the light-skinned offspring of black-white unions. But by the 1790s, with the more widespread emancipation of slaves in the Upper South, not only of mulattos but of persons of pure African descent, there was a body of free African Americans in that region and in some cities of the Lower South that was large enough and dark enough to camouflage individual runaways. In some places there were so many free blacks about that whites could not know every one of them, and enough were dark skinned so that whites no longer could assume that every person of pure African descent whom they did not know was a slave. True, free blacks had to carry papers certifying their freedom, and there were always some whites who were intent on checking

African Americans they did not recognize. But in time the sheer numbers of free African Americans, particularly in the more populated areas, wore down the intentions of the most vigilant whites.

A related change affecting slaves' ability to escape involved the rapid growth of towns and cities to which the fugitives could run, and where they were less likely to be turned in or identified. In the city skilled blacks had reasonable chances of hiring their own time and melding into the growing urban underclass. The back alleys, narrow streets, artisans' stalls, and taverns of the urban areas teemed with whites and blacks, slave and free. If an African-American fugitive could speak reasonably well, feel comfortable in groups, read a little bit, and perform a skill in demand, he (or more rarely she) could take up residence in Richmond or Baltimore, Charleston or New Orleans, and have a chance of not being apprehended. Thus, urban areas became havens for runaways through the early decades of the nineteenth century—so much so that by the early 1830s the Mayor of New Orleans was complaining loudly to the City Council about the runaways who "crowd in the city, hide, and make our City a den."

Even some isolated rural areas of the Upper South became semipermanent homes for runaways. The growing number of white tenant farmers that appeared in Maryland and northern Virginia soon after the Revolution needed cheap labor. Some hired blacks whom they suspected to be fugitives without asking questions and kept them on if they worked well.

Beckoning to slaves further, and increasingly so, was the prospect of running north to freedom. By the beginning of the nineteenth century, many slaves knew that north of Maryland blacks could exist as free persons. From 1793—almost before there was a fugitive slave problem of any significance—there had been a federal Fugitive Slave Law that required extradition and rendition of persons sworn to be runaways, but it never became a truly effective deterrent for persons fleeing north. Pennsylvania became an early target for fugitives from the Upper South—by the 1790s Virginia slave owners knew what it meant for a slave to take "the Philadelphia road"—and in time runaways began to trickle into upstate New York and coastal New England.

The tide of runaways ebbed and flowed into the nineteenth century. Chaotic conditions surrounding the War of 1812, with British troops once again offering African Americans freedom for escape to their lines, induced more slaves to take flight. The increase in the internal slave trade in the 1820s prompted still more to prefer the frightening prospects of flight to sale and separation from loved ones. Some escaped in groups large enough to constitute an exodus. In 1829 several white Accomac County, Virginia, residents wrote their governor that slaves had left the state's Eastern Shore for New York and Philadelphia "in gangs and armed, bidding defiance to the citizens." Another wave of blacks from the same county camped on islands in Chesapeake Bay and fought against anyone coming to apprehend them. A few years later, eighteen slaves commandeered a boat in Northampton County, just south of Accomac, and sailed it from Chesapeake Bay to New York City.

Such boldness frightened and angered white southerners. Those with enough perspective recognized that the trickle of runaways of 1789 had become a noticeable stream by 1830. If African-American rebels and conspirators threatened the institution of slavery and the safety of southern whites, black runaways imperiled the economic well-being of the plantation. Each runaway not captured and returned was another piece of property lost, another cog in the plantation machinery no longer able to turn.

For southern slave owners, the problems they faced due to runaways and rebellions would not go away. When it became evident that the federal Fugitive Slave Law was not deterring runaways, southern state legislatures began strengthening their own fugitive legislation. As they were tightening restrictions and beefing up patrols to prevent rebellions, legislatures were adding penalties for harboring fugitives and raising rewards for informers. When these measures neither cut the number of runaways nor stifled African Americans' general rebelliousness, slave owners began to dig to uncover the deepest roots of the problem: by the second decade of the nineteenth century, many found the free black community at the bottom of their troubles. Only since the Revolution and the appearance of such a sizable number of free African Americans, they believed, had rebellion and flight become such serious social problems. And they thought they understood why. In this age of the "rights of man," slave owners justified holding humans in bondage with the crudest racist arguments. Persons of African descent were different, inferior, not capable to compete successfully in white society, they argued. The institution of slavery insured needed labor for white southerners, whites conceded, but it also was a way to take care of blacks in the United States as it controlled them and thus protected the more civilized white Americans, especially white women, from such dangerous elements. But could slavery ever be secure so long as persons of African descent were going about flaunting their freedom? Their doing so incited slaves to resist or rebel or run away. It also flew in the face of the accepted rationale for their peculiar institution. For many southerners in the years before the strengthening of the abolitionist movement, free blacks were the main cause for the heightened unrest in the slave community. Something, they felt, had to be done.

CHAPTER FOUR

Free African Americans in a Slave Society

"Slaves without masters," "quasi-free blacks," "slaves who were free"—all are phrases coined by historians to describe the persons of African descent who lived outside of slavery before the Civil War. One needs special terms to identify them for they were a distinct group in America—some have labeled them a separate "caste"—legally free but able to experience only a few of the benefits freedom had to offer. They were not widely noticed before the English colonies became the United States of America, but after that they became an important element of American life—to many whites they became a clear "problem"—over a short time.

America first took notice of its free black population during the first two decades of the country's existence, not that there were no free persons of African descent in colonial America. In the middle of the seventeenth century, African Americans on Virginia's Eastern Shore owned property, raised and sold crops, and argued against whites in colonial courts. There were free African Americans in most northern cities for almost as long as slaves lived there, and in Massachusetts, when the "minutemen" awaited the approach of the British in 1775, free blacks stood ready with them. But all along, their numbers were tiny. On the eve of the Revolution there may have been thirty thousand free African Americans—not 5 percent of the black population of the colonies. Most free African Americans were the mulatto children of black-white unions; others were former slaves who had become physically disabled or had grown too old to be useful to their masters and thus were left to their own devices. Until after the Revolution, there simply were not enough persons of African descent who were free, at least in relation to the numbers of whites, to cause much of a stir. It was, again, the Revolutionary era that spawned a quick and steady rise in the number of free African Americans.

United States census figures are notoriously inaccurate on their enumerations of blacks in the country, and especially so when trying to count free blacks in the early period of America's existence. Census marshals were the ones who had to make the racial identification for each individual, and they had no clear guidelines for doing so. The offspring of one white and one black parent, as were many free blacks, were either "black" or "white" on the call of a marshal. Further, the marshals often preferred not to venture along some of the narrow paths, dark streets, and back alleys of the cities in which many free African Americans lived. Even when the marshals did find the courage to enter the innermost urban labyrinths, many was the runaway or person living as free beyond the law who took pains to avoid the prying eyes of the federal government. Ira Berlin in *Slaves Without Masters* estimates that the federal census regularly underenumerated the southern free black population by at least 20 percent, and its count of the same group in the North was not considerably better. Still, the undercounting was fairly constant from one decade to the next, so census figures can provide useful relative data on the size and growth rate of the free African-American community.

What the earliest census figures show is that over the quarter century between 1785 and 1810, there was a virtual explosion of freedom among the African-American population. Then, for two decades after 1810, the number of free blacks continued to grow, but at a more measured pace.

The first census from 1790 lists the number of free blacks in the

United States at about 60,000. (This, and the figures that follow, are rounded for the sake of simple comparison.) Then the number rose steadily to 110,000 in 1800, 185,000 in 1810, 235,000 in 1820, and 320,000 in 1830. Part of this increase was the result of natural population growth, but part was caused also by the abolition of slavery in the North, the greatly increased incidence of manumission in the Upper South, and the growing possibility in the southern states for slaves to purchase their freedom or to run away. The North's free African-American population went from 27,000 in 1790 to 138,000 in 1830; the Upper South's from 30,000 to 150,000 over the same period. Through the first decade of the nineteenth century, there was enough manumission in Delaware, Maryland, and northern Virginia to make this part of the Upper South a focal point of the free black community and to furnish streams of blacks that raised the populations of several northern cities. Such was not the case in the Lower South, however. In 1790 there were just over 2,000 free blacks there, and forty years later—even with the addition of Louisiana, with its large, free mulatto population—the number had grown only to 30,000. Most of the Lower South's free blacks lived in the vicinity of two cities, Charleston and New Orleans.

As with slaves, the lives of free African Americans changed over time, and they varied considerably among sections of the country. One thing that all African Americans everywhere had in common, though, was that they lacked the full privileges of American citizenship.

Freedom in the North

North of Delaware and Maryland, African Americans should have been able to lead normal lives as American citizens. After all, it was in the northern states where slavery had ended earliest, and it was in the Old Northwest where the federal government agreed that slavery would never exist in the first place. These were areas that would produce fiery abolitionists and the dedicated fighter against slavery, John Brown; these were the states that, between 1861 and 1865, sent hundreds of thousands of their men and boys off to fight against the slaveholding South, exalting John Brown's body in song and giving their lives to end the wicked institution that kept millions of humans in bondage. Blacks living north of the Mason-Dixon line and the Ohio River in the years of the early republic should have had the basic rights and privileges of citizens in the Republic: equal treatment, equal opportunity, and respect as human beings. But they did not.

There is no doubt that the Revolution triggered the ending of slavery north of Maryland and Delaware. Antislavery efforts prior to 1770 were mostly in the hands of Quakers and were tame by later standards, but the Revolution brought fire to the moral tinder lying about in the Northern colonies. Vermont wrote a constitution in 1777 that read, "No male person ought to be holden by law to serve any person as a servant, slave, or apprentice after he arrives to the age of twenty-one years, nor female in like manner after she arrives to the age of eighteen years." The Massachusetts Constitution of 1780 that declared "all men are born free and equal" was interpreted in court to include blacks under that maxim. The Declaration of Rights of New Hampshire's 1783 Constitution effectively ended slavery there. And beginning with Pennsylvania in 1780, the remainder of the northern states passed laws abolishing slavery gradually. As mentioned, New York and New Jersey were the last to do so, and they did it in such a way as to allow the most calculating of masters to be compensated beyond their slaves' value and to enable slavery to linger, in declining numbers, until 1827 in New York and until much later in New Jersey. But if one deals with the rule rather than the exceptions, by the 1820s slavery had ceased to exist in the northern states.

The fervor of the Revolution played a role also in limiting the spread of slavery into some of the western lands where new states would emerge. In 1787 the Congress of the Articles of Confederation passed the Northwest Ordinance, a body of laws to govern the Northwest Territory, that vast hunk of land west of the Alleghenies that eventually would be divided into the states of Ohio, Indiana, Michigan, Illinois, and Wisconsin. The spirit of the successful Revolution, many believe, brought the group to include Article VI in the ordinance, which banned slavery or involuntary servitude in the territory. But it was not at all a simple matter. According to Paul Finkelman in "Slavery and the Northwest Territory: A Study in Ambiguity," *Jour-*

nal of the Early Republic, 6 (1986), the antislavery article "was ambiguous, internally inconsistent, and written by men who were uncertain of their objectives." Although Article VI was added to the ordinance just before its passage, meaning it received minimal discussion, although it received votes from southerners because they believed it strengthened slavery's existence south of the Ohio River by limiting it north of there, and although it was fraught with enough problems to allow slaveholders in the territories to keep some blacks in bondage and others in a form of indentured servitude not far removed from slavery into the 1830s, the article set the stage for the eventual existence of five free states. In that alone lies its importance.

To the number of persons freed by the abolition of slavery in the North was added a good-sized body of slaves freed in the South and a smaller group of runaways who ventured north. Between 1790 and 1830, masters in Delaware, Maryland, and Virginia manumitted thousands of slaves. Many of these saw greater opportunity in the northern states, especially in its cities. "For the first time the North Star came to symbolize freedom," writes Gary B. Nash in *Forging Freedom: The Formation of Philadelphia's Black Community, 1720–1840* (1988), and thus fugitives added to the numbers of blacks moving northward. Many came by sea, many by land, all lured by a vague promise of real freedom and a better life.

There seems to have been a small window of opportunity—it varied from place to place and, no doubt, did not exist at all in some locations—through which African Americans emerging from slavery could see opportunity and promise. Between about 1790 and 1815 in New York City, for example, some newly freed blacks recognized a bright side of their existence. Shane White in *Somewhat More Independent* shows that although most of New York's free African Americans who were no longer residing with whites lived in deplorable conditions, many in crowded cellars and attics, a number of them pieced together jobs of one sort or another, sold items on the street, found markets for their skills, and believed generally that they were living in a climate in which they could improve their lives. When New Yorkers feared a British invasion of the city in the summer of 1814, a large group of former slaves and sons of slaves met at 5:00 AM and crossed the East River to Brooklyn Heights, where they spent the day building fortifications. It was the "duty of every colored man resident in this city to volunteer," wrote a "Citizen of Color" to the *New York Evening Post*, because "we dwell in safety and pursue our honest callings, none daring to molest us, whatever his complexion or circumstances."

But northern blacks who were free by law or southern blacks who came north and overcame the initial obstacles—the trials surrounding flight and establishment of residence among strangers in a new location—must have realized before many years that substantial barriers blocked their pursuit of honest callings and that gaining freedom was not gaining citizenship. Leon F. Litwack writes in *North of Slavery: The Negro in the Free States, 1790–1860* (1961), "No statute or court decision could immediately erase from the public mind, North or South, that long and firmly held conviction that the African race was inferior and therefore incapable of being assimilated politically, socially, and most certainly physically with the dominant and superior white society." Thus, when John M. Duncan traveled through the northern states in 1818 and 1819, he would find "chains of a stronger kind still manacled [blacks'] limbs, from which no legislative act could free them; a mental and moral subordination and inferiority, to which tyrant custom has here subjected all the sons and daughters of Africa."

And it was not only "tyrant custom" that took an early toll. Many of the blacks who migrated into the northern cities around the turn of the century suffered from physical ailments. Chronic respiratory problems plagued African Americans who moved from southern states into the colder North, and the often poorer living conditions, especially the dank cellars that collected water and refuse, posed serious health problems for the new arrivals. "Out of the 48 blacks, living in ten cellars, 33 were sick, of whom 14 died;" read one early-nineteenth-century medical report from New York City, "while, out of 120 whites, living *immediately over their heads* in the *apartments of the same houses, not one* had the fever."

Also troubling to the free African-American population were the North's poor economic conditions generally. Seaborne commerce collapsed in the first decade of the nineteenth century, largely because of the Embargo of 1807 and the Nonintercourse Act that followed, and with it fell seamen's wages. For many African-American men, this was a vital blow. Numbers of them had come to northern cities because of the promise of getting maritime work or labor in the associated docks and warehouses. Moreover, out-of-work seamen on the larger labor market brought wages down across the board, and at the same time the cost of living rose. In the cities, new industries were beginning in response to the ending of British imports, but the new industrial jobs were usually reserved for whites. Finally, not enough white households needed servants to meet free blacks' demands for work. All of this meant that most new black arrivals had to scratch up what jobs they could find, usually on the lowest rung of the common-labor ladder—digging, loading, carrying, sweeping, or tending.

Studies of later periods have suggested that African-American women had an easier time than did African-American men in finding employment in the northern cities, mostly as domestics. But these studies do not reflect periods in the early nineteenth century during which men and women probably had nearly equal work opportunities, nor do they tend to focus on the taxing nature of the work African-American women ended up performing. The early republic was a time when being a domestic servant meant being a person who worked strenuously, on her feet, from before most whites got up and until they went to bed. Cooking, cleaning up after meals, and cleaning house were physically demanding tasks. Merely heating water necessitated hauling wood for a fire (and carrying out ashes). Monday was "wash day" because doing a family's laundry—from the heating of water to scrubbing with the washboard to hanging to dry to folding—while still cooking for the household and cleaning up afterwards took all day. Many African-American women in northern cities who could not find regular work in a white household "took in" washing—that is, they brought whites' laundry to their homes, washed the clothes, and returned them a day or two later. One enterprising African-American woman in turn-of-the-century New York City sold milk, butter, and eggs out of her basement, along with "cookies, pies, and sweetmeats of her own manufacture," and she took in washing for "several bachelor gentlemen in the neighborhood." Some black women worked as seamstresses, a job that was tedious but required less standing than most domestic work. Perhaps more fortunate still were the few African-American women who were proprietors of boarding houses for single men. Philadelphia had five such women in 1816. And whether from necessity or by choice, some African-American women joined white women in prostitution. Médéric Moreau de St. Méry noted in her *American Journal, 1793–1798* (1947) that "women of every color can be found in the streets, particularly after 10 o'clock at night, soliciting men and proudly flaunting their licentiousness in the most shameless manner."

On top of these general hardships, free black women who were not themselves heads of families lived with the knowledge that they would almost certainly outlive their husbands and thus face especially difficult years in widowhood. Women past middle age found it hard to keep the long hours of hard work required of domestics, and there were not many alternatives. The particularly difficult problems of widowhood for blacks explain the existence of a plethora of women's benevolent societies that appeared in the second and third decades of the nineteenth century. The preamble of one in Philadelphia read,

> Reflecting on the vicissitudes of life to which the female part of the community are continually exposed, and stimulated by the desire of improving our condition, [we] do conclude that the most efficient method of securing ourselves from the extreme exigencies to which we are liable to be reduced, is by uniting ourselves in a body for the purpose of raising a fund for the relief of its members.

If poor health, early death, and general problems finding work were not enough to dampen the hopes of newly freed African Americans, the real tyrant of custom, white racism, joined to do the job thoroughly. Simply because many northern whites condemned slavery did not mean that they cared at all for persons of African descent. The general feeling among whites in America at the start of the nineteenth century was that African Americans were different, inferior, and in many ways a kind of nuisance. Whites characterized blacks as shiftless, uneducated (perhaps uneducable), unproductive, and unpleasant to be around. With more African Americans arriving into northern cities, more northern whites recognized problems associated with racial differences. The common fear among whites was that African Americans who had rights and privileges equal to theirs would quickly step out of their "place," bring roguishness and incivility to gatherings, and most serious in tight economic times, compete for economic opportunities with persons of European descent. It was not something northern whites wanted to see happen.

The cleanest way to prevent such things was to exclude free blacks from the state, and a surprising number of northern states attempted to do so. New Jersey passed a law in 1786 that prohibited free African Americans from entering the state to reside there. A 1788 Massachusetts law that dealt with "Rogues, vagabonds, common beggars, and other idle, disorderly, and lewd Persons" identified African Americans with such types; one clause of the law excluded all blacks from the state if they could not prove their citizenship. And as the size of the free black populations rose in cities along the eastern seaboard, more eastern states tried to keep blacks out. Even Pennsylvania, the center of early antislavery activity, belied its image of being benevolent toward African Americans. The state legislature barely defeated restrictive legislation in the first decade of the nineteenth century, and Philadelphia's white leadership continued to petition the state to close Pennsylvania borders to blacks, who were "becoming nuisances."

New states entering the union were in positions to deal quickly and decisively with the "free-black problem." Ohio had been a state barely a year when, in 1804, its legislature required free African Americans in the state "to give bond and security for the sum of $500 for their good conduct." The first Illinois legislative assembly in 1819 passed a series of "Black Laws" that made it nearly impossible for African Americans to enter the state: a free black wanting to live in the state had to post a $1,000 bond, guaranteeing that he or she would not become a public charge; all free blacks in Illinois had to register and obtain certification; anyone employing an uncertified African American was subject to a fine; and black persons living in the state without the necessary certification were deemed runaway slaves and so treated. The enforcement of such laws was seldom careful and rigid, but their existence had the effect of keeping African Americans out of the states through the middle of the nineteenth century—just the effect the states' leaders had intended.

In places where free blacks could enter and reside in the North, they had few rights and privileges. Litwack's book is a detailed catalogue of the varied proscriptions the northern states reserved for African Americans. Northern restrictions on black voting grew with potential black voting strength, to the point that, by the end of the early republic, some 80 percent of northern free blacks lived in states that disallowed them to exercise the fundamental right of democracy. Social custom in most northern states prevented blacks from serving on juries, and some states refused to admit the testimony of blacks in courts of law. This latter fact prompted an Ohio judge to declare, "The white man may now plunder the Negro, he may abuse his person; he may take his life: He may do this in open daylight . . . and he must go acquitted, unless . . . there . . . be some white man present."

If the absence of political and judicial rights and privileges was not a daily thorn in the side of free African Americans in the North, segregation was. Forced separation of black from white served as a public expression of the social inferiority of African Americans. By the second decade of the nineteenth century, racial segregation, driven by the force of white public opinion, had crept into most aspects of northern life. Litwack summarizes the separate treatment:

> [African Americans] sat, when permitted, in secluded and remote corners of theaters and lecture halls; they could not enter most hotels, restaurants, and resorts, except as servants; they prayed in "Negro pews" in the white churches, and if partaking of the sacrament of the Lord's Supper, they waited until whites had been served the bread and wine. Moreover, they were often educated in segregated schools, punished in segregated prisons, nursed in segregated hospitals, and buried in segregated cemeteries.

Some northern states feared racial mixing enough to outlaw interracial marriage. And residential segregation was a fact of life in most cities. Economic conditions and social pressures shunted poor African Americans off to live in various "Little Africas" or "Nigger

Hills," the forerunners of the larger black ghettos of a century later. It was such conditions that prompted an English traveler, Henry B. Fearon, to observe in 1818 that all of northern society was divided into dichotomous groups—"Brahmins and Pariahs." No one had to guess which group included free blacks.

Where legislation and more subtle social pressures failed to exclude free African Americans or to keep them in a sufficiently subordinate position, mob violence succeeded. Mobs had long been crude instruments for expressing and manifesting a perceived common interest. In the unsettling times of the early nineteenth century, popular disorder could take on an air of legitimacy, giving the mob a "proper social function." Among most whites in America's cities, controlling the rapidly growing group of free blacks, whom whites considered potentially unruly, was such a function. Whites of the lower class, who competed with African Americans in the labor market, regarded persons of African descent as threats to racial purity and liked having an identifiable group that was below them in status; hatred and fear combined to provide a host of reasons for mob activity aimed at blacks.

In the early years of the free black community's formation, the important social institutions of African Americans—their churches, mutual aid societies, and schools—seemed to symbolize independence and upward mobility to whites, so they became the major focus of disruptive activity. Churches were singled out the most, probably, explains Paul A. Gilje in *The Road to Mobocracy: Popular Disorder in New York City, 1763–1834* (1987), because "whites understood the strength and solace blacks received from . . . their own religious exercises . . . [and] feared the sense of moral equality, even superiority, enjoyed by blacks through regular religious worship." Independent black churches in New York and Philadelphia have left records from early in the nineteenth century of regular white harassment—doors broken in, services disrupted. Once, in Philadelphia, whites threw cayenne pepper and salt into a church's wood-burning stove during a Sunday evening service, causing a rush to the door that left two of the African-American parishioners dead. After a virtual race riot following a black church service in Philadelphia in

1829, a local newspaper wrote that "on Sundays, especially, [blacks] seem to think themselves above all restraint, and their insolence is intolerable."

White rioting in black sections of northern cities became frequent in the 1820s. In 1824 a mob of sixty whites spent over four hours tearing down all twenty buildings in a black section of Providence, Rhode Island. In 1826 a Boston mob demolished several houses in the city's "Negro Hill" section. Riots in Philadelphia, Portsmouth, Ohio, Hartford, Connecticut, and Providence between 1829 and 1831 pitted white mobs against free blacks.

The episode that had the most telling results was the riot in Cincinnati, Ohio, in the summer of 1829. It was then that the city's government, hoping to reduce the size of Cincinnati's growing black population, attempted to enforce the state's twenty-two-year-old black laws that required African Americans to post a $500 bond for their good behavior. Large numbers of the city's African-American men and women planned to move to Canada in response, as many of the city's whites had wished, but when the evacuation did not proceed as quickly as some believed it should, mobs of angry whites got involved. For four nights in mid-August a group of several hundred whites assailed Cincinnati's black west end, according to a contemporary newspaper account, "throwing stones, demolishing houses, [and] doing every other act of violence." The targets of the riot remained inside through most of the activity, but on the fifth night, tired of waiting for police protection, some African Americans fought back, shooting into the white mob and killing one man. This halted the rioting but speeded the African-American exodus. Between July and December of 1829 more than one thousand black Cincinnatians made the northward trek to Canada. Charles Hammond, who edited the Cincinnati *Gazette*, wrote in September of that year that the riot "has driven away the sober, honest, industrious, and useful portion of the coloured population . . . [and] has demonstrated the humiliating fact that cruelty and injustice, the rank oppression of a devoted people, may be consummated in the midst of us without exciting either sympathy, or operative indignation."

One particular danger that free blacks faced in the North—and one that hung over the heads of many an African American as he or she went about business—was kidnapping. Most African Americans in northern states had been slaves; most had gained their freedom legally, but some had not. As part of the effort to appease disaffected southern interests, the United States Constitution included a fugitive-slave clause in Article IV, Section 2, which read, "No person held to service or labour in one State, under the laws thereof, escaping into another, shall, in consequence of any law or regulation therein, be discharged from such service or labour, but shall be delivered up on claim of the party to whom such service or labour may be due." In 1793 Congress passed an act to bring about such "delivery." It allowed slave owners or their agents to seize a fugitive slave and take him or her before a judge or magistrate. The judge could allow the master to remove his human property on the basis of the testimony of the master only that the slave had escaped. Persons caught harboring fugitives could be fined five hundred dollars. The law was absent of penalties for kidnapping freed persons and selling them into slavery.

Under the broad umbrella of this law, kidnapping of African Americans became common. Authorized agents of slave owners were not always careful about the identity of the persons they seized—sometimes they had never cast eyes on the fugitives they were seeking. Worse yet, persons of bad character frequently posed as slave owners or agents in search of fugitives. They roamed the streets and back alleys of cities, waiting for the opportunity to nab an unsuspecting free black. Because of the law, such kidnappers could rather easily receive a certificate to transport the man or woman "back home" toward the South. Or a kidnapper might forego legal particulars altogether and simply abscond with the victim; once into Maryland or Virginia, he could sell his captive to a slave trader. Black mutual benefit societies and churches worked to help the victims of such illegal treatment, and so did some of the whites who opposed slavery. In the mid-1820s, Pennsylvania and New York began a trend among northern states by passing "personal-liberty laws," which attempted to safeguard the personal liberty of free blacks by interposing state regulations that went beyond the requirements of the federal law for seizing suspected fugitives. But so long as persons of African descent were bringing good prices, with few questions asked, in the cities of the Upper South, kidnapping remained a serious threat to free African Americans.

Thus, by 1830 the prospects for free blacks in the north were dim. The bevy of state and federal legislation, social custom, and popular pressure that bound free blacks to membership in a lower social, economic, and political order prompted Philadelphia Quaker Roberts Vaux in 1831 to write,

> The popular feeling is against them—the interests of our citizens are against them. The small degree of compassion once cherished toward them in the commonwealths which got rid of slavery, or which never were disfigured by it, appears to be exhausted. Their prospects either as free, or bond men, are dreary, and comfortless.

Freedom in the South

The situation was different and generally worse south of Pennsylvania and the Ohio River, where slavery continued to exist and grow. In the Upper South, the rush of emancipation and hope that came in the wake of the Revolution lasted about a generation before it declined, leaving a sizable black community, especially in rural areas but also in several cities. In the Lower South, the free black population started small and grew much more slowly: it was unique in being light skinned, urban centered, privileged, and conservative. Across the South generally the larger the free African-American population became, the more restrictions followed closely in its wake.

As in the North, independence brought a nascent abolition spirit in the states of the Upper South. Between 1782 and 1790, every southern state except North Carolina altered its laws to permit owners to manumit their slaves, and the new southern states, Kentucky and Tennessee, followed suit. With liberation in the wind (and with slave prices falling by about half over the decade following the Revolution), a wave of manumission broke across the Upper South. There was less emancipation from Virginia's Southside on into North Carolina, but even there masters subverted the law and turned slaves over to Quaker "trustees" or simply let them go as they pleased. As freedom spread in the Upper South, African Americans in slavery took initiative and brought suit to obtain it, or purchased it, or simply stole away as fugitives. Thus came the dramatic rise in the numbers of free blacks, especially across Delaware, Maryland, and northern Virginia. There may have been between 4,000 and 5,000 African Americans in the Upper South who were not slaves in 1780. In 1790 there were 30,000, in 1800 57,000, and by 1810, when there were 94,000, free African Americans were the most rapidly growing segment of the Upper South's population. Moreover, these were not just light-skinned people, the injured, the chronically infirm, or the elderly. The early-nineteenth-century free black population of the Upper South included persons who were as dark skinned as most slaves and who were young and vigorous.

The especially rapid growth of the Upper South's free black population lasted for about a quarter of a century. After 1810 the rate of growth dropped dramatically—to 20 percent between 1810 and 1820—and although it rose again slightly in the 1820s, it continued to fall steadily thereafter. The primary source of the early increase, manumissions, dwindled as legal restrictions and popular pressure cut into masters' freedom and willingness to emancipate their slaves. By the 1820s, such manumission that occurred in the Upper South was mostly in single numbers. By then, those being freed were slaves who, for whatever reasons, had become their masters' favorites. These included more women than men, for more women worked close to whites (as domestics) and tended to gain their favor more (and probably threatened them less) than did men. More slaves who were house servants and who possessed artisanal skills were freed than those who were field hands. Later, manumission occurred more frequently in or around the growing southern cities. Thus, by 1830, the free black community of the Upper South had an important urban and skilled element, and the urban portion of the community was disproportionately female.

In spite of the steady movement of free blacks to the Upper-South cities, the region's free African-American population remained largely rural. Like newly emancipated African Americans in the North, those in the Upper South made a quick break with their former owners. They removed themselves from their former masters' property as quickly as practicable, taking into consideration the pull of the kin and community to remain.

The urban element of the Upper South's free African-American population followed certain patterns that were similar to their counterparts' in northern cities. They tended early on to look to the waterfront and the sea for employment, they took up many of the same trades—wood cutting, carpentry, smithing, tailoring, and baking, for instance—and over time they formed their own neighborhoods and communities.

The sexual imbalance among free blacks in the cities of the Upper South, however, caused African-American women serious problems that may not have been shared to the same extent by their northern counterparts. Most southern African-American women were manumitted separately from their husbands, yet half of them were freed with their children. This meant that many black women in the southern cities were the heads of households who had no choice but to work. Poor women, black or white, found it nearly impossible to land jobs beyond the most menial—working most commonly as housekeepers, cooks, laundresses, seamstresses, street peddlers. Some with special skills or resources might run small grocery stores or taverns or become medical practitioners or midwives. And as in so many urban locales, prostitution was a resort of the destitute.

Suzanne Lebsock includes information on southern African-American women during the early republic in *The Free Women of Petersburg: Status and Culture in a Southern Town, 1784–1860* (1984). Petersburg, in southern Virginia, grew rapidly with the new nation. It boasted around three thousand people in 1790 and almost twice that many in 1810. By early in the nineteenth century, free black women outnumbered free black men in Petersburg by a ratio of three to two, they were the heads of over half of the town's free black households, they made up nearly half of the paid free black labor force, and they lived in grinding poverty. As late as 1860, half of the free African-American women heads of households in Petersburg owned no property whatsoever, not a stick of furniture. As Lebsock puts it, when speaking of Petersburg's free black women, "[t]here is not much material for romanticizing."

Still, most newly emancipated men and women continued to work in agriculture, as they had in slavery. The region's burgeoning cereal cultivation lent itself to wage labor; freed African Americans could find themselves harvesting or threshing alongside blacks still in slavery, sometimes even living in or next to a slave quarter. Such contact sometimes led to intermarriage between free persons and slaves, and there were instances of masters allowing slaves to cohabit with free persons. In this way and others, Upper-South free blacks and slaves continued to have much in common. While some newly freed African Americans did indeed move away, begin to collect wages, and mold a new life based on the freedom to go and do as they pleased, many remained tied by kinship, experience, and even material existence to those still in bondage. And for most, slave or free, there remained the common bond of having white oppressors.

Much of this was different in the Lower South. The Revolutionary ideology failed to convince many slaveholders in South Carolina and Georgia to free their slaves. Those who manumitted did so for paternalistic reasons—they freed individual slaves to whom they were most closely connected, sometimes by blood. But the small number of free blacks that existed in the Lower South by the 1790s, almost exclusively in such cities as Charleston and Savannah, was augmented by an influx of skilled, mostly light-skinned persons who were fleeing from the revolution on Saint Domingue. Then, too, when Louisiana was added to American territory in 1803, it contained more than two thousand *gens de couleur* (people of color) who were products of extramarital black-white unions in the time of Spanish or French rule, a liberal Spanish policy for self-purchase, or voluntary immigration from Saint Domingue. Thus, by 1810 the Lower South had its own free African-American population of more than fourteen thousand, concentrated heavily in the coastal cities.

Unlike in the North and Upper South, free blacks in the Lower South, from the beginning, were different from other African Americans in the region—and from nearly all blacks in the country. The selective manumission, coupled with the influx of artisans from the West Indies, had produced a largely mulatto group whose members were wealthy, educated, well connected, and relatively privileged. They appreciated their special place as a kind of third and middle caste in the slave society, and they recognized the effort that would be necessary for them to preserve that place. They thus became a conservative force, fearing that change of any kind for them could be only in a negative direction.

Free African Americans in the Lower South manifested their conservative outlook in nearly every aspect of their lives. If blacks in the rest of the country left their residences, changed their names, and sought new work almost as soon as they were freed, often to the chagrin of their former masters, the free persons of color in the Lower South did the opposite: they remained close to the white upper class, cultivating their friendship and showing their loyalty; they kept the surnames of the great slaveholding families; and they tried to work as close to and be as social with influential whites as they could. Of course, this did not always win white favor. White planters remained wary of the threat that people of color posed to their elite social and economic position. In a recent article, "Free Blacks in a Slave Society: New Orleans, 1718–1812," *William and Mary Quarterly*, 3rd series, 68 (1991), Thomas N. Ingersoll argues that neither their relative large numbers, their economic importance, nor their loyal service to the state in an organized militia brought free African Americans in New Orleans significantly higher status or better treatment. In that southern city, writes Ingersoll, "by concerting the powers of the local, state, and federal governments against free blacks to degrade them and limit their numbers, planters ensured the system of racial supremacy that allowed them to exploit blacks and command the loyalty of nonslaveholding whites."

Still, living and working in a part of the country where the economy and society rested squarely on African-American chattel slavery, the free people of color in the Lower South had a constant reminder of how much worse their lives could be. Establishing their identity as separate from slaves was a necessity that required their serious effort and constant attention. When whites did not want to congregate with them, they formed their own institutions, like Charleston's Brown Fellowship Society and its Free Dark Men of Color. They wanted no part in an organization that had the word "African" in its title and no membership in a community that included slaves—unless they owned them. Some free blacks in the Lower South did grow wealthy enough to own slaves. In 1830, approximately 3,700 free African Americans, mostly in the Lower South, owned nearly 12,000 slaves. And it was no protective and benevolent form of ownership as existed here and there in the Upper South. According to Loren Schweninger in *Black Property Owners in the South, 1790–1915* (1990), most of the free people of color who owned slaves "considered their blacks primarily as chattel property. They bought, sold, mortgaged, willed, traded, and transferred fellow Negroes, demanded long hours in the workshops and fields, and severely disciplined recalcitrant blacks." Schweninger mentions two African-born mulatto brothers who owned rice plantations in South Carolina worked by one hundred slaves and who made a "substantial fortune" off the Atlantic slave trade before 1808. Another free African American from Alabama, A. F. Edwards, participated in the domestic slave trade. He used the Mobile *Advertiser* in 1835 to inform potential customers, "I have a regular correspondence with gentlemen in the market where Negroes are bought as well as where they are sold."

The fact that a good number of free blacks in the Lower South owned African-American slaves underscores the distance that freedom placed between the free and the enslaved there. In the North and Upper South, free blacks remembered their roots, continued to empathize with the slaves' plight (which in freedom was still not always worlds apart from their own), and participated in community activities with those still in slavery. But in the Lower South, little of this was the case. There, freedom had spawned a small, wealthy, light-skinned, privileged class, who knew that any expansion of slaves' liberties would probably mean a contraction of their own.

With the possible exception of some of the most privileged free persons of color, nearly all newly emancipated African Americans throughout the South faced difficult times. Beginning independent living with minimal resources was everywhere a tall order, but making times worse was the body of restrictions and prohibitions that southern states began to place on free blacks. As the size of the southern free black population grew, and as its nature changed from being largely that of persons of lighter skin to persons of generally darker complexion, whites began to question long-standing colonial policies that gave free African Americans a good portion of the rights held by whites. Racial subordination was still vital to control in a slave society, so equality between individual members of the races was threatening. New legislation had to overturn the old colonial practices and ensure the subordination of free blacks.

Controlling the growth of the free African-American community was an important first step. Beginning in the 1790s, state laws limited the work of the small southern abolitionist societies, and popular pressure forced evangelical Christians to back away from antislavery activities. Then, systematically, southern state legislatures began whittling away at free blacks' rights. Most southern states banned African Americans from voting in the early part of the nineteenth century. Fearing the intermingling of slaves and free blacks, states began restricting the latter's mobility. Virginia was the leader, prohibiting free African Americans from entering the commonwealth in 1793 and then, in 1806, requiring newly freed African Americans to leave the state. Not wanting to be warders for Virginia's fleeing blacks, other states followed the Virginia model. To control free African Americans within their borders, states passed new legislation requiring all free blacks to register their existence. North Carolina made free African Americans wear a shoulder patch with the word "Free" inscribed on it; in Virginia, urban free blacks had to reregister each year. Such new states as Kentucky and Tennessee merely borrowed many of these laws from the older states.

At the bench, justice was not long blind for free blacks. A free African American in seventeenth-century Virginia could sue a white under the law, but by the nineteenth century not only was such a suit impossible, but in some states persons of African descent were not allowed to have a jury trial. White justices of the peace, in touch with the will of the local gentry, handled such procedures. Of all the southern states, only Delaware allowed free blacks to testify against whites, while all allowed slaves to testify against free blacks. Free persons of African descent regularly received punishments not meted out to whites—most notably sale into servitude that was tantamount to a return to slavery. An 1811 Delaware law, for instance, dealt with free blacks convicted of stealing horses by selling those found guilty to the West Indies for up to fourteen years.

Without the law on their side, free African Americans in the South had to live in fear of being kidnapped and returned to slavery. Being unable to testify against whites stymied justice for most of the black men and women who were stolen, for the simple reason that in most cases of kidnapping the only witnesses were blacks. As prices for slaves in the Lower South rose steadily through the first third of the nineteenth century, so did incidents of kidnapping in the Upper South. Free black communities banded together and formed organizations to thwart kidnappers, like Baltimore's Society for Relief in Case of Seizure, but with prosecution of kidnappers remaining difficult and with public apathy toward the kidnapping of free blacks that seems to have grown with the years, being captured and returned to bondage was a free African American's nightmare that could quite possibly come true.

Whites also quickly eroded whatever competitive chance free blacks had in the southern economy. Of particular importance was keeping the newly emancipated African Americans under white economic control. Vagrancy laws became standard devices for extorting free-black labor, and when those were insufficient, states began to find ways to "bind out" free blacks between the ages of eight and twenty-one so that they would work for whites and learn "proper" respect and behavior. By the beginning of the nineteenth century, writes Berlin in *Slaves Without Masters*, "At any time, any white could demand proof of a free Negro's status; even if his papers were in order, an unemployed free Negro could be jailed and enslaved and his children bound out to strangers."

In the few places where African Americans found economic opportunity, southern legislators found ways to stifle it. Maryland prohibited free African Americans from selling agricultural produce without a special permit; Virginia and Georgia prevented free blacks from becoming riverboat captains or pilots; and some cities barred free blacks from specific occupations. Virginia, Georgia, and South Carolina levied special taxes on free persons of African descent.

Fears generated by the Haitian Revolution and by the widespread unrest surrounding Gabriel's insurrection further eroded free blacks' rights and privileges. Some of the laws entered into the realm of the ridiculous. Maryland required African Americans to license their guns and dogs; Delaware barred blacks from towns on election day; and in various places free blacks were fined or whipped for entertaining slaves, meeting in groups of more than seven, attending school, or holding church meetings. Some slave codes were not so strict.

Still, the law was not always the final word. When in the eyes of white southerners free African Americans had forgotten their "place" in society, or when whites felt uneasy from the mere presence of "too large" a number of free blacks in their midst, extralegal action was sometimes the result. In 1821, in Amelia County, Virginia, a vigilante band came together "for the purpose of chastising a set of free negroes in the county who were of bad fame and who had associated with them a white woman of foul character." "Chastising" was little more than a euphemism for brutal punishment that kept blacks intimidated and docile. A white Virginian wrote in the *Richmond Enquirer* early in 1831,

> who does not know that when a free negro . . . has rendered himself obnoxious to a neighborhood, how easy it is for a party to visit him one night, take him from his bed and family, and apply to him the gentle admonition of a severe flagellation, to induce him to *consent* to go away? In a few nights the dose can be repeated, perhaps increased, until . . . the fellow becomes perfectly willing to go away.

African Americans who were slaves had protection from their masters from such extralegal terror, for masters cared for their property and had means of defense, but free blacks by themselves had no such means. Their only recourse was an ounce of prevention in the form of established relationships with important white people. Free African Americans wisely sought and kept on their persons certificates of good character from white employers or customers, so when vigilantes came "chastising," the word of a powerful white might lead them to pass over the certificate's bearer.

Berlin summarizes the difficult circumstances of free blacks in the South and the broad movement in the southern states to hamstring the free African-American population:

> By the beginning of the nineteenth century, the ambiguity that characterized the status of the free Negro during colonial years was gone and the equalitarian enthusiasm of the Revolutionary years had run its course. Whites had pushed free Negroes into a place of permanent legal inferiority. Like slaves, free Negroes were generally without political rights, were unable to move freely, were prohibited from testifying against whites, and were often punished with the lash. Indeed, the free Negro's only right that escaped unscathed was his ability to hold property—a striking commentary on the American idea of liberty.

Freedom's Struggle

For a number of years, historians examining the lives of free African Americans before the Civil War focused on the myriad of proscriptions the lower-caste-like group faced. It was the ever-broadening body of economic, social, and political restraints that made the group of persons of African descent only *quasi*-free, and indeed, in some instances placed them in positions not far removed from bodies of slaves. But in recent years a handful of historians have suggested that focus on all that was done unto the free blacks distorts a balanced view of them and, in effect, relegates them to a mass of humanity defined by the objective case. According to Shane White in *Somewhat More Independent*, New York City's newly emancipated blacks, for instance, "were not passive ciphers, helplessly swept along by currents of repression and discrimination and controlled solely by whites." Instead, they were "exceptional men and women," whose story "illustrates their ingenuity and strength." All up and down the eastern seaboard, it was the free African Americans over the generation immediately following the Revolution who separated themselves from slavery forever and survived the difficult transition to freedom with a sense of optimism intact. It was this group that struggled to create or maintain black family life and ultimately established the basic institutions—churches, schools, self-help societies—that would join with the family in forming and holding together the free African-American community.

Across the northern states and through much of the Upper South, once African Americans gained their freedom they went through a process of cultural transformation and creation that was remarkably similar. Speaking generally, only the timing of the process seems to have varied between the regions and among specific locales.

One of the first things newly emancipated blacks did was to terminate their most obvious links with the past. Coming up with new names was an important first step. Berlin writes, "A new name was both a symbol of personal liberation and an act of political defiance; it reversed the enslavement process and confirmed the free Negro's newly won liberty." Within a generation of emancipation, free blacks had cast aside the supposedly comic, classical or derisive forenames of the days of slavery. By 1800 it was rare to find a young, free African American named Caesar or Pompey, Mistake or Moody. Also rare was the free black who clung to the surname of the former master. Early-nineteenth-century city directories show that African Americans in their freedom preferred common English forenames—John, William, Thomas, and such surnames as Johnson, Brown, and Smith.

Once freed, African Americans tended to want to leave the site of their enslavement. Slavery had always restricted men and women's physical mobility. A true test of their freedom was in their ability to take to the road and go elsewhere. But practical considerations often affected the former slave's decision to get away. In the states where slavery remained a legal institution, freed persons often had family and friends still in bondage, and even when that was not the case, ties to old homes could remain strong. Naturally, one of the first considerations upon leaving was finding the means to subsist. Masters who had been moved by the libertarian ideology to manumit the men and women they held in bondage rarely felt any compulsion to see that their former slaves had a way to make a living. Few left slavery with more in their possession than the clothes they were wearing, a few rough pieces of furniture, some cooking pots, and a tiny bit of money. Some had no alternative but to hire themselves back to their former masters under conditions that approximated slavery. Even skilled slaves had initial problems leaving home and finding good jobs.

But ties to the community and practical matters did not always carry the day. The desire to move from the place that held the memory of servitude weighed heavily. Sooner or later, most free blacks moved away. They went in all directions, a few over long distances to Canada or Haiti, many more on short treks to neighboring counties. A steady number of freed blacks in the border regions of Delaware, Maryland, and northern Virginia traveled the relatively short distances north, where in Pennsylvania, New York, or New England their freedom would be more secure. But it was most common for former slaves to remain in the general latitudes of their bondage. In the Upper South, where opportunities existed for wage labor or tenant farming, many free blacks found work in rural areas.

Yet, if there was a trend in the free black movement across the land, it was toward the growing urban areas, where they believed the greatest number of opportunities existed. From Boston to Savannah, free African-American populations grew at astonishing rates between 1790 and 1810. Philadelphia's black population was just over 2,000 in 1790; it was nearly 10,000 in 1810. New York's jumped from 1,000 to 7,500 over the same period. And Baltimore's free black growth rate was even more phenomenal—from 323 in 1790 to 5,671 in 1810—an increase of 1,655 percent. Although more free blacks remained outside the cities in the South, by the end of the first decade of the nineteenth century it was clear that an important center of the free African-American community would be the country's urban areas.

It would be naive, of course, to believe that all African Americans who gained their freedom launched themselves onto paths of hard work and clean living. As in all groups, the growing number of free blacks had an irresponsible element. Some newly emancipated persons left their families, took to the sea, traveled for years, and never settled down. Because slavery was so closely associated with working, some equated freedom with never having to toil, and these went down a road of idleness and shiftlessness that often ended in the public almshouse or jailhouse; worse yet, some ended up like John Richards, who, according to the coroner's report, died in New York in January 1804, "from want of Bedding, Cloathing, and the Common Necessaries of Life. . . ." And like whites of the same time (and before and since), some members of the free African-American community stole money and goods from whites and other blacks (forcing historians to recognize limits on any concept of black community), overindulged in alcohol, had children out of wedlock, and scrapped and fought over slights, real and imagined. (One real slight that erupted into a brawl occurred in a New York tavern in 1802 after one black man stubbed out his "segar" in another man's drink.)

But a remarkable number of newly emancipated African Americans faced life's challenges soberly and got about the business of making their existence as good as it could be. The first generations of free blacks were particularly intent on perpetuating or creating the family life that had been important in bondage. In the North or in the South, this was hard to do. Men and women in the southern states, plus some in northern states where emancipation was gradual, faced the added problem of having loved ones who remained in slavery. Former slaves entered freedom without means, but many devoted years of hard work and austere living to accumulate enough money to purchase the freedom of their kin. Petersburg, Virginia, may have been typical of the experience in other Upper-South cities. Between 1784 and 1820, free blacks were responsible, through purchase, for one-sixth of all manumissions there (and one-half of these black emancipators were women). Petersburg shoemaker Graham Bell worked long hours, saved carefully, and between 1792 and 1805 purchased the freedom of seven family members and three others. When purchase for the sake of manumission became more difficult, African Americans found other options. Philip J. Schwarz in "Emancipators, Protectors, and Anomalies: Free Black Slaveowners in Virginia," *Virginia Magazine of History and Biography*, 95 (1987), shows how some Virginia free blacks before 1830 became, in effect, masters themselves as they purchased as slaves their own family members who could not otherwise be freed and kept them in a form of bondage that was "fraternal, protective, and benevolent by design."

Emancipated blacks in the North faced difficulties trying to maintain or create new families, for migration to cities and a subsequent life in poverty made family life a struggle for all. Reporting on studies of several hundred African-American households in each of three northern cities in the 1820 census, Gary B. Nash in "Forging Freedom: The Emancipation Experience in the Northern Seaport Cities, 1775–1820," in Berlin and Hoffman, *Slavery and Freedom in the Age of the American Revolution* identifies a process of household formation that commonly occurred:

> Emancipated Afro-Americans first extricated themselves from white households; then often combined households, with relatives, friends, and boarders intermingling; and finally, as they were able, established nuclear households. . . . The process proceeded at different rates . . . , but everywhere black family life grew more secure.

Not all urban black families went through the process described above at the same time or at the same pace: slavery ended at different times in various cities, and economic and social pressures were not the same from city to city. But given their past in slavery and the obvious economic difficulties African Americans faced in trying to secure monogamous families, the change to nuclear or at least stable families took place relatively rapidly. In fact, it is remarkable how successful the earliest generations of free blacks were at creating family structures. Through the first two decades of the nineteenth century, over 85 percent of black children in Philadelphia grew up in male-headed, and in most cases two-parent, households. "Black sojourners in Philadelphia constructed and reconstructed families very quickly and maintained them through the first quarter of the nineteenth century," Nash maintains, "with at least as great success as white families of the working class." Free blacks in the South moved toward family households and stable, nuclear families in much the same fashion and speed. One suspects that the cyclical nature of the slave family—the destruction, construction, and dispersal—had left the newly emancipated African Americans with useful experience at reestablishing family structures.

The free black households that were forming in urban locations gradually moved to areas of the cities where other blacks were located, and thus clusters of black residences emerged. In southern cities these clusters seem to have remained small and separate. In some of the largest northern cities, however, with black family incomes low, these clusters often formed where housing was cheapest—in southern Philadelphia, for instance, or around the "Five Points" district in New York—and grew to some size. It was these clusters and neighborhoods that came to be the centers of the free black community. What followed in fairly close order in these locations was the establishment of the extrafamilial organizations—African-American churches, mutual benefit societies, and schools—that would serve as the community's institutional foundation.

African Americans did not enter freedom intent on establishing their own, separate, distinct social institutions. Most welcomed the opportunity to attend Christian worship services in established congregations and to have their children benefit from existing schools. But in these white-dominated institutions, blacks were denied admission or segregated and treated as inferior. The alternative, therefore, was for African-Americans to create their own institutions.

Mutual aid societies and independent black churches were the first social institutions to appear in the rapidly growing free black community of the late eighteenth century. They were closely associated in many cases and became important, first in the urban areas, at about the same time.

Poor African Americans first formed mutual aid societies to perform collectively those vital functions that they could not afford to carry out individually—burial of the dead, care for the sick, and the support of widows and orphans. These societies entered onto the urban scene over the first decades of the early republic and soon filled a social and economic niche in free black communities. The Newport, Rhode Island, African Union Society was the first black mutual benefit society; it began in 1780. Philadelphia's better-known Free African Society came into being in 1787. Thereafter, more of such societies appeared in northern cities, and their numbers grew, especially over the decade between 1802 and 1812. Nine new benevolent societies appeared in Philadelphia between 1810 and 1812, and by 1830 the city had over one hundred such organizations, with an average membership of 175. Southern free blacks formed mutual aid societies, too, but southern whites' fears of African Americans in any size assembly, for whatever reason, often limited these organizations' ability to grow or function. Baltimore had more black mutual aid societies than any other southern city—thirty by the 1830s; Charleston had two major societies, one for the light-skinned (the Brown Fellowship Society) and one for the dark (the Free Dark Men of Color). Many mutual aid societies had close ties to the spreading black churches; some had bases in occupations (the Coachmen's Benevolent or the Humane Mechanics Society, for example); and many attempted to maintain an identity with blacks' African heritage through their names—the Daughters of Ethiopia, the Daughters of Samaria, the Angola Society, or the Sons of Africa. African Lodges of the Masons, all outgrowths of the activities of Massachusetts African American Prince Hall, who received an English charter for a Boston lodge in 1784 when he could not get one from American Masons, lent secrecy, ritual, regalia, ceremony, and prestige to the usual economic and social functions of the societies.

At the heart of the credo of free black mutual aid societies were a moralistic ideal, a middle-class outlook on getting ahead, and a desire to assist those African Americans in desperate need. Members of Philadelphia's Free African Society had to pay one shilling per month for redistribution to those who needed assistance, "provided the necessity is not brought on them by their own imprudence." The ranks of the societies were almost universally closed to those unable to lead sober and respectable lives. Enforcement of these strict codes was important, members believed, for those not long out of bondage needed good models of behavior and rules for living if they hoped to gain acceptance in American society. As the societies became more firmly established, their functions expanded. Some lent money to worthy members, invested in black businesses, or formed the equivalent of insurance companies.

The independent black church also existed to help its members—socially and economically, as well as spiritually. White racism prompted their separate and independent existence. Through the late eighteenth century, white congregations admitted African Americans to worship services. Most blacks gravitated toward the evangelical denominations, where the only demand for salvation was acceptance of the gospel. Some white congregations even allowed black preachers to conduct services, and in some mixed congregations blacks and whites shared control of church business. But the trend in white-controlled, interracial churches was to include rules and customs that separated the races. When they were permitted to attend the same services as whites, African Americans were often seated separately in "Africa corners." And blacks often had to hold baptisms, take communion, or attend Sunday school with members of their race only. Rankled by all this, free African Americans began forming their own congregations. Separate black churches popped up here and there across the South, beginning with the Silver Bluffs (South Carolina) Baptist Church and the First African Baptist Church of Savannah in the mid–1770s. Separate services for southern free blacks proved possible in some locations, but independence from white control turned out to be more difficult to achieve. The initial movement toward fully independent black churches took place in northern and border-state cities. Two Philadelphia free blacks, Richard Allen and Absalom Jones, were pioneers in the movement.

Allen was born a slave of a Philadelphia lawyer in 1760 and was sold to a middling farmer in Delaware when he was an adolescent. Allen's financially troubled new master sold off Allen's parents and younger siblings in 1777. It was about then that the saddened youngster listened to the call for spiritual rebirth from evangelical preachers and embraced Methodism. Allen's master allowed him to purchase his freedom in 1780—he took the name Richard Allen to signify his free status—and after several years of riding the Methodist circuits, he settled in Philadelphia. Once there, he drew blacks into the St. George's Methodist Church, a small building with a dirt floor where the white membership permitted him to preach to blacks at 5:00 A.M. It was here that Allen met Jones, also a former slave from Delaware, and with him soon established the Free African Society.

Older than Allen by thirteen years, Jones had been a household slave in a prominent Delaware merchant-planter family. He learned to read and write, and in 1762, when his master decided to move to

Philadelphia, he took Jones with him. Jones's mother and six siblings were sold away. In the city, Jones worked long hours, saved money, and attended school at night. He married, purchased his wife's freedom, bought a house, and then, in 1783, was allowed to buy his own freedom. A few years later he found himself listening to Allen in St George's church.

Allen, Jones, and a number of other free blacks soon came to understand that it was impossible for a truly biracial church to exist, even in the "City of Brotherly Love." They had been collecting small amounts of money to begin a racially separate, nondenominational church, while still attending services with whites at St. George's in 1792, when an event in the church convinced them, in Allen's words, of the immediacy of establishing a place "to worship God under our own vine and fig tree." Black worshippers had contributed money and labor to an expansion of St. George's, but on the first Sunday following the work's completion, whites decided to segregate the congregation, then and there. Allen relates the experience in *The Life Experiences and Gospel Labors of Rt. Rev. Richard Allen* (1960):

> We expected to take the seats over the ones we formerly occupied below, not knowing any better. We took those seats; meeting had begun, and they were nearly done singing, and just as we got to the seats, the Elder said, 'Let us pray.' We had not been long upon our knees before I heard considerable scuffling and loud talking. I raised my head up and saw one of the trustees, H— M—, having hold of the Rev. Absalom Jones, pulling him off his knees, and saying, 'You must get up, you must not kneel here.' Mr. Jones replied, 'Wait until the prayer is over, and I will get up, and trouble you no more.' With that he beckoned to one of the trustees, Mr. L — S—, to come to his assistance. He came and went to William White to pull him up. By this time prayer was over, and we all went out of the church in a body, and they were no more plagued by us in the church.

Subsequent construction of a new "African Church" was slowed by the influx into Philadelphia of sugar planters from Saint Domingue (for they siphoned off money of the city's white philanthropists that might otherwise have gone to the blacks' project) and the worst epidemic of yellow fever ever to hit Philadelphia (which brought the city's free blacks into service as auxiliary doctors, nurses, carters of the dead, and grave diggers). But by the spring of

1794 the blacks' own church building was completed. When the majority of the African-American worshipers agreed to make it an Episcopal Church, Allen, who "could not be anything else but a Methodist," again withdrew. Jones became the minister of the African Episcopal Church of St. Thomas. Allen and a group of his followers purchased and renovated a blacksmith's shop and moved it to a corner lot on Sixth Street in Cedar Ward, where many free blacks were residing, for use as their church. The wooden building, replaced by one of brick in 1805, served as the "Mother Bethel" of the African Methodist Episcopal Church. In 1815 the Bethel Church had 1,400 members, and St. Thomas's, in the midst of a schism in the congregation, had 600.

These were truly independent black churches. Allen's was open only to "descendants of the African race." Only members could nominate ministers for ordination, and these could be "any persons endowed with the gifts and graces to speak for God." Members also reserved for themselves the right "to call any brother that appears to us adequate to the task to preach or exhort as a local preacher, without the interference of the Conference or any other person or persons whatsoever." St. Thomas's and Bethel became models for free blacks wanting to worship as they chose, where they chose, and under the direction of whom they chose.

Ill feeling between black and white worshipers in many cities from Baltimore northward led African Americans to form independent churches, much as the Philadelphia blacks did. Some of the best-known African-American churches of today have their roots in this separatist movement during the early republic—the AME Zion (1800), Abyssinian Baptist (1804), and St. Philip's Episcopal (1820) in New York; the African Baptist (later the First Independent Baptist Church of People of Color) (1805) and the AME (1818) in Boston; the Bethel AME (1797) and the Sharp Street AME Church (1799) in Baltimore; and more. In 1816 delegations from African Methodist churches in several mid-Atlantic cities met in Philadelphia to confederate their congregations and form the African Methodist Episcopal Church. This was the final act of emancipation of the black Methodists from the jurisdiction of whites, and it stood as the first all-black, independent church body, not only in the history of the United States, but in the history of Christendom.

African Americans in the southern states found rougher going in their attempts to form separate and independent churches. White southerners' fears of slave insurrection, coupled with their notion that blacks in the pulpit liked to preach a revolutionary doctrine, led southern state legislatures to keep black churches under strict control. The one AME church below Maryland, founded by the Rev. Morris Brown in Charleston in 1817, was closed by the state in the wake of the Vesey Conspiracy in 1822, and Brown had to flee to Philadelphia. White Baptists held tight control over the "colored branches" in the South, retaining ownership of church property, appointing church leaders, and making sure that all pastors were white males. Once Nat Turner's rebellion took place, even stricter state laws checked black preaching and insured white control.

Black churches and mutual aid societies played important roles in establishing schools for the children of newly emancipated slaves. The importance of education, especially for former slaves needing to bridge the gap between bondage and freedom, was evident to the emerging class of black leaders. After all, men like Philadelphia's Jones and Allen were successful in large part because of their learning. Many of the schools set up by white philanthropists and abolition interests prior to the Revolution had disappeared by the end of the century, however, and the growing spirit in the North to provide free public education for all youth did not include young African Americans. In the few places public education existed for blacks, it was separate, of a short term, and unequal. It was soon clear to free blacks that if they were to rise through education, they would have to provide for it largely by themselves. The churches and aid societies were the organizations best suited to begin the task.

Between 1800 and 1820, in city after city between Maryland and Massachusetts, black church leaders and officers in mutual benefit societies solicited funds and began schools for young blacks. Uniformly, they encountered problems. Acquiring money for buildings and teachers was always difficult. So was convincing parents of free black children that education was useful, given that, as headmaster Charles C. Andrews put it in *The History of the New-York African Free-Schools* (1830, 1969), after graduation the African American found "every avenue closed to him, which is open to the white boy, for honourable and respectable rank in society." For parents who believed in education but who needed to indenture their children at an early age, merely getting the children released by their masters to attend school was a struggle. Success came slowly. By 1813, when Philadelphia had a black population of between ten and eleven thousand, only 414 African-American youths were in school. Problems were greater, of course, in the Deep South. The Brown Fellowship Society began a school in Charleston in 1790, and the free persons of color of New Orleans supported several schools for their children. But opposition appeared early and was strong. In 1811, when a free black, Christopher McPherson, established a night school in Richmond "for male adults of colour" and opened with twenty-five pupils, the city's whites drove the teacher out of town, jailed McPherson, and shipped him off to the asylum in Williamsburg. Once white southerners had reacted strongly to Vesey's conspiracy and Turner's rebellion, there was no real chance for southern schools or churches. Too many slave owners held the position that education was not only wasted on blacks but might even prove dangerous to the slave system and orderly society.

But the schools for free blacks that existed through the early republic trained the leaders of the antebellum period and pointed many African Americans toward new and important roles. Between 1826 and 1828 the New York African Free School, for example, listed among its students Henry Highland Garnet, the radical abolitionist and political organizer of the 1840s; Samuel Ringgold Ward, another antislavery intellectual; James McCune Smith, a physician and perhaps the best-known African-American scholar before the time of W. E. B. Du Bois; and Ira Aldridge, a Shakespearian actor. Whites were correct in some of their thinking on the subject—education was subversive.

Mutual aid societies, independent black churches, and schools for African Americans became essential elements in the free black community during the years of the early republic. They were the central institutions of the free blacks' culture; they appeared wherever the free black community developed, and they grew with surprising speed, especially given the constraints under which free blacks functioned. By the 1820s, writes Nash in "Forging Freedom," Philadelphia blacks "had created an institutional life that was richer and more stable than that of the lower-income whites with whom they shared neighborhoods."

Part of the importance of the institutions was to the newly emancipated African American. In *The Philadelphia Negro* (1900), Du Bois refers to the Free African Society as "the first wavering step of a people toward an organized social life." Such organizations lent the African Americans not long out of bondage support, confidence, a sense of security, camaraderie, helpful role models, a chance for some formal education, and a place to develop self-esteem. But part of their importance was to those free blacks who had already achieved some distance from slavery. The mutual aid society, the church, and the school were where the established core of the free black community exercised leadership and pursued lofty goals. By the second decade of the nineteenth century, the institutions were the practice grounds and playing fields of the small but growing free black elite.

Not all free blacks had equal advantages in their quest for full and creative lives. Some gained their freedom early—by the 1790s, in fact—and thus had the experience of life in freedom. Others had professions or special skills that gave them economic advantage. In most of the early free black communities a group of professionals, almost all ministers and teachers, dominated society. Below them in status were the self-employed (often in such personal services as hairdressing or barbering, or as shopkeepers). Once the black community grew large enough to support a body of skilled craftsmen, African-American artisans began to find sufficient work for themselves and systematically took on apprentices to help them meet the market's growing demand for their services. By early in the nineteenth century most good-sized northern cities, several in the Upper South, and Charleston and Savannah had a body of reputable black carpenters, tailors, cobblers, bakers, and painters, as well as plasterers, cigarmakers, carters, caterers, sawyers, wheelwrights, jewelers, and more.

Slowly, the small, free black elite gained a measure of wealth and status. Across the country in the half-century following the Revolution, there was a steady rise in the number of free African Americans who owned property. Berlin cites Talbot County, Maryland, which had 18 free black property owners in 1793, 88 in 1803, and 102 in 1813. Results of the growth were more dramatic in northern cities. By the 1830s in Philadelphia, 282 free blacks owned, in aggregate, over $300,000 worth of real estate alone. The educated property owners, professionals, business people, and skilled artisans became the backbone of an urban black middle class.

Who were these African Americans of note in the early nineteenth century? Philadelphia's Allen and Jones are good examples, and there are others. Daniel Coker, born in Maryland to a slave and a white indentured servant, rose to become first a highly regarded teacher and then leader of Baltimore's black religious community. John Chavis studied under the president of Princeton University and then began a school in Raleigh, North Carolina, attended by prominent white children as well as free blacks.

James Forten was probably the most noteworthy free African-American entrepreneur in the early nineteenth century. The great-grandson of an African brought to the Delaware River valley by the Dutch and the son of a Philadelphia free black, Forten learned to read and write in Anthony Benezet's Quaker school, then fought at sea for the patriot cause in the Revolution. After the war he took a job with a white sailmaker. Twelve years later, when he was thirty-three, he purchased the business. By 1807, in spite of the decline in maritime trade, Forten was employing a white and black work force of thirty men. Many of the grandest merchant ships that sailed from Philadelphia's shipyards in the early decades of the nineteenth century caught the wind in sails fabricated in Forten's shop. He owned two large houses on the city's Lombard Street and was almost certainly the wealthiest African American of his time.

The relationship between this budding free black elite and the masses of African Americans who were poor and uneducated, slave or free, is enigmatic. Although, again, it was not the same across space and over time, the relationship shows the effects on free blacks of tugs and pulls in different directions by practical considerations relating to class issues and personal feelings relating to race.

Class was a major divisive factor. Some members of the early generation of free blacks saw opportunity to get ahead through emulating the white, middle-class world they looked upon. They became literate, gained wealth and property, and associated broadly with whites in their business dealings. Getting ahead often meant separating themselves from the poor, uneducated slaves and free blacks upon whom whites looked with disfavor. Successful free mulattoes looked "upwards, not downwards," wrote a Baltimore minister, "constantly seeking, and acquiring too, the privileges of whites." This probably remained the case longer in the southern states, and in the Lower South in particular, where free blacks' social and economic success remained tied to their ability to distinguish themselves from the mass of slaves. In the northern states and, more slowly and perhaps to a lesser extent in the Upper South, the identity of free blacks with all persons of their race, even those below them in wealth, education, and status, grew with the years of the early republic. The feeling seems to have begun with the separation of the black church from white control, but it was heightened steadily by the changing white attitudes toward free blacks and the repressive legislation and social customs that curtailed the activities of the free black community. As more free blacks gained wealth, rose in society, and dressed and acted as they thought befit persons of their social rank, the more whites began to resent them for "putting on airs." It seems that no sooner did free blacks succeed within the rules of advancement and acceptance than whites changed the rules and refused to accept them. It was the same winless situation of assimilation that, from then on, would continue to plague African Americans attempting to get ahead in a world controlled by whites.

CHAPTER FIVE

New Directions

A pivotal event of the movement in America to abolish slavery was the beginning of publication of the *Liberator* by the twenty-six-year-old William Lloyd Garrison on January 1, 1831. Garrison emerged from a childhood of poverty in Massachusetts to become a middling-successful printer and journalist. Slight, bespectacled, and balding, his appearance belied the intensity of his passion over issues involving injustice. Louis Filler writes in *The Crusade Against Slavery, 1830–1860* (1960) that as Garrison entered his twenties, "piety, peace, total abstinence, and a general search for reform issues characterized his work and reflected his need for a moral universe." His search ended when he came to abolition.

Organized efforts to end slavery up to that time had been scattered and weak. If they had a general thrust, it was toward gradual abolition with compensation for slave owners and the removal of the former slaves to lands outside the United States. Garrison's focus in 1831 was different. His desire was to end slavery immediately without payments to the owners or removal of those liberated. And he was forceful. "I will be as harsh as truth, and as uncompromising as justice," he wrote on page one of the *Liberator*'s first edition.

> On this subject I do not wish to think, or to speak or write, with moderation. No! No! Tell a man whose house is on fire to give a moderate alarm; tell him to moderately rescue his wife from the hands of a ravisher; tell the mother to moderately extricate her babe from the fire into which it has fallen—but urge me not to use moderation in a cause like the present. I am in earnest—I will not equivocate—I will not retreat a single inch—and I WILL BE HEARD.

Heard he was, eventually. Appearance of the *Liberator* symbolized the start of a shift of direction and intensity in the abolition movement. It marked the beginning of a broader and more serious offensive against slavery that would build until the Civil War.

Garrison has had his detractors among historians. Some have portrayed him as arrogant, egotistical, fanatical, narrow minded, stubborn, and vindictive. But only a handful downplay his importance in changing the abolition movement. Where the popular image of Garrison seems poorly formed is in the idea that the young journalist cut the immediate-emancipation design solely from his own moral fabric, with minimal assistance or influence from others, and then rallied blacks and whites to take up his cause. Like the ideas of most reformers, Garrison's were the product of his time and place. He did not invent the strident tone of militant abolitionism nor the sense of urgency to end slavery by himself in the weeks or months before turning out the first number of the *Liberator*; he developed his ideas in reaction to contemporary events involving slavery and broad contacts with black people and white people over the first third of the nineteenth century. Garrison's real formative period was the time between 1815 and 1830. It was a time when white Americans generally were becoming increasingly racist and when whites formed arguments in support of African-American slavery and the colonization of free blacks. It was a time when events on the local, state, and national levels were drawing increasingly more attention to slavery and related issues. And perhaps most important, it was a time when free African Americans were becoming more militant in their opposition to slavery, for they were beginning to see more clearly than ever that their fate and that of slaves were connected by race.

White Racism and Proslavery

The half-century between 1780 and 1830 was important in the development of a number of basic beliefs, attitudes, and assumptions held by Americans. The United States Constitution, the Bill of Rights, and the American political system all came into being during this period. So did some of the fundamental modes of American political thinking—the conservatism of Federalists, the republicanism of Jeffersonians, the broader democracy of Jacksonians. But of particular importance for this study was the development during the early republic of increasingly rigid thoughts and feelings concerned with racial difference, along with assumptions about the inferiority of persons of African descent.

Questions about the beginnings of racism in English-speaking North America are hard ones to answer. There is no doubt that the early English colonists in the New World had strong, negative preconceptions of persons who differed from themselves physically or culturally. Indeed, they used racist notions concerning Native Americans—that they were a "brutish" sort of people, lacking religion, nearer to beasts than to humans—to justify taking their land. And the early English had negative preconceptions of persons of African descent, who through English eyes appeared to have no religion, to wear few clothes, to eat odd foods with their hands, and to live close to nature with strange animals. But more and more historians are doubting that racial prejudice was the main reason why English colonists elected to use African men and women as slaves for their permanent labor force in mainland North America. Instead, they believe that the settlers' inability to find any other long-term stable supply of laborers (and, indeed, through much of the seventeenth century they tried—and even seemed to prefer—indentured servants from the British Isles), coupled with the availability of large numbers of Africans at low costs, brought the English colonists to turn almost exclusively to black slavery by the start of the eighteenth century.

Of course, the fact that slavery became a permanent condition for persons of African descent in America only strengthened existing racial prejudices. It was hard to enslave another distinctive group of people without developing negative feelings for them—especially when it proved necessary to punish them beyond the limits of the law or common decency in order to extract work from them. Thus, if racism made it easier for Englishmen to enslave blacks when economic necessity warranted it, slavery made it easier and in some sense necessary to strengthen whites' racist notions about blacks.

What had the potential to break this negative spiral of white attitudes toward African Americans was the ideology of the American Revolution. When the American patriots asserted in the Declaration of Independence that "all men are created equal," they were setting forth a doctrine into which slavery did not fit. Nothing in the document suggested that "all men" meant merely all white men. It was the spirit of egalitarianism, spreading with the Revolutionary ideology, that led to the ending of slavery north of Maryland and Delaware and to the wave of manumissions in the Upper South, as noted in earlier chapters. Gary B. Nash in *Race and Revolution* (1990) makes clear how strong the post-Revolutionary consensus was—not just in the North—for at least gradual emancipation. But where slavery became the real dilemma for the country based on democratic principles and individual freedoms was in the South. In the wake of the Revolution, southern whites believed that their economic prosperity and social stability lay in the slave system. There was no question in the minds of most prominent whites in South Carolina and Georgia about perpetuating black slavery in the new country. Sylvia R. Frey in *Water from the Rock: Black Resistance in a Revolutionary Age* (1991) contends that "a desperate effort to reassert their hegemony over their slaves and thereby preserve their fragmented world" was a major reason why the white gentry of the Lower South supported American independence and the war against Great Britain. Planters from the two southernmost states probably would have made national acceptance of slavery a clearly stated prerequisite for their joining the Union had they not so drastically needed the military might of the federal government to help them repel active Creek war parties and the potential threat from Spanish Florida. But the question that did come up for so many white southerners, again and again, was how to rationalize the continuing existence of slavery in a country in which all men had those clearly stated and widely accepted inalienable rights. The only possible approach to forming an answer was to separate those in slavery from the group of "all men." And the only way to do so was to fall back on racist assumptions about the "nature and character" of persons of African descent.

Fortunately for those wishing to justify slavery by degrading African Americans, entering onto the intellectual stage at about the same time as the philosophy that asserted Man's natural rights were scientific studies of physical differences among humans and related attempts to classify humans according to their race. Into the Revolutionary years, educated Americans held to the basic Enlightenment ideas that all humans were of the same species, that all were capable of indefinite improvement, and that obvious physical and cultural differences among humans were the result of environment. But beginning in the 1770s, a steady pecking away at the "environmental theory" of difference took place. In 1774 in his *History of Jamaica*, Edward Long argued that blacks were of a lower order of humanity than whites, "a different species of the same GENUS," and that "the ourang-outang and some races of men are very nearly allied." Long's theories spread rapidly in the United States after the influential *Columbian Magazine* printed two extracts from his book in 1788. The magazine followed with a portion of Thomas Jefferson's *Notes on the State of Virginia* (1785). Jefferson did not agree with Long on a number of points concerning persons of African descent, but he provided fuel for racist fires in the United States with his *Notes*. Jefferson suspected "that the blacks, whether originally a distinct race or made distinct by time and circumstances, are inferior to whites in the endowments of both body and mind." From "scientific observation" Jefferson testified to blacks' laziness and slowness, their inability to reason, their lack of imagination, and their unsightly appearance set off by "wooly hair" and an "ungainly" physique. Implied in the arguments was the idea that blacks did not need to—indeed, should not and probably could not—live in a free society as equals to whites because of their racial inferiority. Slavery thus was the proper institution for dealing with such different creatures. If slavery was evil, then it was a "necessary evil."

With the founding of the new nation came further refinement of these ideas. It became clear almost immediately that the Founding

Fathers, whose wisdom some considered to be guided by Providence, intended the United States to be a "white man's country." This was made evident during the first session of Congress when it passed a naturalization law limiting acquisition of citizenship to white immigrants, and again in the second session when it limited participation in the militia to white men. Most whites justified these acts by arguing that a homogeneous and intelligent citizenry was necessary for a republic to function smoothly. Blacks could not assume such citizenship, they argued, because whites would never accept them as equals, thus allowing them to assimilate, and because persons of African descent did not possess the intelligence needed to be effective citizens. African Americans not in slavery thus had no place in the country, and their continuing existence might prove dangerous should they become restless in their subordinate position. Virginian St. George Tucker echoed this voice in *A Dissertation on Slavery* (1796). "If it is true, as Mr. Jefferson seems to suppose," wrote Tucker,

> that the Africans are really an inferior race of mankind, will not sound policy advise their exclusion from a society in which they have not yet been admitted to participate in civil rights and even to guard against such admission, at any future period, since it may eventually depreciate the whole national character? . . . Though I am opposed to the banishment of Negroes, I wish not to encourage their future residence among us.

Such racist arguments for slavery proved to be heavy intellectual ammunition for weapons that were temporarily stacked.* In spite of the wave of egalitarianism and individual manumission that continued to wash over the North and Upper South past the turn of the century, no serious and concerted attack on the Deep South's slave system materialized for some time after the country's beginning. Most agitation relating to slavery during the country's first two

* In *Somewhat More Independent*, Shane White argues that it was primarily the intellectually influential, urban, white elite whose racial attitudes hardened in late-eighteenth-century America. From a reading of almanacs, which circulated among "the lower orders of society," White concludes that the treatment of African Americans by whites who were predominantly rural, less well-to-do, and less literate was, "on the whole, sympathetic and relatively benign."

decades of existence focused on halting American participation in the Atlantic slave trade, and by the time the Constitution permitted Congress to act against the trade in 1808, only a minority of southerners cared to resist. In those instances when persons with libertarian sentiments mounted a reasoned criticism of slavery, apologists for the institution could trot out their racist notions, that most white Americans of the time probably shared, that slavery was a necessary evil. Otherwise, they simply did not have to mount a broad defense of slavery. Belief about black inferiority could remain a shared assumption in no need of more complete articulation—and it could remain that way until the attack against slavery strengthened.

For some time, most students of proslavery thought in America have believed that white southerners did not generate thinking on the subject beyond the "necessary-evil" argument until the 1820s. William S. Jenkins set out the basic thesis in *Pro-slavery Thought in the Old South* (1935) that only in reaction to a series of threatening events of the 1820s—the debates in Congress over slavery in Missouri, Denmark Vesey's conspiracy, discussions surrounding the activities of the American Colonization Society, and the growing amount of propaganda coming from abolitionist groups—did white southerners begin marshaling their intellectual forces for a stronger defense of slavery. To do so, they refined their old racist thinking and came up with a new belief that slavery was, more than a necessary evil, a "positive good." The argument seemed simple to them. If one assumed that persons of African descent were innately inferior to persons of European descent, as most whites did, then one could argue that slavery was the Africans' proper and natural status. Because masters took care of blacks better than they could take care of themselves, the argument went, slavery was actually beneficial for those enslaved. Slavery was also good for the slave owners and, by extension, the country, for the persons in bondage produced crops that sold well, giving the slave owner profit and status while helping the country's economy. Thus evolved the South's main proslavery argument for the antebellum period.

But in a book published in 1987, *Proslavery: A History of the Defense of Slavery in America, 1701–1840*, Larry E. Tise analyzes the contents of proslavery arguments, studies some of the individuals who made the arguments, and asserts that most historians of the defense of slavery have been off base, especially in their sense of how and why proslavery arguments developed and who first came up with them. Tise contends that the most pervasive and long-lasting proslavery arguments arose as part of a conservative reaction to the social and political convulsions that rocked the country repeatedly between 1790 and 1830. And these arguments were articulated throughout the period not by southern slave owners but almost solely by "natives of New England, sons of staunch Federalists, and the products of Congregational religious training." Tise's argument suggests more about how a country grounded in liberty could continue to practice slavery and justify doing so, and it emphasizes the critical effect that the events of the early nineteenth century had on the hardening of white attitudes toward African Americans and slavery.

The time of the early republic was disruptive to the extreme. The ideological basis of the country was still in ferment after the era of the Revolution and the subsequent period of constitution building. Then, radically new, potentially subversive ideas gushed out of the hydrant that was the French Revolution, frightening those, particularly the New England Federalists, who longed for order and stability in society. Order and stability were not easily found, however, for wars and threats of war were almost constant, and society itself was in flux, with new lands opening, people moving about more widely than before, and old moral and religious tenets frequently being discarded. Furthermore, the thrashing out of American politics and the rapid rise first of Jeffersonian Republicanism and then of Jacksonian Democracy left many wondering if the greatest danger to the country were not from within.

Through the long, chaotic generation following the country's beginning, conservative Americans fashioned an ideology—one that supported law, order, tradition, and a social and economic system that included slavery. Influential white Americans, with a number of New England clergymen in the forefront, reacted strongly to persons or groups whom they perceived as disruptive and subversive. The reactions normally involved linking the perceived causes of turmoil to French infidels, crazed democrats, or others who cared not about the country, religious orthodoxy, public order, or other elements that had made American society strong. It was, writes Tise, a "conservative counterrevolution" against what many believed to be the forces of anarchy and disruption.

These conservative ideas were hatched in the North by 1800, and they moved southward in the early decades of the new century, largely with itinerant clergymen who were intent upon spreading Christianity. When the events of the 1820s and 1830s spawned the greatest questioning of slavery that had occurred since the Revolutionary era and increasing amounts of antislavery propaganda emerged from abolitionists to threaten southern slaveholders, the latter already had the conservative underpinning for their proslavery arguments. Abolitionism was a subversive conspiracy, they argued, a threat to the established order and to the country's working, hierarchical society. Slavery was a "positive good" because it preserved order and maintained the social hierarchy. Abolitionists were wild-eyed radicals cut from the mold of the French Revolutionary. And the conservative arguments were not simply those of white southerners who owned slaves. The "conservative republicanism" that supported and justified slavery, Tise contends, was a sentiment probably held by a majority of white Americans by 1830.

Tise's argument is useful because it shows how much of the country accepted the basis for the defense of the South's peculiar institution, but it directs attention away from a still more broadly held assumption—the racist one—the growth of which after 1790 was essential to the overcoming of the lingering egalitarianism and the support of the proslavery arguments. A strong belief in the inferiority of persons of African descent helped weaken the movement to spread natural rights to African Americans. It was the belief that underlay both the "necessary evil" and the "positive good" arguments in defense of slavery. In a review of Tise's book in the *Journal of Southern History*, 5 (1989), Leland J. Bellot underscores the importance of the seldom-questioned racist assumptions that spread widely among the country's white population in the time of the early republic: "[R]acism—particularly the assumption that black people, whether slave or free, could not be assimilated into white society—was the common thread running through the fabric of American proslavery thought, whether it arose from *northern* or *southern* sources, from clergy or laity, in democratic or conservative contexts."

The same racist assumptions had crept into the thinking of whites who opposed slavery and of those who merely saw it as an institution that eventually would cease to exist in America. If the descendants of Africans, once freed, remained inferior and could not be assimilated, what could be done with them? For many in the first third of the nineteenth century, colonization was the answer.

Colonization

There is a "chicken-or-egg" quality to the question about the origins of the idea of African-American colonization. Did American blacks, who saw no future in remaining in a country in which the racism of whites kept them in a degraded position, first suggest removing themselves to the land of their ancestors where prospects were better? Or did whites, who judged persons of African descent to be inferior, who did not want to live among free blacks, and who believed that African Americans' only chance for advancement was to leave America, make the initial suggestion for removal? The answer, it seems, is that northern slaves were the first to bring up the idea, but that Virginia slave owners, apparently independently, followed quickly with a different version.

In 1773, four bondsmen living near Boston asked the Massachusetts legislature to allow them to work one day each week for themselves in order that they might purchase their freedom and, "as soon as we can from our joynt labours procure money to transport ourselves to some part of the coast of Africa, where we propose a settlement." Four years later, libertarians in the Virginia legislature introduced a plan to free the state's slaves born after a certain date, make the freed youth apprentices until they reached adulthood, and then remove them from the country. In *Notes on the State of Virginia*, Jefferson explains why removal of the free black was necessary:

> Deep rooted prejudices entertained by whites; ten thousand recollections, by the blacks, of injuries they have sustained; . . . the real distinctions which nature has made; and many other circumstances, will divide us into two parties and produce convulsions which will probably never end but in extermination of one or the other race.

So before the Revolution was over, some of the cards of the African-American emigration or colonization schemes were on the table. Some blacks were so hopeless about their future in America that they wanted to leave. Some whites were so opposed to living with free blacks that they wanted to be rid of them. These two strains of thought would remain prominent in the minds of some blacks and whites for more than a century.

Before the eighteenth century was over, events across the Atlantic provided focus for the colonization idea. In 1787 a group of British philanthropists sent four hundred of London's "Black Poor" to what is now Sierra Leone, on Africa's West Coast, to begin a colony. In the minds of many British humanitarians, the black colonists, in addition to enjoying land ownership and free lives, were to bring Christianity to the indigenous Africans, work toward ending the slave trade, and in time replace the trade in humans with a commerce lucrative to the colonists and, of course, to the commercial interests of the colony's philanthropic supporters back in England. (It was, remarked one wag, "philanthropy plus six per cent.")

The first ships carrying the black English colonists were out in the Atlantic, on their way toward the site of the colony, when a Quaker physician from the West-Indian island of Antigua, William Thornton, broached the idea of colonization to African Americans in Boston and Newport, Rhode Island. Blacks in these areas had already been discussing the issue, so Thornton found numbers of them who were seriously interested. But when Thornton presented the idea to the Free African Society in Philadelphia, the response was different. Thornton came to Philadelphia just as the Pennsylvania Abolition Society was reorganizing and making plans to take broader and bolder action against slavery and in support of newly emancipated African Americans. Philadelphia blacks had rising hopes for better lives in America. The Free African Society wrote to black supporters of Thornton's idea in Newport about "persons who are sacrificing their own time, ease, and prosperity for us, the stranger and the fatherless, in this wilderness." Many free blacks in Philadelphia still believed that the Lord, with help from well-meaning whites, would "break every yoke and let the oppressed go free" in the United States.

If the opposition of African Americans in Philadelphia did not squelch the enthusiasm for emigration of blacks in New England, lack of funds did. Newport's African Union Society sent a lone emissary to Sierra Leone in 1795 to size up prospects for emigration, but it could afford nothing more. By the end of the century, the voices supporting emigration had quieted, not to be heard again until a free black from Massachusetts, an entrepreneur cut in the true Yankee mold, sailed for West Africa in 1811.

Paul Cuffe might be more widely known for his principled refusal, around 1780, to pay poll and property taxes in Massachusetts, where, because he was African American, he was not allowed to vote. Like many other Massachusetts citizens at the time, he believed taxation without representation was illegitimate. Cuffe was the offspring of a freed slave, originally from the Gold Coast of Africa, and a Native-American woman. His home was the southern edge of Massachusetts. Though lacking formal education, Cuffe and his brother, after some years of sailing and whaling, began a maritime commercial business that seemed to grow in size every year. By early in the nineteenth century, Cuffe owned one sloop, two brigs, and several schooners, and he was transporting cargo to Philadelphia and Baltimore, with occasional trips to the Caribbean and Europe. He raised the eyebrows of many in American and foreign ports, for his vessels sailed with all-black crews.

In 1808, Cuffe turned his attention to Africa. He had come to believe that participation in the sinful slave trade had degraded indigenous Africans and stripped them of their moral foundation. But he reasoned that if African Americans brought Christianity and legitimate trade to the peoples of Africa they could "uplift" those living in the lands of their ancestors. Cuffe believed that he could transport moral, religious, and propertied African Americans across the Atlantic in order to begin the process. He joined the Society of Friends and worked to persuade Quakers to support his idea. They, in turn, notified leaders of Britain's philanthropic institutions, who encouraged Cuffe to make an inspection of the functioning Sierra Leone colony. Once America's trade embargo with Great Britain ended, in 1810, Cuffe readied for the inspection voyage, his first to West Africa.

Cuffe's impression of Sierra Leone was positive. He liked its prospects for settlement and trade, and he felt that the colonists there were indeed useful links in the bringing of Christianity and commerce to the indigenous population. In 1811 while still in Sierra

Leone, Cuffe helped prompt The Friendly Society of Sierra Leone, a cooperative black trading organization. Members of the society were to act "for the beneficial good of the universe and the glory of God," but their activities were to have the effect, as the organization's full title suggests, "of Encouraging the Black Settlers of Sierra Leone, and the Natives of Africa generally, in the Cultivation of their Soil, by the Sale of their Produce." Black colonists, English philanthropists, the British government—all were supporters of Cuffe's "civilizing mission."

Cuffe returned to the United States in 1812, intent on sending at least one vessel each year to Sierra Leone, transporting free African-American settlers and goods to the colony, and returning with marketable African products—camwood, ivory, cowhides, palm oil, peanuts, and rice. His ideas caught the attention of African Americans and infused new energy into old thoughts of emigration. But Cuffe's immediate problem was the pending war with Great Britain and the resultant disruption of commerce. Cuffe petitioned Congress for a license to conduct a small amount of trade with Britain's West African colony, but the House of Representatives denied his request. If he was to take African Americans to the British colony, Cuffe would have to wait out the War of 1812.

Within less than a year of the signing of the Treaty of Ghent in 1814, Cuffe organized his first voyage of colonization and commerce. On his brig *Traveller*, which left Boston on December 10, 1815, was a cargo of tobacco, flour, soap, candles, naval stores, hats, shoes, tools, and iron. Also aboard were fifty-eight African Americans—thirty-eight adults and twenty children—intent on settling in Sierra Leone.

Cuffe judged the voyage a partial success. Although he failed to make money on his commercial ventures in Sierra Leone, he obtained land there for the African-American settlers. After his return to the United States in the spring of 1816, he grew even more enthusiastic over the prospects of African colonization. As he read of slave insurrections in the American South and of increasing racial tensions in the North where poor whites did not take kindly to having to compete with free blacks for jobs, Cuffe came to believe that only in Africa, away from white animosity, could America's blacks "rise to be a people." The United States ought to free its slaves and then colonize them on "their own soil," he believed. As he waxed enthusiastic over large-scale African-American colonization, Cuffe found his ideas paralleling those of some white Americans, who were working at that time toward the same ends with a new organization, the American Colonization Society.

The Virginia legislature continued to think and speak of colonization following its early discussions. Immediately after Gabriel's plot in 1800, the legislature, in secret session, brought up colonization and asked Governor Monroe to consult President Jefferson on the matter. Jefferson inquired about the British venture in Sierra Leone, but he found no interest there in any massive infusion of American blacks. For the next decade, colonization was a dead issue in the minds of whites. But once the War of 1812 had ended, the growing size of the free African-American population, the plight of many poor free blacks, and increasing racial tensions made dealing with the free black "problem" seem more urgent to many whites. Early in 1816, Virginia legislator Charles Fenton Mercer got the colonization "bug." Mercer was convinced that racism would forever keep blacks at the bottom of America's class structure and thus make them a threat to the wealthier elements in American society. He feared that African Americans would prove to be a permanent "banditti, consisting of this degraded, idle, and vicious population, who sally forth from their coverts . . . and plunder the rich proprietors in the valleys." When he argued in Congress, in December of 1816, that the federal government ought to colonize free blacks on Africa's west coast, more whites than ever before thought it was an idea whose time had arrived.

New Jersey Presbyterian clergyman Robert Finley, who headed Princeton's Theological Seminary, took up Mercer's idea and pressed its merits with a number of prominent religious leaders and politicians. "We would be cleared of them," he argued bluntly; "we would send to Africa a population partially civilized and christianized . . . [and] blacks would be put in a better condition." Finley sought Cuffe's advice and received assurance that Cuffe, the only person in America who had experience in taking blacks to an African colony, was prepared "to be made use of in any way, which may forward the plan . . ." Finley's campaign culminated in a meeting in Washington's Davis Hotel on December 21, 1816, where a group of prominent ministers and government leaders agreed to form the American Society for Colonizing the Free People of Color in the United States. A week later the American Colonization Society was organized formally in the United States House of Representatives, with Supreme Court Justice Bushrod Washington as its president, its rank and file including such notables as Henry Clay, Daniel Webster, Francis Scott Key, Andrew Jackson, and John Tyler.

Members of the society emphasized publicly their humanitarian motives. Their major interest, they said, was to improve the lives of persons of African descent who were existing in a degraded position in the United States. But humanitarian proclamations could not hide what was at the heart of the society's existence. African Americans were at the bottom of America's social structure because the racist attitudes and actions of whites relegated them to that position. Rather than working to end the racism of whites, the society preferred to remove the objects of the racism.

And it was not only "humanitarians" who supported the society. Many southerners would not have participated in the organization from the beginning had they not been told that it would pay no attention, in the words of Henry Clay, to "any question of emancipation, or that which was concerned with the abolition of slavery." If some society members believed that establishment of a colony in Africa for freed slaves might eventually lead more masters to emancipate their slaves, others thought that ridding the United States of its "troublesome" free blacks would make the institution of slavery more secure. Thus, for a time many whites who opposed the existence of slavery joined forces with prosperous and influential slave owners to support the efforts of the American Colonization Society.

In the northern states and in those of the Upper South, sentiment for colonization of free blacks spread rapidly. Branches of the American Colonization Society appeared in cities from Baltimore to Boston; states established their own colonization societies; and some state legislatures even endorsed these efforts and voted them funds. Maryland and Virginia eventually enacted legislation designed to colonize their newly emancipated African Americans. Agents for the

American Colonization Society fanned out into small towns and rural areas of the Upper South in particular, soliciting funds and trying to interest free blacks in colonization.

With support from powerful figures in government, the society moved quickly. When its emissaries met a cool reception in Sierra Leone, the society decided to seek its own location for a "homeland." In 1821, President James Monroe approved use of the United States Navy to support such activity. The next year, Lieutenant (later Commodore) Matthew C. Perry, in command of the U.S. schooner *Shark*, selected a site on Cape Mesurado, south of Sierra Leone, and negotiated with the indigenous Africans for its sale. African-American colonists sent over by the American Colonization Society soon established a settlement there, naming it Monrovia after the president, and America's grandest colonization scheme was under way.

Yet, in spite of the strong governmental support and the flurry of activity, relatively few African Americans ever participated in the colonization effort. Over the forty years between the settlement of Monrovia and the outbreak of the Civil War, only 15,000 black Americans—not four hundred annually, on average—made the Atlantic crossing and attempted to become permanent residents of what would soon be called Liberia—the "land of freedom."

The main reason the society never transported more African Americans to Liberia was a simple one. American blacks regarded the country of their birth, rather than the land of their ancestors, as their home. The feeling was never universal, but it grew in that direction. From the start, colonization was of real interest to only a portion of the free black community. Among African Americans not long out of slavery or those living in rural areas and poorer economic conditions, the appeal of African colonization grew out of discouragement and hopelessness. Such people held a stronger sense that emigration to Africa was preferable to life in the United States, where racial distinctions permanently relegated persons with African ancestry to a lower caste. "I am an African, and in this country, however meritorious my conduct and respectable my character, I cannot receive the credit due either," wrote Virginia minister Lott Cary in 1821, as he was preparing to leave for Africa. "I wish to go to a country where I shall be estimated by my merits, not by my complexion." The white husband of a Tennessee free black woman, noting that "*Coloured* . . . is a word of tremendous impact in North America," feared "bequeathing to my children a hopeless degredation! I will go *anywhere*," he wrote, "to avoid so hateful an attitude."

But, as we shall see, another strain of thought strongly opposed to colonization came to predominate in the free black community. And in the 1820s the whole colonization issue would help clarify free African Americans' ideas about the future for blacks in America, whether for themselves or for those still enslaved. Still, none of this would happen before some of the earliest white abolitionists latched onto colonization and made it a part of their program for ending slavery in the United States.

White Antislavery Sentiment

White efforts to end slavery in the United States had their intellectual roots in Christian religious principles and the egalitarianism of the Western world's Enlightenment. Antislavery sentiments emerged in continental Europe and spread to England, where by 1750, philanthropists began to devote large amounts of money and time toward ending the slave trade and slavery itself. In 1772 they succeeded in getting slavery abolished in England in the celebrated case, *Somerset* v. *Stewart*, and they pressed on to attack the slave trade and human bondage around the British empire.

Most eighteenth-century residents of British North America were less concerned about the issue. There had long been scattered handfuls of people in the colonies who deemed chattel slavery immoral and unchristian and who said so, but it was the members of the Society of Friends, more commonly called Quakers, who were the most frequently outspoken on the subject. After the middle of the eighteenth century, Quakers became even more vociferous in their antipathy toward slavery. Such men as John Woolman and Anthony Benezet first pressed for disowning Friends who continued to hold slaves. Then they broadened their efforts to direct a more frontal assault on the slave trade and to bring thoughts about the immorality of slavery itself before the educated public.

The same impulse that had led American colonists to rise up

against what they considered economic and political enslavement to mother England brought many of the same people to question the propriety of holding persons of African descent in bondage. Indeed, many of the most prominent American patriots—Benjamin Franklin, Alexander Hamilton, Patrick Henry, John Adams, Thomas Paine—declared their belief that slavery contradicted the principles of the Revolution. The Quakers did not ease off, either. In conjunction with British humanitarians, Benezet coordinated an assault on slavery's existence throughout the New World.

Once the Revolutionary War ended, even though slavery continued to exist in the country, many victorious Americans from all parts of the land looked forward to the day of complete emancipation, and some began to work toward its realization. There had been a formal antislavery organization in Philadelphia since 1775, and a decade later antislavery societies began to sprout up in every state north of Virginia. In 1794, delegates from several of the state antislavery societies met in Philadelphia to form a national federation, the American Convention for Promoting the Abolition of Slavery and Improving the Condition of the African Race. Even persons with antislavery sentiments in Virginia, emboldened by the 1782 state law allowing manumissions, petitioned the General Assembly in 1785 to require the freeing of slaves, thus gradually ending the ownership of humans in the state. Although this activity served to marshal the state's proslavery forces, and the latter, managing to work up broad support, had carried the day in the Assembly, neither Virginians who wanted to end slavery nor others around the country who favored abolition abandoned hope. The steady demise of slavery in the northern states and the regular occurrence of individual manumissions in the Upper South confirmed existing beliefs that slavery was slowly dying in the country that had been founded on the principles of liberty.

But activities and events that took place over the decade following the start of the Constitutional Convention in 1787 altered the course of slavery in the United States and made persons opposed to the institution assume a different outlook on the future. In spite of the number of Constitutional Convention members who had antislavery leanings, the Founding Fathers did not attempt to abolish slavery in the United States Constitution. The overriding concerns of the Founders were to bring stability to the country, to guarantee private property, and to install a truly national government with authority over the states and localities. Attacking slavery would have made all of that much harder to achieve, so even those in the convention who seemed to dislike slavery the most agreed quietly to set the issue aside and ignore memorials asking them to deal decisively with the institution.

The events of the early years of the nation's existence were more bothersome to those who considered slavery anathema to the country. In 1789, North Carolina ceded its western lands to the United States with a stipulation that "no regulation made or to be made shall tend to emancipate slaves," and Congress accepted the cession. In 1791 Kentucky entered the union with a state constitution that permitted slavery; in 1793 Congress enacted a fugitive slave law, as the Constitution authorized, that denied alleged fugitives due process of law and thus violated the Constitution's Fifth Amendment; in 1801 Congress allowed slavery and slave trading to exist in the newly formed District of Columbia; and throughout the 1790s and early 1800s scores of thousands of African slaves poured into several southern ports to be sold throughout the Deep South. Moreover, the economic expansion of slave-based agriculture, which the invention of the cotton gin had helped to foster, further obscured the hopeful outlook that had once existed that slavery would eventually wither away of its own accord. By the start of the new century it must have been clear to all but the most optimistic opponents of the institution that slavery was more thoroughly entrenched in the country than it had been a generation earlier.

Not that antislavery activity was dead in the water. In the last years of the eighteenth century, some evangelical Protestants joined the ubiquitous Quakers in antislavery activities. Evangelicals had begun to recognize slavery as a wrong against humanity during one of the various waves of revivalism between 1740 and the early 1800s. As they continued to spread their word around the country, the wrongs of slavery were never far from their thinking. These feelngs were heightened during the rapidly changing times of the early republic, when evangelicals were especially both-red by what appeared to be a turning away from God on the part of so many Americans. They saw increasing secularism and self-indulgence as highlighting their countrymen's growing sinfulness—and it all tempted a wrathful God. Some even saw the millennium at hand and wished to right society's wrongs before it was too late. Reforms of all sorts proliferated—there were Bible societies, peace societies, temperance societies, even antismoking societies.

Some reformers believed that the worst of Americans' sins was holding blacks in bondage. With the institution flourishing in the southern states, they wondered if punishment by God could be close at hand. In the minds of some, it was their religious duty to work to end slavery. Not to do so would be to abdicate one's responsibility to virtue and right. Seeing signs of Divine repayment in kind in the slave unrest on Saint Domingue and even closer to home in Richmond, evangelicals had come to believe that doing God's will was closely tied to the long-term stability of American society. It all made good religious and social sense. Speak out they must.

Virginia Baptists adopted an official resolution condemning slavery in 1789, the Presbyterian General Assembly did so in 1795, and Methodists, who had been working at such resolutions for a number of years, adopted the final one in 1796. Then in 1800, Methodist bishops met in Baltimore and decided to redouble their efforts to promote emancipation. They called on all elders, deacons, and itinerant preachers to collect signatures on petitions that would be sent to southern state legislatures, asking them to enact emancipation laws. And other religious elements continued to press an antislavery message, particularly in the South. But such activities, occurring in the wake of the Saint Domingue revolution, Gabriel's rebellion, and broad fears of slave unrest in many parts of the country, merely brought out popular opposition of an imposing kind. White Charlestonians mobbed Methodist preachers in the city, burning their antislavery petitions and nearly killing one church leader. Across the South in the early years of the nineteenth century, evangelical preachers found themselves threatened with bodily harm if they continued to rail against slavery. Those with the strongest feelings left the South, often for lands being settled in the western territories. Most of the others quieted down.

Any antislavery feeling that remained in the second decade of the nineteenth century seemed narrow and weak in comparison to that espoused by the earlier generation. With a few exceptions, antislavery organizations—more of which could be found in the southern states into the mid–1820s than in the North—avoided being provocative. Their intent was to conciliate slave owners, to argue in temperate language that slavery was a national problem that required a reasonable solution that would do little harm to anyone. Over time, antislavery groups in cities in the North and Upper South tended to do less petitioning and agitating to end slavery and to become more involved in helping newly freed blacks through the difficult transition from bondage to a viable existence in freedom. Protecting free African Americans from kidnappers and collecting funds to begin schools for black children were high on abolition society agendas.

The existence of the newly formed American Colonization Society after 1816 provided what James B. Stewart in *Holy Warriors: The Abolitionists and American Society* (1976) calls "a respectable outlet for misgivings about slavery in an era which demanded ideological moderation." Thus, although there was no formal consensus among the abolitionist groups, into the 1820s many whites who were against slavery moved toward the idea that the gradual approach to abolition, with colonization as the end, would be the most acceptable and thus most effective tack to take into a pretty strong prevailing wind. Reasoned arguments about the immorality of holding persons in bondage might ultimately convince southern slave owners to manumit their slaves, many believed. Providing masters just compensation for their financial losses would make manumission more palatable, as would the idea that the freed slaves would not remain in the United States, where they were inassimilable and likely to be a dangerous element for generations.

White Americans who wished to abolish slavery in the country at some point in the future tended to focus their energies on particular issues or problems. They wrote or voiced strong opinions as Congress was debating the extension of slavery into Missouri in 1820, or when southern settlers in Illinois tried to legalize slavery there in 1823. Many worked also to gain more rights and greater opportunities for free blacks. But in spite of the growing volume of their writings, into the middle 1820s abolitionists still did not pose a serious threat to southern slave owners, who had heard most of the moral arguments before.

If there was a promising element among abolitionists in the 1820s, it involved those who carried on with one or another strain of the religious argument. Not surprisingly, Quakers remained the most numerous in this group. Small pockets of religion-inspired abolitionism began to gain at least regional notice. In the hill country of western North Carolina and eastern Tennessee, for example, Quakers and evangelicals turned out letters and pamphlets that showed up regularly in newspapers with antislavery leanings. Their writings could be direct and their language strong. One Tennessee Quaker, Elihu Embree, began his own abolitionist paper, the *Emancipator*, in Jonesborough in 1820. "The Slavery of the Africans in the United States, if continued a few generations longer, will produce such scenes of misery and destruction for our posterity as have not been exceeded in the history of man," he wrote in an early issue. And when he learned that, as part of the Missouri Compromise, slavery would be permitted in Missouri and in states formed out of the southern portion of the Louisiana Purchase, Embree wrote, "Hell is about to enlarge her borders; and tyranny her domain."

An area of eastern Ohio where southern Quakers had settled was another center of antislavery activity. Just across the Ohio River from Wheeling, Virginia, was where Benjamin Lundy, the most prolific abolitionist writer of the 1820s, began his antislavery activities. Lundy was a Quaker from New Jersey, a saddler by trade, who observed a coffle of slaves moving south out of Wheeling and soon thereafter devoted himself to the cause of abolition. From his home in St. Clairesville, Ohio, Lundy in 1815 organized the Union Humane Society, an antislavery group that would grow rapidly to have a membership of five hundred. Then Lundy joined Charles Osborn, a former associate of Embree in Tennessee, in publishing the *Philanthropist*, a journal backing antislavery among other reforms. In 1821, after extensive travels and some pointed writings on slavery and the Missouri question, Lundy decided to begin his own antislavery newspaper, the *Genius of Universal Emancipation*. Ultimately to be published wherever Lundy happened to be living—and he was a remarkably peripatetic individual—the *Genius* continued to appear, sometimes irregularly, until Lundy died in 1839. It was an important organ for disseminating ideas about abolition among sympathetic whites and free blacks through the formative years of the abolition movement.

Lundy's message in the *Genius* did not differ significantly from those of other Quaker and evangelical abolitionists in the middle 1820s. He favored gradual emancipation, Congressional limitation of the spread of slavery, elimination of restrictions on free blacks, and colonization. His hope remained to persuade masters of the immorality of slave ownership, prompting them to take individual action to emancipate their slaves. To better spread his message, Lundy moved his paper to Tennessee in 1822; then he relocated again, this time to Baltimore. On a trip to Boston in 1828, where he was trying to drum up support for his struggling newspaper, Lundy was introduced to William Lloyd Garrison, who, though but twenty-one, was already an established editor for a reformist journal. Lundy convinced Garrison to come to Baltimore to work with him on the *Genius*. It was there, over several months, that Garrison saw for the first time the difficult circumstances of the city's four thousand slaves. It was there, too, that Garrison got to know a number of persons in Baltimore's large free black community. He talked with them, read what they were reading, and slowly altered his views on ending slavery. Before coming to Baltimore, Garrison had been interested in abolition as one of several reform issues, and he had termed the idea of immediate emancipation "not desirable" and a "wild . . . vision." Like Lundy, he had been a supporter of colonization. But when he left Baltimore in June 1830, he was intent on beginning a paper to push his only cause, abolition, and he favored neither colonization nor the gradual approach nor compensation for the former slave owners.

Slavery in the Limelight

The years following the War of 1812 were good ones for many Americans. International peace was at hand for the first time in years, a spirit of rapprochement was descending on Anglo-American relations, Spain agreed to a southern border favorable to the United States, the country seemed more united than ever before, and its economy was prospering. Following the unsettled quarter-century since the nation's beginning, the period after the War of 1812 seemed especially tranquil, and the tranquility showed in the American people's outlook and demeanor. Historians refer to the two-term presidency of James Monroe, between 1817 and 1825, as the Era of Good Feelings.

But the period of Monroe's presidency and the half dozen years that followed were not full of good feelings all around. This was a time when stormy national issues drew the public's attention to the very existence of slavery and to the future of the institution in the United States. The disagreement over these issues brought out fundamental differences between various elements of the white population, but between northerners and southerners generally, with frightening portents for the future. In the Era of Good Feelings lay some of the early groundwork for the disruption of the Union that ultimately would end slavery.

If slavery had been removed from the public eye during the years of the war, it came back into sharp focus after 1815. With the war's end and the annihilation or forced removal of most of the major Indian groups in the South, new lands for cotton growing opened and the domestic slave trade began to operate at unprecedented levels. It did not take long for the inhumane treatment of black men and women through their sale and relocation to catch humanitarians' attention. Then, with the rapid movement of planters and slaves into the Deep South, Mississippi and Alabama entered the Union as slave states in 1817 and 1819. Northerners, who had come to consider the Ohio River as the unofficial northern limit of slavery in the West, did not object. But when Missouri Territory petitioned for statehood as a slave state, a controversy arose first in Congress and then across the nation that awakened many persons, as it did Thomas Jefferson, "like a fire bell in the night." The Missouri question, Jefferson wrote to Massachusetts Congressman John Holmes, ". . . filled me with terror. I considered it at once the knell of the Union."

Whites in the North were alarmed at the rapid growth of the

slave population—a dangerous, inassimilable element in the country's core, or so many of them believed, and a cheap labor force that might give the southern economy an advantage—and were still annoyed by the three-fifths compromise of the Constitution, which allowed a slave state to count 60 percent of its slave population in determining its due number of representatives in Congress. Once Alabama became part of the Union in 1819, there were eleven free and eleven slave states. Admission of Missouri as a slave state would give slave interests control of the Senate and still more disproportional weight in the House of Representatives. Who knew where the trend would stop?

It was with these matters in mind that New York Representative James Tallmadge, in February 1819, introduced an amendment to the Missouri Enabling Act to cease the further importation of slaves into the territory and to free all slaves in the new state once they reached the age of twenty-five. The amendment frightened and angered most southern congressmen, who were wary of losing their political influence and fearful of racial conflict that might occur if the South's fast-growing African-American population was confined to the present slave states. Some were probably concerned as well over what restricting slavery would do to slave prices over the long run. The House passed the act with Tallmadge's amendment, but the Senate, where southern influence was stronger, did not. Arguments in each chamber grew heated; congressmen and senators recklessly tossed about threats of disunion and civil war.

Then, between March and December 1819, while Congress was out of session, the "Missouri Question" became a national cause. State legislatures, counties and towns, antislavery groups, and southern apologists sent memorials to Congress, pressing one or another point of view. When the lawmakers reconvened in December, the tone of debate grew angrier still. Senator Rufus King of New York went beyond discussion of slavery's extension; he attacked the institution itself as "contrary to the law of nature, which is the law of God." (John Quincy Adams wrote in his diary that "the great slaveholders of the House gnawed their lips and clenched their fists as they heard him.") New Hampshire's Arthur Livermore showed how the Missouri debates prompted some of slavery's opponents to bring to full boil their long-simmering thoughts on the Constitution, slavery, and its extension into new territories. "Slavery is not established by our Constitution," Livermore argued. Instead he asserted, "a part of the States are indulged in the commission of a sin from which they could not at once be restrained, and which they would not consent to abandon." Congress had to allow slavery to continue where it existed, Livermore concluded, "for our boasted Constitution connives at it." But, he concluded, "liberty and equal rights are the end and aim of all our institutions, and . . . to tolerate slavery beyond the Constitution, is a perversion of them all."

Southerners rose to the occasion, defending their Constitutional guarantees of property rights and insisting that Congress lacked the authority to prohibit slavery's extension. The debates raged for months at unprecedented levels of intensity and employing language seldom heard before in either chamber.

Eventually, congressmen worked out a compromise that, as we now know, served to put off the question of slavery's extension into new territories for a generation. (Jefferson recognized that the compromise was "a reprieve only, not a final sentence.") When Maine petitioned to enter the Union as a free state in 1820, the possibility of a compromise was apparent. Maine and Missouri could enter as free and slave states respectively, preserving the balance in the Senate. To make the compromise more palatable for House members and to prevent further conflict, Congress adopted Illinois Senator Jesse B. Thomas's proposal to prohibit slavery forever in all of the Louisiana Purchase north of Missouri's southern boundary (thirty-six degrees, thirty minutes north latitude). President Monroe signed the compromise legislation on March 6, 1820.

But that was not the end. The compromise nearly fell apart when Missourians drafted a state constitution that called for laws prohibiting free blacks from entering the state. This made for particularly thorny debate in Congress, because some northern states had laws that virtually did the same thing. More argument and delay ensued until, in an act that defied logic, Congress permitted Missouri to keep its constitutional clause excluding blacks so long as it would "never be construed to authorize the passage of any law discriminating against the citizens of another state" as Article IV, Section 2 of the federal Constitution prohibited. Thus did Missouri enter the Union in August 1821.

The Missouri question gave long pause to many thoughtful Americans. John Quincy Adams called it the "title page to a great tragic volume." Southerners had gained admission of Missouri and with it the extension of slavery into land that stretched northward to the same latitude as New York City—precisely where many northerners did not want it to go. Also, southerners had agreed to keep slavery out of a vast hunk of unorganized Indian territory that many thought impractical for slavery anyway. The only thing, then, that northerners gained was reinforcement of the principle, set down in the Northwest Ordinance of 1787, that Congress could prohibit slavery in the territories.

But the Missouri controversy had effects beyond the most obvious. For the first time since the country was formed, slavery was the topic of open, national debate. Although Congress focused only tangentially on the morality of slavery or the institution's right to exist where it was already established, persons away from the capitol did not limit their discussion. Budding abolitionists leaped into the debate; opinions on slavery filled newspaper columns across the country; and common people discussed it wherever they met—in general stores, livery stables, along the docks, or in drinking establishments. It turned out that southerners were right about one issue—such open questioning of slavery could indeed "contaminate" the minds of slaves. As noted, Denmark Vesey read about the Missouri debates and spoke his approval of King's strong speech before the Senate. Vesey began conspiring with Charleston blacks within months of the time Missouri had become a new slave state.

Moreover, the Missouri debates gave free blacks further reason to question their position in society. Free African Americans in the North were generally dismayed by approval of slavery's extension in Missouri. The compromise not only gave slavery new life in their eyes, but it practically prohibited any of their number from entering the state. And could they help but to recognize the hypocrisy of all the northerners who wished to prohibit slavery's extension but cared little for African Americans as people and for the rights of free blacks as citizens in the country?

The Missouri issue had a way of lingering, too. It seemed to convulse the internal politics of other states and to lie not far in the background when additional sectional matters caught the nation's attention. It clearly influenced happenings in Illinois. The state, whose southern half lay just east of Missouri, had entered the Union in 1818. A good portion of its population had proslavery leanings. Although the Northwest Ordinance forbade slavery in Illinois, the state's constitution contained elements that fairly defied that prohibition. The Illinois Constitution freed not one of the nine hundred slaves already there when the state entered the Union, leaving open the possibility of a future amendment to legalize slavery. With the debate over Missouri fresh in their minds, slave interests in Illinois in 1822 attempted to call a state legislative convention to make slavery legal. For nearly two years, proslavery and antislavery advocates from inside and outside Illinois fought over the effort. In the end a popular vote defeated the convention proposal by a margin of almost two thousand votes out of 11,500 cast. By the middle of the 1820s, while Illinois was no bastion of sentiment for black rights—it still carried "Black Codes" on its books that required free African Americans to register and carry certificates—it would not join the group of southern states that allowed slavery.

The nullification controversy that arose several years later was technically about South Carolinians' efforts to keep heavy federal tariffs from being levied within their state's borders. Slavery did not seem to be a major factor in the controversy. But just below the surface, the fear of a federal effort to abolish slavery was the fundamental issue that kept the South Carolinians riled and prompted them to fight a battle over tariffs that, if won, might one day help them preserve their cherished institution of slavery.

The tariff conflict was sectional to its core. Since the beginning of manufacturing in the United States earlier in the century, northerners had been beseeching Congress to enact tariffs to protect their budding industries from foreign competition. No sooner had tariff laws been passed in 1816 than southerners began to complain about the higher prices the tariffs caused them to pay for manufactured goods. It was sectional favoritism, they complained, and should be done away with. Such bickering was going on behind the scenes during the Missouri controversy. But when Congress, on the eve of the presidential election of 1828, raised tariff rates to unprecedented levels, southern leaders complained more bitterly than ever about the pain inflicted upon them by the "Tariff of Abominations." Mired in a decade-long economic decline, South Carolinians went beyond the usual complaints. The state's legislature endorsed an anonymous statement (known widely to have been written by the state's favorite son, Vice-President John C. Calhoun) that proclaimed a state's right to nullify a federal law—declare it void within the state's boundaries—if it deemed the law harmful to its citizens. President Andrew Jackson and many others opposed the doctrine of nullification, viewing it as a threat to the Union. The controversy gained increased public notice in January 1830 when senators Daniel Webster of Massachusetts and Robert Y. Hayne of South Carolina debated the nullification theory and the nature of the Union, with slavery thrown in. Then, in May 1832, after Congress lowered the tariff but not nearly as much as South Carolinians wanted, the state's legislature called a special convention, which voted overwhelmingly to nullify the 1828 and 1832 tariffs and to forbid their collection within the state. Jackson asked for and received congressional approval to use the army to enforce the tariff, but he also sought lower rates. When Congress enacted the latter in 1833, South Carolina rescinded its earlier nullification and the crisis abated.

Over this period of four years, South Carolina had taken an extreme stand against federal action that appeared harmful to state interests. Was it all because of the tariff issue and the principle of protecting minorities from tyranny of the majority, as Calhoun implied? William W. Freehling in *Prelude to Civil War* argues that it was not. While South Carolinians were indeed suffering economically, as much from their inability to compete with new cotton lands in the southwest as from the federal tariffs, Freehling contends "that the nullification impulse was to a crucial extent a revealing expression of South Carolina's morbid sensitivity to the beginnings of the antislavery campaign." The abolitionists of the 1820s were faint shadows of what they would become, but that did not matter to established planters of South Carolina's lowcountry. Since the Missouri debates and reactions to Denmark Vesey's conspiracy, South Carolinians had seen a growing disposition in the country to question slavery's future. What could affect that future most directly was the will of the nation as reflected by Congress. They therefore preferred to fight Congress over the tariff now than over slavery later, should Congress indeed decide to question their cherished institution.

While some historians have criticized Freehling for overstating South Carolinians' fears of the threat to slavery (and Freehling has modified his argument somewhat in the intervening years), it seems clear that from the time of the Missouri Compromise on, southerners were aware that their institution *was* peculiar and that it faced the possibility of limitation, even abolition, by a government that expressed the popular will. By 1830, slavery lurked behind many testy issues, waiting to channel argument into sectional dispute, waiting to expand debate into national controversy, waiting to force otherwise reasonable persons to take extreme measures to support their positions.

At the same time that South Carolina planters were threatening to nullify the federal tariff, Virginians were keeping the slave issue more directly before the public. In 1829, delegates convened in Richmond to draw up a new state constitution. Rumors spread that the document might include provisions for gradual emancipation. Although the convention never took up the matter, the rumors of state action to end slavery persisted into 1830 because of the election of a new governor, John Floyd. Floyd was a states'-rights man in the mold of South Carolina's Calhoun, but he was no supporter of slavery. Convinced that slavery was a wasteful labor system that retarded economic growth, Floyd supported gradual emancipation and colonization of the state's African Americans. In November of 1830, Floyd even scribbled in his diary, "Before I leave the Government, I will have contrived to have a law passed gradually abolishing slavery in the state, or at all events to begin the work by prohibiting slavery west of the Blue Ridge Mountains." In this goal he was supported by whites in the state's western counties. Long opposed to slavery because they found it difficult to compete against the tidewater and piedmont planters, the western Virginians regularly sent memorials to the state legislature supporting emancipation with colonization.

Naturally, the state's wealthier slave owners raised their voices in opposition.

Nat Turner's rebellion in August of 1831 turned out to be the catalyst for open debate of slavery in the Virginia legislature. In the wake of the rebellion, whites across the state demanded action to ensure that such an incident never recurred. But should they take action to end slavery and remove the blacks or tighten the reins on the slave population as never before? Virginia legislators argued these matters over the last weeks of 1831 and the first few of 1832. Thomas Richie of the *Richmond Enquirer* thought it remarkable that "we now see the whole subject ripped up and discussed with open doors, and in the presence of a crowded gallery and lobby." Most southerners from outside the state were aghast over Virginia's open discussion, with broad press coverage, of emancipation, colonization, and the economic, social, and moral pros and cons of holding humans in bondage. They believed it all to be fuel for the fires being lit by abolitionists or, worse yet, for those always flickering in the slave quarters. But the Virginia legislators stormed and ranted and pressed the debate nonetheless.

In the end, as most had suspected, the proslavery forces won out. The legislature proceeded to reinforce the state's slave codes to ensure that blacks never again could mount a rebellion like Turner's. They beefed up state militias and slave patrols, took away most of the rights of free blacks (whose very presence stirred up the slaves, most believed), and curtailed slaves' religious activities. Long since shelving his vision of ending slavery in the state, Governor Floyd called on a professor with proslavery leanings, Thomas R. Dew of William and Mary University, to furnish an analysis of the legislative debates along with conclusions and recommendations. Dew's *Review of the Debates of the Virginia Legislature of 1831 and 1832* (1832) was the fullest justification of slavery that the South had yet produced. If it caused widened debate in the North, it helped solidify those southerners who had no intention of ending slavery. According to Oates in *The Fires of Jubilee*, in the wake of the Virginia debates, white southerners "closed ranks behind Dew and dug in, inflexibly determined that slavery would remain."

If these were the major discussions and debates that kept slavery and African Americans in the national limelight, they were hardly the only ones. It seemed that over the decade following the Missouri controversy, new issues involving slavery, abolition, colonization, and related topics were regularly being aired, shooting up and attracting instant notice like flares in a night sky before dying away in the darkness. Freehling cites half a dozen lesser-known episodes of controversy involving slavery that kept South Carolina (and no doubt other) slaveholders on edge through the 1820s. These included: the Ohio legislature's recommendation in 1824 of a plan for gradually freeing and colonizing all American slaves—a recommendation that eight other states endorsed; Rufus King's resolution in the United States Senate in 1825 to use money gained from the sale of public land to emancipate slaves; President Adams's 1826 proposal to send a delegation to the Panama Congress of Spanish-American Nations, where they would have to consort with black revolutionaries from Haiti and perhaps sit through "incendiary" deliberations; the American Colonization Society's petition to Congress in 1827 for a federal appropriation to support its activities, an act some southerners saw as an "entering wedge" for abolition; South Carolinian Marigny D'Auterive's request of Congress in 1828 to compensate him for war-damaged property, which happened to be a slave—a request that forced some northern congressmen to suggest that recognizing humans as property went against the country's libertarian foundations while leading southerners to point out how the Constitution sanctioned chattel slavery and private property; and Charles F. Mercer's reintroduction in 1830 of the American Colonization Society petition, this time asking for the appropriation of between twenty-five and thirty-five dollars for each free black's colonization. Stretching across most of the 1820s was the debate, mostly among lawyers and eventually settled to the satisfaction of few by Supreme Court Justice John Marshall, over what to do with 280 Africans who had been taken from an intercepted slaver off the Florida coast. ("Why were they not instantly liberated and sent home to Africa . . . ?" asked John Quincy Adams. "Is it possible that the President of the United States should be ignorant that the right of personal liberty is individual?") Each of these issues was set on a background of faint, but sometimes effective, abolitionist propaganda, the appearance of, and argument over, personal liberty laws, and the constant fear of slave insurrection.

These issues that kept some southerners worried about the security of their slave institution were having effects on others. In particular, free African Americans in the North and Upper South were reading and listening and wondering all the more about their future and that of blacks in bondage. Could their lives improve? Would slavery persist? Were African Americans better off in America than they would be elsewhere? And were they obliged to try to affect the answers to these questions?

Black Abolitionists

The early republic was the time when the intellectual leadership of the young African-American community first confronted the conflict that W. E. B. Du Bois described in *Souls of Black Folk* (1903)—a conflict over feelings of "twoness—an American, a Negro, two souls, two thoughts, two unreconciled strivings; two warring ideals in one dark body, whose dogged strength alone keeps it from being torn asunder." In the second and third decades of the nineteenth century, free African Americans in the North and Upper South were forced to come to grips with the difficulties and contradictions of their dual identity and to seek ways to survive as persons of African descent in America. It was the beginning of an effort that has not ended.

Those who were freed from slavery in the wake of the Revolution were perhaps among the first blacks to relish their American nationality. For many, the ideology behind the country's existence was behind their freedom; they were grateful and proud. A primary idea that they held was to succeed as rapidly as they could on the terms of American society: as we have seen, such success came hard.

The generation to mature in the first third of the nineteenth century found greater reason to recognize and appreciate its *black* nationality. The frustrations of the rising black middle class in the cities were important in broadening their perspective on race. The years after 1815 were pivotal times for the ideological development of America's free black leadership. These were the years when members of the black middle class of the North and Upper South, affected deeply by the increasingly evident racism in the country, by efforts to remove free blacks from the land of their birth, by the growing legal repression and social rejection of all African Americans, and by how all this belied the promise of America's republican spirit, began to question their definition of success and to doubt the correctness of the path they had chosen for personal betterment. Between 1815 and 1830, more free blacks were beginning to wonder if their long-term well-being might not lay in channeling their energies toward improving the lot of all African Americans, those in bondage as well as those in freedom. National issues involving slavery and local issues concerning hatred of and violence toward free blacks helped expand their race consciousness. By 1830, more free African Americans would be thinking first about abolition and full equality for all blacks and only second about individual and class advancement.

From about as soon as a free African-American community existed—even back into colonial times—some of its members were working to end slavery. Their efforts usually involved petitioning governing bodies: most of the early petitions sought abolition in a particular state. But by the end of the eighteenth century, small numbers of blacks were broadening their efforts. In 1797 Prince Hall addressed the principle of abolition before a meeting of the Boston African Masonic Lodge, and eleven years later, as the Atlantic slave trade ended legally, the lodge published a formal antislavery statement. In the same year, black Philadelphians petitioned the United States Congress to end slavery in the country. The early petitions took a standard form—they were polite and direct. Some expressed the petitioners' gratitude for their own freedom before making their case.

As the free African-American community matured, more of its members became openly concerned with the problems blacks continued to face in slavery, and more became involved in working to terminate the institution. With the ending of the Atlantic slave trade to the United States in 1808, the focus of the energies of many northern black leaders turned to abolition. Mixing Revolutionary ideology with Christian principles, African-American ministers led an oratorical onslaught against slavery. According to Nash in *Race and Revolution*, these arguments nurtured a tradition of protest for African Americans that they saw stretching back to the deliverance of the Israelites out of Egypt, and they kept "reminding white Americans of the installments on the revolutionary mortgage on which they were defaulting."

Ironically, what served initially as the catalyst for this reaction was the idea held by some blacks, and many more whites, including noted "friends of the Negro," of removing free blacks from this country and taking them to Africa—their "homeland." On a cold night in the dead of winter, January 15, 1817, three thousand black Philadelphians crammed into the city's big Bethel African Methodist Episcopal Church on Sixth Street. They sat shoulder to shoulder on the main floor and filled the balcony that extended around three sides of the church. They were responding to a call from the city's black leaders for a general meeting to address African colonization. James Forten chaired the meeting and posed the question: Should Philadelphia's African-American community support the idea of the recently organized American Colonization Society to transport free blacks from the United States to Africa. Of course, implied in the question was a broader one: Was there hope that African Americans would ever experience the blessings of liberty in the country of their birth?

Philadelphia's free blacks knew the factors bearing on the problem. Many remembered lives in slavery and could reflect on the heady early days of freedom, when the promise of full citizenship seemed real. But all were aware of the proscription, segregation, ostracism, lack of opportunity, and for many abject poverty that persons of African descent experienced—even in states where slavery no longer existed. Was there reason to hold out hope for better lives? Might moving to Africa, away from whites, hold more promise than continuing to live in the United States?

Philadelphia's black community agreed on the answers. Of the three thousand people packed into the Bethel Church, "there was not one sole that was in favor of going to Africa," wrote Forten. One of the resolutions passed that night expressed the sense of the congregation:

> whereas our ancestors (not of choice) were the first successful cultivators of the wilds of America, we their descendants feel ourselves entitled to participate in the blessings of her luxuriant soil, which their blood and sweat manured; and that any measure . . . having a tendency to banish us from her bosom, would not only be cruel, but in direct violation of those principles which have been the boast of the republic.

In the same year, free African Americans in Richmond declared that they would rather be "colonized in the most remote corner of the land of our nativity, than to be exiled to a foreign country."

Such anticolonization thinking from 1817 gained adherents and emerged as an almost orthodox position of free black leaders over the dozen years following the formation of the American Colonization Society. Free African Americans did not want racist whites telling them where to live, especially under the guise of benevolence. As more whites, and more white southerners in particular, pushed colonization, more blacks grew suspicious of their motives. They came to recognize that many of the strongest voices for colonization were southerners who desired to rid the country of free African Americans only in order to strengthen their hold on the slaves left behind.

At least partly for this reason, alongside free blacks' anticolonization sentiment grew an increasing awareness of their responsibility for those still in slavery. "We never will separate ourselves voluntarily from the slave population of this country," resolved the African Americans in Philadelphia in their winter meeting in 1817. They are "our brethren by the ties of consanguinity, or suffering, and of wrong."

Six months later, Philadelphia's blacks met again to protest the formation in the city of a branch of the American Colonization Society. Addressing the "humane and benevolent Inhabitants of the city and county of Philadelphia," they wrote,

> . . . *We humbly*, respectfully, and fervently intreat and beseech your disapprobation of the plan of colonization now offered . . . ; let not a purpose be assisted which will stay the cause of the entire abolition of slavery in the

United States, and which may defeat it altogether; which proffers to those who do not ask for them what it calls benefits, but which they consider injuries; and which must insure to the multitudes whose prayers can only reach you through us, MISERY, *sufferings*, and *perpetual slavery*.

It was not long after this that the Missouri question arose, with its several years of debates, followed regularly by the well-publicized controversies over issues concerning slavery, abolition, and colonization. These matters, which historians most often consider first in terms of how they heightened sectional feelings, had important effects on the thinking of educated African Americans. Through the 1820s, a certain militancy entered into the tone of free blacks' opposition to colonization. By 1830 the cities of the Upper South were centers of black anticolonization activity. Free African Americans from urban areas moved throughout the countryside, sometimes on the heels of colonization agents, arguing with blacks who were leaning toward emigration. In southern cities, where groups of African Americans gathered before embarkation for Liberia, free blacks harangued and cajoled and often got takers for alternate transportation to New York or Philadelphia. Free African Americans in Baltimore left evidence of their new assertiveness when they declared in 1831, "We consider that land in which we were born our only 'true and appropriate home' and when we desire to remove we will apprise the public of the same, in due season."

The more assertive action and language were not confined to stances against colonization. Evidence begins to appear in the late 1820s of new ways of thinking on the part of some free blacks concerning the abolition of slavery altogether. Free blacks began forming their own antislavery organizations—there were nearly fifty of them in existence by 1830, disguised somewhat by such names as the Massachusetts General Colored Association or the New York African Clarkson Association—and African-American opposition to slavery gained new voice. In 1827, tired of criticisms of blacks in New York newspapers, African Americans in that city raised money to begin publication of *Freedom's Journal*, under the editorship of Samuel E. Cornish and John B. Russwurm. The opening words of the paper's first edition were, "We wish to plead our cause. Too long have others spoken for us." Primarily an organ for the growing black urban community, the paper promised not to be "unmindful of our brethren who are still in the iron fetters of bondage." The first issue contained a critical article on "The Church and the Auction Block," and an early editorial stated bluntly: "We abominate slavery, and all its advocates." The paper was one of the first voices in the country to support immediate emancipation. When Benjamin Lundy's the *Genius of Universal Emancipation* spoke out against "immediatism," the editors of *Freedom's Journal* asserted, "We shall only be throwing dirt in other's eyes, if we talk of anything short of this. It is just one simple thing and is to be taken so, as much as a declaration of war." With agents in seventeen East Coast cities between Washington and Portland, Maine, *Freedom's Journal* reached literate members of the free African-American community.

As *Freedom's Journal* was circulating through the streets of New York, students at the New York African Free School talked over schemes "for the freeing and upbuilding of our race." Alexander Crummell remembered that in 1828 he and a group of fellow students made a pact "that when we had educated ourselves we would go South, start an insurrection and free our brethren in bondage." It may have been the reckless vow of adolescents, but among the group was young Henry Highland Garnet, who, at a national convention of African Americans fifteen years later, would urge slaves to kill masters unwilling to liberate them.

Such militancy existed among older persons in other segments of the African-American community. David Walker was such a person. Walker was a clothing salesman who also served as an agent for *Freedom's Journal* in Boston in the late 1820s. His background had acquainted him with the lives of blacks in slavery and in freedom and with ideas about overcoming African Americans' lowly condition. Walker was born free in Wilmington, North Carolina, in 1785—his father was a slave, his mother free—but he had spent time in Charleston, South Carolina, as a young man and probably experienced some of the same bitter feelings that led Denmark Vesey to conspire to end slavery there. Perhaps the young Walker had known the elder, outspoken Vesey. When he was thirty, Walker left the South. "If I remain in this bloody land I will not live long," he later wrote.

In the mid–1820s Walker settled in Boston, opened a clothing store, and married. He was a good Methodist, and he quickly became a noticeable person in Boston's free African-American community. He joined the Massachusetts General Colored Association in 1826 and spoke to the group about the "two hundred and eighty years of very intolerable sufferings" persons of African descent had experienced in America. "Shall we keep slumbering on," he asked the membership, "with our arms completely folded, exclaiming every now and then, against our miseries, yet never do the least thing to ameliorate our condition, or that of posterity?" It was a question he would answer himself.

In September 1829, Walker published his famous *Appeal, in Four Articles Together with a Preamble to the Coloured Citizens of the World, but in Particular, and Very Expressly to those of the United States of America*. The pamphlet was the boldest call for direct action against slavery yet made. It would have influence on whites and blacks far beyond its innocuous title or its seventy-six pages of dense prose and imperfect grammar. Its message was hard to miss. African Americans were "the *most wretched, degraded* and abject set of beings that ever *lived* since the world began," Walker argued. The reason for this was white exploitation of slaves and free blacks, which kept African Americans poor, socially ostracized, and without political rights. Colonization would not help; mere espousal of the idea made blacks' lives worse. Walker asked, "Can our condition be any worse? Can it be more mean and abject?"

It was Walker's solution to the problem that frightened southern whites and drew special attention to the *Appeal*. From the depths of the social and economic order, African Americans had little to lose in fighting for their rights, he reasoned. If whites would not change their ways and end slavery immediately, then black men in bondage should rise against their masters. And once the fight had begun, Walker counseled blacks to "make sure work—do not trifle, for they will not trifle with you—they want us for their slaves and think nothing of murdering us in order to subject us to that wretched condition—therefore, if there is an *attempt* made by us, kill or be killed."

Going along with Walker's encouragement of African Americans to strike against slavery was a call for black unity and a special appeal to free blacks to recognize their bonds with those in slavery. The *Appeal* was one of the earliest printed assertions that feelings akin to nationalism underlay the African-American community. Walker was critical of most African Americans because they were slow to realize a common bond and duty. Blacks in freedom were selfish and apathetic, he charged. They organized themselves into benevolent societies and Masonic lodges that might aid them socially but did nothing for fellow African Americans in bondage. Worse still, they curried favor with whites, their "natural enemies," and thus strengthened slave owners' grip on their property by letting them think that free blacks approved of their actions. Walker advised free blacks that

> your full glory and happiness, as well as all other coloured people under Heaven, shall never be fully consummated, but with the *entire emancipation of your enslaved brethren all over the world*. You may therefore, go to work and do what you can to rescue, or join in with tyrants to oppress them and yourselves, until the Lord shall come upon you all like a thief in the night. For I believe it is the will of the Lord that our greatest happiness shall consist in working for the salvation of our whole body.

Near the end of the pamphlet he tied black unity to the call to rebellion with a warning to white Americans: "My colour will yet, root some of you out of the very face of the earth!!!!!!"

Walker's pamphlet found many readers. It went through three printings (with Walker revising his message slightly each time) before a year was up. It passed easily among African Americans in the North, and Walker apparently had an idea for spreading his *Appeal* in the southern states—through seamen who visited southern ports and then in the hands of black southerners for further distribution. The southern reaction was swift. White southerners had found the polemics of white abolitionists hard to take, but at least they had possessed the mitigating quality of being moral arguments, conciliatory in tone and directed at other whites. In Walker's *Appeal* southern whites encountered the words of a black revolutionary who was urging other blacks to rise up in rebellion. It was shades of Toussaint, or

Gabriel, or Denmark Vesey; it played to their greatest fears. Southern officials went about searching for other subversive writings while state and local governments beefed up laws against free blacks.

No one is likely to know what effect the publication of Walker's *Appeal* had on Nat Turner, whose bloody rebellion cut through southeastern Virginia within two years of the pamphlet's appearance. Many southerners were convinced that the *Appeal* and sentiments expressed in Garrison's *Liberator* were behind the slaughter in Southampton County. But Walker's effect on the thinking of others is more evident. The years on either side of 1830 seem to have been particularly formative ones for Garrison. From 1826 until August of 1829, just a month before publication of the *Appeal*, Garrison lived in or kept in close contact with Boston. He may have known Walker among the city's African-American residents. He was familiar with the problems of free blacks that led Walker to hold some of his sentiments. When Garrison first read the *Appeal*, while working with Lundy on the *Genius of Universal Emancipation*, he withheld comment for several months. Then he expressed a certain ambivalence toward the pamphlet, recognizing the author's "most impassioned and determined spirit" and his "bravery and intelligence," but condemning the publication as "injudicious." But thereafter, Garrison's attacks on slavery in the *Genius* gained strength. It was in the summer of 1830 that Garrison decided to move back to the North and to begin his own newspaper, this time espousing the immediate abolition of slavery without colonization or compensation. The *Liberator*'s first edition would be in the mail in a matter of months.

It would be wrong to assert that Walker's *Appeal* had some kind of pivotal effect on Garrison's thinking, just as it was wrong for many to speak with authority on its influence over Turner. Evidence for either assertion is circumstantial. But it is reasonable to suggest that Garrison's ideas were formed in part by the milieu in which he operated, which for five years prior to publication of the *Liberator* was the Boston of David Walker or the Baltimore of a lively free black population with strong feelings against colonization and slavery. Garrison admitted that the free blacks in his acquaintance in Baltimore had changed his mind about colonization. Walker did not convince the young, white, peace-loving editor to call for a slave rebellion, but he may have made Garrison consider more seriously the urgency of ending slavery given the growing militancy of African Americans that Walker so forcefully expressed.

The change in the free black community over the 1820s was far from total, and Walker's was not a typical expression of that feeling, for, clearly, he was at the radical end of a continuum of belief about race, slavery, and ways to effect abolition. But between 1815 and 1830 there had occurred the beginnings of a movement of opinion within the free black community toward an awareness of what today one might call "black consciousness." Borne out of the memories of slavery and the frustrating experiences of free persons of African descent in the young United States, the new black consciousness forced free African Americans to accept the reality that their fate and that of the two million persons still in bondage were tied together by race. By 1830, growing numbers of free blacks were ready to put their energies toward hurrying the end of slavery as well as toward improving their own living conditions. This could only have pushed white abolitionists toward an immediatist position and, over the following decades, brought militancy into the outlook of those who today get greater notice for working to abolish slavery in America. Thus, abolition was a slowly rolling bandwagon, propelled initially as much by African Americans as by white Quakers and evangelicals, that Garrison jumped onto in 1831.

EPILOGUE

No startling changes for African Americans came along soon after 1831. The movement to end slavery immediately, without compensation or colonization, grew only slowly in spite of Garrison's impassioned statements and the predictable support he garnered from African Americans. Garrison and his supporters formed the American Antislavery Society in 1833, which set about coordinating abolitionist activities and disseminating propaganda in a broad effort to convince Americans that slavery was immoral. The spirits of many free blacks especially were buoyed by the new thrust of abolitionism. They were the major group of subscribers to the *Liberator*, and they held meetings and mustered support as best they could. But most white northerners remained apathetic, and many of them remained threatened enough by immediate abolitionism to slow the movement considerably. Abolitionists often ran into hostile opinion; sometimes they met mob violence. Internal dissension among white abolitionists and a tendency on the part of many of their leaders to support the idea of freedom and civil rights on the one hand, while being paternalistic, condescending, and outwardly prejudiced toward African Americans on the other, helped keep a united antislavery front from forging ahead. Abolitionism probably achieved some success in the 1830s, convincing a growing number of northerners that slavery was an immoral institution that needed to be done away with, but this success was so slow in coming and so limited in extent that it was difficult to discern at the time.

Turner's rebellion did not spark more and greater uprisings among slaves, either. On the contrary, the rebellion brought such a tightening of the South's reins on slaves' activities that no African Americans were either inclined or able to mount an uprising that approached the ferocity of Turner's rebellion or the scope of Gabriel's or Denmark Vesey's plans. In a sense, as cotton production soared in the 1830s and 1840s, and as the Lower South grew more into the shape of the image most people today tend to hold of it, with more large plantations, seemingly endless fields of cotton, and large gangs of slaves, the region's peculiar institution seemed just as secure as it had in the first decade of the country's existence.

But neither the black nor white community was a stagnant entity over the years that followed the onset of militant abolitionism and Turner's rebellion. The slave population continued to grow—to well past three million by 1850—and the domestic trade of humans increased still more rapidly in the 1830s and 1840s. By 1840 the Lower South would have 55,000 more African Americans in bondage than the Upper South; by 1850 over 410,000 more. Those in slavery continued to chafe at their bonds, but as fewer slaves looked upon rebellion as a reasonable solution to their situation, more simply thought of escape. With the North existing as a haven of sorts, growing numbers of African-American men and women in the South began attempting the hazardous journey toward freedom. Contrary to what nostalgic abolitionists remembered in the half-century following the Civil War, and to what southern slave owners thought at the time, only a small percentage of those who attempted escape made it to freedom in the North or Canada. But whatever Underground Railroad existed in the three decades before the Civil War did so almost solely because of African Americans. It was the men and women fugitives who accomplished the most arduous and dangerous part of the escape on their own, and it was to other persons of African descent that they turned most frequently for assistance once across the Ohio River or the Mason-Dixon line.

Over the same time, free African Americans continued to increase their activities on behalf of blacks in slavery and in freedom. The early 1830s saw the beginning of a National Negro Convention Movement, wherein northern free black leaders met to protest slavery and the difficult circumstances of African Americans' lives in freedom. The new American Moral Reform Society dominated these efforts in the middle and late 1830s. Its African-American membership believed that blacks' lives would improve once the whole human race was uplifted. But the Moral Reformers received criticism from a number of free African Americans, who charged that the Moral Reform Movement lacked practical objectives, race awareness, and race pride. As the Moral Reformers' influence waned after 1840, its critics revitalized the Negro Convention Movement with a new series of meetings and a militant tone that was a loud echo of black voices from the late 1820s. At an 1843 conference in Buffalo, several free blacks from New York openly advocated violence to end slavery. It was then that Rev. Henry Highland Garnet, addressing slaves as "Brethren," urged them to

> arise, arise! Strike for your lives and liberties. Now is the day and the hour. Let every slave throughout the land do this, and the days of slavery are numbered. You cannot be more oppressed than you have been—you cannot suffer greater cruelties than you have already. *Rather die freemen than live to be slaves.*

The convention failed to agree by one vote to print and distribute Garnet's address, but a subsequent convention in Troy, New York, published the address, and two years later a group of free African Americans in Ohio printed and distributed five hundred copies of Garnet's address bound with a fresh printing of Walker's *Appeal*.

Free blacks became increasingly involved with helping runaways, too. In several northern cities in the middle 1830s, African Americans formed "vigilance committees," whose members collected money from other blacks used to feed, clothe, and shelter fugitives from slavery. Vigilance committees helped blacks who had escaped from slavery find safe places to settle, and they remained vigilant indeed in their efforts to prevent kidnappings of fugitives and free blacks.

But the efforts of slaves to escape in the 1830s and 1840s and the increasing race consciousness and antislavery militancy among free blacks of the same time were not the most telling changes for African Americans over the long run. It is ironic that changes in the attitudes of the white population of the South may have been the ones most influential in making the 1830s and 1840s particularly fateful for African Americans and for the nation as a whole.

In the wake of the immediatist thrust of abolitionists in the North and Turner's bloody uprising in Virginia, white southerners began a psychological withdrawal into a position that defended their section and their way of life. They grew increasingly frightened of the slaves in their midst, suspicious and angry about the spreading abolitionist propaganda, and afraid generally that the federal government one day might enforce a national will to abolish slavery. These fears and animosities were heightened by the growing incidence of slave escapes and the southerners' notion, however poorly founded, that a conspiratorial "Underground Railroad" was manned by white abolitionists to spirit away the South's valuable property. Backed into their section of the country, with their economy rooted in export agriculture that rested on their peculiar institution, the white South became, in the words of Stephen B. Oates, "a closed, martial society determined to preserve and perpetuate its slave-based civilization come what may."

Come what may involved a good deal more contention. As the country endured past midcentury, more white southerners reacted to further conflict over slavery—including continuing attempts to restrict the institution geographically, growing northern sentiment to assist fugitive slaves, the appearance in Kansas of northerners who were willing to shed blood in order to keep slavery from expanding, the existence of a new Republican party that had roots in the abolitionism of the 1840s, and an ever-broadening public debate over slavery's future. John Brown's raid into Virginia in an attempt to foment a slave rebellion in 1859, followed by the election of Republican Abraham Lincoln as president in 1860, brought one southern state after another to secede from the Union in an attempt to preserve their economy, their wealth, and their way of life, all of which were based on keeping African Americans as slaves. The South's secession led to the Civil War, of course. And it was that destructive and devastating war that ended slavery in the United States, as perhaps only a war of its magnitude could have, and started African Americans along their long road toward better lives than the ones they had led during the early republic.

BIBLIOGRAPHICAL ESSAY

If the period between the end of the American Revolution and Nat Turner's rebellion is a particularly important and formative time for the history of black Americans, as this study contends, it is a fact that is hidden in African-American historiography. There is no single treatment of black history limited to the period and, indeed, there is considerably less focus on the 1789–1831 period in African-American historical literature than on the three decades that follow, which make up the more traditional antebellum period. Thus, overviews of black history in the early republic are available mostly in selected chapters of broader works, including African-American texts. It is fortunate that some of these are quite good.

John B. Boles's *Black Southerners, 1619–1869* (1983) is a carefully written book that treats many of the important themes and topics of this period in detail—though, as the book's title suggests, its focus is on African Americans in the South. Two volumes of Philip S. Foner's *History of Black Americans* contain a large amount of useful information, much of it in welcomed detail. Volume I, *From Africa to the Emergence of the Cotton Kingdom* (1975), has ten chapters on relevant topics, and Volume II, *From the Emergence of the Cotton Kingdom to the Eve of the Compromise of 1850* (1983), begins with a clear discussion of American historians and slavery and has an excellent chapter on the rise of cotton production and the domestic slave trade, several on free blacks, and others of considerable use. The detailed bibliographical essays in the books by Boles and

Foner are probably the best entrances into the historical writing on the period. John Hope Franklin and Alfred A. Moss, Jr.'s *From Slavery to Freedom: A History of Negro Americans*, 6th ed. (1988) treats many of the basic issues of the period and offers good bibliographical essays; and Ira Berlin's "Time, Space, and the Transformation of Afro-American Society in the United States: 1770–1820" in *Autre Temps, Autre Espace/An Other Time, An Other Place: Études sur l'Amérique pré-Industrielle*, edited by Elise Marienstras and Barbara Karsky (1986) is a clear, concise overview of the changes that affected the lives of slaves and free blacks living in the various African-American societies during the early republic.

It is probably important to note here several books that are widely known (and justly so) but that must be used in a particular way—with attention to citations for the dates of the primary sources—to glean information on black history in the early republic. The standard treatments of antebellum slavery—Kenneth M. Stampp's *The Peculiar Institution: Slavery in the Antebellum South* (1956), Stanley M. Elkins's *Slavery: A Problem in American Institutional and Intellectual Life* (1959), John W. Blassingame's *The Slave Community: Plantation Life in the Antebellum South* (1972), Eugene D. Genovese's *Roll, Jordan, Roll: The World the Slaves Made* (1974), and Leslie Howard Owens's *This Species of Property: Slave Life and Culture in the Old South* (1976)—take much of their evidence from the post–1830 period and, in a larger sense, are discussions of slavery and African-American society in slavery from a time when southern plantation agriculture was more fully developed than it had been during the early republic.

Two well-known books that contain information on the period are among the most controversial studies in all of African-American historiography. The jury is no longer out—in fact, it returned a verdict some time ago—on Ulrich B. Phillips's work. Phillips was thorough in his research and a good writer, but he was a product of his time (the post-Reconstruction period, when racist ideas of African-American inferiority were widespread) and place. (Phillips was a Georgian who had, as he put it, "inherited southern traditions".) Thus, when he examined select plantation records, it is not surprising that he found evidence supporting his ideas that African Americans were by nature shiftless and sensual, loyal but lazy, and that the plantation was, "in fact, a school constantly training and controlling pupils who were in a backward state of civilization." One must always bear Phillips's biases in mind as one reads his *American Negro Slavery: A Survey of the Supply, Employment and Control of Negro Labor as Determined by the Plantation Regime* (1918), which contains otherwise useful chapters on "The Introduction of Cotton and Sugar," "The Westward Movement," "The Domestic Slave Trade," and "The Cotton Regime."

A book that remains the subject of argument and debate nearly two decades after its publication is Robert W. Fogel and Stanley L. Engerman's *Time on the Cross: The Economics of American Negro Slavery* (1974). The authors draw their conclusions from interpretations of quantitative data, and they boldly present their evidence and methods in a companion volume. All of this is good, but many of their conclusions run counter to historians' long-held assumptions about life in slavery. In their treatment of "The Interregional Redistribution of Slaves," for example, they state that "84 percent of the slaves engaged in the westward movement migrated with their owners," rendering the domestic slave trade a relatively insignificant part of the redistribution, and they state that only "about 2 percent of the marriages of slaves involved in the westward trek were destroyed by the process of migration." These were not the boldest of their assertions; they struck many nerves. Not surprisingly, attacks on Fogel and Engerman have been legion. Herbert G. Gutman, for one, in *Slavery and the Numbers Game: A Critique of Time on the Cross* (1975), charged that the two authors were guilty of (in the words of a useful summary by Philip Foner) "frequent and shocking errors, fabrication of facts, dubious quantitative data, exaggerated rhetoric, flawed assumptions, faulty inferences, inept research, incompetent reading, confused thinking, vague generalizations, and unfair treatment of abolitionists and historians." A good summary of the reviews of and reactions to Fogel and Engerman's work is Charles Crowe's, "*Time on the Cross*: The Historical Monograph as Pop Event," *History Teacher*, 9 (1976).

Two books that deal with blacks in the age of the American Revolution come closest to being surveys of African Americans in the early republic. Chronological limits of several of the studies in *Slavery and Freedom in the Age of the American Revolution*, edited by Ira Berlin and Ronald Hoffman (1983), extend to 1810 or 1820, allowing them to serve as useful introductions to the period. Allan Kulikoff's chapter, "Uprooted Peoples: Black Migrants in the Age of the American Revolution, 1790–1820," is important for calling attention to the migration theme and providing details of the earliest years of the uprooting. Sylvia R. Frey's *Water from the Rock: Black Resistance in a Revolutionary Age* (1991) covers a long period before and through the Revolutionary War, but the last three chapters treat in detail the chaos in the war's aftermath, the great movement of African Americans into "the Christian social order" between 1785 and 1829, and the role Afro-Christian churches played in unifying the African-American community. Frey's book does not attempt to deal with free African Americans living outside the South.

The best studies of slave society before the rapid expansion of cotton production include Allan Kulikoff's *Tobacco and Slaves: The Development of Southern Cultures in the Chesapeake, 1680–1800* (1986); the chapters by Richard S. Dunn ("Black Society in the Chesapeake, 1776–1810") and Philip D. Morgan ("Black Society in the Lowcountry, 1760–1810") in *Slavery and Freedom in the Age of the American Revolution*, edited by Berlin and Hoffman; Philip Morgan and Michael L. Nicholls's "Slaves in Piedmont Virginia, 1720–1790," *William and Mary Quarterly*, 3rd series, 46 (1989); Lorena S. Walsh's "Rural African Americans in the Constitutional Era in Maryland, 1776–1810," *Maryland Historical Magazine*, 84 (1989); and Walsh's "Plantation Management in the Chesapeake, 1620–1820," *Journal of Economic History*, 49 (1989). Two studies that do not focus on blacks or slavery but add nevertheless to knowledge of the spread of slave society into southern Virginia are Richard R. Beeman's *The Evolution of the Southern Backcountry: A Case Study of Lunenburg County, Virginia, 1746–1832* (1984); and Frederick F. Siegel's *The Roots of Southern Distinctiveness: Tobacco and Society in Danville, Virginia, 1780–1865* (1965). The latter book describes the enormous amount of labor required on tobacco plantations, and it shows how rapidly the African-American population grew in a Virginia piedmont county after 1812. A similar, shorter treatment of another area in Virginia is John T. Schlotterbeck's "The 'Social Economy' of an Upper South Community: Orange and Greene Counties, Virginia, 1815–1860" in *Class, Conflict, and Consensus: Antebellum Southern Community Studies*, edited by Orville Vernon Burton and Robert C. McMath, Jr. (1982).

Joseph Clarke Robert's *The Tobacco Kingdom* (1965) is useful for the post-Revolutionary spread of tobacco production, arguing that the extent of tobacco's decline has long been exaggerated. Rachel N. Klein's *Unification of a Slave State: The Rise of the Planter Class in the South Carolina Backcountry, 1760–1808* (1990) shows how the plantation model, with slave labor as its basis, took root in western South Carolina before the demand for cotton fiber proved its efficacy.

A fine, new overview of the early growth of an inland cotton kingdom is Joyce E. Chaplin's "Creating a Cotton South in Georgia and South Carolina, 1760–1815," *Journal of Southern History*, 57 (1991). Chaplin details how the Revolution spurred domestic cotton production and charts cotton's early, rapid growth onto the Georgia frontier. Volume two of Lewis C. Gray's *History of Agriculture in the Southern United States to 1860* (1941) remains the standard work on the development and expansion of cotton and sugar production in this country. An interesting article on the early ginning of cotton is Daniel H. Thomas's, "Pre-Whitney Cotton Gins in French Louisiana," *Journal of Southern History*, 31 (1965). There are two good books on Whitney and his invention: Jeanette Mirsky and Allan Nevins's *The World of Eli Whitney* (1952) and Constance McLaughlin Green's *Eli Whitney and the Birth of American Technology* (1956). For the origin of Sea Island cotton see S. G. Stephens's article by that name in *Agricultural History*, 50 (1976). J. Carlyle Sitterson's, *The Cane Sugar Industry in the South, 1753–1950* (1953) can supplement Gray for the growth of sugar production.

Parts of several studies treat the coming of plantation agriculture to particular states or regions. John H. Moore's *The Emergence of the Cotton Kingdom in the Old Southwest: Mississippi, 1770–1860* (1988), the most recently published of these, is an excellent model for much-needed work on other states. Not nearly so useful for African-American history is Thomas P. Abernethy's *The Formative*

Period in Alabama, 1815–1828, 2nd ed. (1965), which treats only whites in the chapter on "Immigrants" during Alabama's formative period. James B. Sellers's *Slavery in Alabama*, 2nd ed. (1964) includes discussion of the growth of cotton agriculture and the interregional trade. John Mills Thornton III's *Politics and Power in a Slave Society: Alabama, 1800–1860* (1978) is good, but its clear focus is on the state's political history. Mary C. Young's "Indian Removal and Allotment: The Civilized Tribes and Jacksonian Justice," *American Historical Review*, 74 (1971), treats the sad story of the way in which much of the Lower South, where Indians had prior claim, became available for white and black settlement.

For the more involved growth of slavery, as well as of sugar and cotton plantations in Louisiana, see Joel Gray Taylor's *Negro Slavery in Louisiana* (1963). Anita S. Goodstein's *Nashville, 1780–1860: From Frontier to City* (1989) includes information on African-American migration into central Tennessee. Juliet E. K. Walker's *Free Frank: A Black Pioneer on the Antebellum Frontier* (1982) is the story of a remarkable slave, born in 1777, who experienced the migration to Kentucky and fifteen years of clearing wilderness to establish his owner's tobacco, corn, and wheat farm. Studies containing information on the early years of slavery in states on the edge of the cotton kingdom through the time of the early republic are Julia Floyd Smith's *Slavery and Population Growth in Antebellum Florida, 1821–1860* (1973) and Randolph B. Campbell's *An Empire for Slavery: The Peculiar Institution in Texas, 1821–1865* (1989).

Kulikoff's "Uprooted Peoples" is good for the post-Revolutionary Atlantic slave trade. Kulikoff points out that a large majority of imported slaves after 1790 went to the spreading backcountry farms and plantations of the Lower South. Darold D. Wax shows how Georgia's slave population doubled over the last decade of the eighteenth century as a result of the reopened Atlantic trade in "'New Negroes Are Always in Demand': The Slave Trade in Eighteenth-Century Georgia," *The Georgia Historical Quarterly*, 68 (1984). Michael E. Stevens's "'To Get As Many Slaves As You Can': An 1807 Slaving Voyage," *South Carolina Historical Magazine*, 87 (1986), covers the last years of the Atlantic trade to the United States as well as one of the last legal voyages to Africa.

For over half a century, Frederick Bancroft's *Slave Trading in the Old South* (1931) was the standard work on the interregional movement of slaves. Bancroft was one of the grand figures among American historians of his time, and his study of the domestic slave trade was scholarly, authoritative, and respected. For Bancroft, who was arguing against Phillips's treatment of slavery as a benign and humane institution, economics won out over humanity in the trading of slaves. Slave trading was much more extensive than Phillips had allowed, Bancroft argued. He found that a number of Upper-South planters probably practiced some form of "slave breeding," that families were separated regularly (rather than practically never, as Phillips averred), and that most planters cared less about slave families than they did for expanding the institution of slavery. In recent years, a few historians have argued for and against some of Bancroft's interpretations. Richard C. Sutch's "The Breeding of Slaves for Sale and the Westward Expansion of Slavery, 1850–1860" in *Race and Slavery in the Western Hemisphere*, edited by Stanley L. Engerman and Eugene D. Genovese (1975), supports Bancroft's ideas about slave breeding—at least during a later period of the trade; while William Calderhead's "How Extensive was the Border State Slave Trade? A New Look," *Civil War History*, 18 (1972), argues against the breeding hypothesis and suggests Bancroft's estimates on numbers of slaves traded was too high. Fogel and Engerman in *Time on the Cross* support Calderhead's conclusions with additional statistical data.

But Michael Tadman's *Speculators and Slaves: Masters, Traders and Slaves in the Old South* (1989) has quickly replaced Bancroft as the standard treatment of the subject, and it seems likely the book will remain as such for some time. Tadman relies on examination of an exhaustive amount of documentary and quantitative data to draw conclusions that support in general many of Bancroft's less-thoroughly grounded conclusions. One cannot read *Speculators and Slaves* without getting a sense of the important, long-term consequences of the trade for African Americans and for black-white relations for years after the trade ceased. Though one can never predict how a new book will continue to be received, it is possible that Tadman's work will do for the interregional slave trade what Philip D. Curtin's *The Atlantic Slave Trade: A Census* (1969) did for the trans-

Atlantic trade—that is, spawn new studies and attract broad criticism, but stand up well as a standard reference for a long time.

Other studies of the interregional slave trade offer insight into particular aspects of the traffic. Herman Freudenberger and Jonathan B. Pritchett in "The Domestic United States Slave Trade: New Evidence," *Journal of Interdisciplinary History*, 21 (1991), use certificates of good character from the New Orleans slave market for 1830 to draw a number of interesting conclusions on sex and age distribution, family separation, the duration and seasonality of the slave trade, and costs and profits. Donald M. Sweig studies twenty-eight ship manifests from the Alexandria, Virginia-to-New Orleans route of the slave trade between 1828 and 1836 in "Reassessing the Human Dimension of the Slave Trade," *Prologue*, 12 (1980). Focusing on John Armfield, Sweig concludes that the trader separated families when it was good business to do so, but he recognized the importance of good public relations and thus attempted to give the impression that his firm, Franklin and Armfield, took pains to avoid family separation. Wendall H. Stephenson's *Isaac Franklin: Slave Trader and Planter in the Old South* (1938) is a good study of Armfield's partner, who conducted the end of the trade in Natchez. Dickson J. Preston in *Young Frederick Douglass: The Maryland Years* (1980) gives a lengthy description of the activities of Baltimore-based slave trader Austin Woolfolk. For a wealth of statistical data relating to the domestic slave trade, birth and death rates, manumissions, and much more, see Peter D. McClelland and Richard J. Zeckhauser's *Demographic Dimensions of the New Republic: American Interregional Migration, Vital Statistics, and Manumissions, 1800–1860* (1982).

Among the useful primary sources on slave trading during the time of the early republic, all written from a variety of biased viewpoints, see Ethan A. Andrews's *Slavery and the Domestic Slave Trade in the United States* (1836); George Featherstonhaugh's *Excursion Through the Slave States* (1844); and Joseph H. Ingraham's *The South-West, by a Yankee* (1835). Charles Ball's *Slavery in the United States: Narrative of the Life and Adventures of Charles Ball*, edited by Isaac Fisher (1837), contains an excellent account of life in a slave coffle. Josiah Henson's account of the sale and separation of his family is in *Father Henson's Story of His Own Life*, edited by Walter

Fisher (1962). John Blassingame's *Slave Testimony: Two Centuries of Letters, Speeches, Interviews, and Autobiographies* (1977) includes a number of accounts of slave sales and movements from the first third of the nineteenth century.

Few of the best-known books about antebellum slavery contain extended discussions of the way the institution changed over the period between the American Revolution and the Civil War. These books define "antebellum" broadly and thus do not make distinctions between the nature of slavery over a fifty- or sixty-year period. Nevertheless, most of the books mentioned in the first part of this essay contain pieces of information from the early republic.

The place to begin examination of the various slave systems in the United States at the time of the country's beginning is Ira Berlin's essay, noted above, in *Autre Temps, Autre Espace*. Gray's *History of Southern Agriculture*, though half a century old, still contains some of the best information on methods of producing the various southern crops with slave labor.

Edgar J. McManus's *Black Bondage in the North* (1973) is the broadest treatment of the subject, while William D. Piersen's *Black Yankees: The Development of an Afro-American Sub-Culture in Eighteenth-Century New England* (1988) examines how New England blacks had created a viable folk culture of their own by the time of the Revolution. Arthur Zilversmit's *The First Emancipation: The Abolition of Slavery in the North* (1967) follows the progress of northern slavery to its end several decades into the nineteenth century. Gary B. Nash's "Forging Freedom: The Emancipation Experience in the Northern Seaport Cities, 1775–1820" in *Slavery and Freedom in the Age of the American Revolution*, edited by Berlin and Hoffman; Nash and Jean R. Soderlund's *Freedom by Degrees: Emancipation in Pennsylvania and Its Aftermath* (1991); Nash's *Forging Freedom: The Formation of Philadelphia's Black Community, 1720–1840* (1988); Shane White's *Somewhat More Independent: The End of Slavery in New York City, 1770–1810* (1991); and Carl Nordstrom's "Slavery in a New York County: Rockland County, 1660–1827," *Afro-Americans in New York Life and History*, 1 (1977) show how long slavery thrived in certain parts of the North.

Richard S. Dunn's "Black Society in the Chesapeake"; Walsh's "Plantation Management in the Chesapeake"; and Carole Shammas's "Black Women's Work and the Evolution of Plantation Society in Virginia," *Labor History*, 26 (1985) are the best starting points for understanding the direction and pace of change in Maryland and Virginia's slave society following the Revolution. Dunn's "A Tale of Two Plantations: Slave Life at Mesopotamia in Jamaica and Mount Airy in Virginia, 1799–1828," *William and Mary Quarterly*, 3rd series, 36 (1977), adds information from later in the period. The first chapter of Barbara Jeanne Fields's *Slavery and Freedom on the Middle Ground: Maryland During the Nineteenth Century* (1988) shows how dramatically Maryland's slave population and the state's views on slavery and freedom changed between 1790 and 1850. The books or portions of books noted earlier by Beeman, Siegel, and Schlotterbeck are case studies of how slave holders took their property and knowledge of commercial agriculture into areas of Virginia away from the Tidewater.

For slavery on the rice plantations of the South Carolina and Georgia lowcountry, see two works by Philip D. Morgan, "Black Society in the Lowcountry," noted above, and "Work and Culture: The Task System and Lowcountry Blacks, 1700–1880," *William and Mary Quarterly*, 3rd series, 39 (1982); Joyce E. Chaplin's "Tidal Rice Cultivation and the Problem of Slavery in South Carolina and Georgia, 1760–1815," *William and Mary Quarterly*, 3rd series, 69 (1992); and Julia Floyd Smith's *Slavery and Rice Culture in Low Country Georgia, 1750–1860* (1985). Charles Joyner's *Down by the Riverside: A South Carolina Slave Community* (1984) is a reconstruction of slaves' lives on a large rice plantation on the Waccamaw River, where the heaviest concentrations of blacks in the country created the most African of African-American cultures.

There is no recent work on sugarcane production along the lower Mississippi. Sitterson's *Sugar Country* remains useful and Joe Gray Taylor's *Negro Slavery in Louisiana* (1963) includes more about the African Americans who worked the sugar.

The development of cotton production on small farms and large plantations across the Deep South is covered thoroughly in several of the works cited above. Moore's *Emergence of the Cotton Kingdom* is an excellent new study that depicts the process of cotton farming coming to Mississippi and the effects the various stages in this process had on the African Americans who worked in the fields. Studies like Moore's for other southern states would be welcome. One other book, Terry Alford's fascinating *Prince Among Slaves: The True Story of An African Prince Sold Into Slavery in the American South* (1977), provides a glimpse of the life of an atypical enslaved African who lived on one of the early cotton plantations in the vicinity of Natchez, showing indeed the variety of the person's experiences.

Owens's *This Species of Property* and Boles's *Black Southerners* contain good information on the working lives of slaves. Persons interested in the working patterns of men and women in slavery should read Joyner's *Down by the Riverside* and Mechal Sobel's *The World They Made Together: Black and White Values in Eighteenth-Century Virginia* (1987), for both books emphasize how much the persons of African descent brought *their* ideas about communal labor and a reasonable pace of work to the fields of the American South.

Richard C. Wade's *Slavery in the Cities, 1820–1860* (1964) remains the standard work on urban slavery. It is thorough, carefully researched, and well written. However, some of Wade's conclusions have been challenged effectively by Claudia Dale Goldin's statistical analysis, *Urban Slavery in the American South, 1820–1860* (1976). Goldin's book is especially useful for its charting the growth of the slave and free black populations of southern cities and for its concise treatment of the lives led by African Americans in the urban milieu. Goldin and Wade do not agree on why urban slavery declined, in relative terms, in the decade preceding the Civil War. Useful articles on particular cities or aspects of urban slavery include Marianne Buroff Sheldon's, "Black-White Relations in Richmond, Virginia, 1782–1820," *Journal of Southern History*, 45 (1979), the reading of which helps explain generally how Charles Ball could walk through Richmond on a normal Sunday without raising any suspicion; William L. Richter's, "Slavery in Baton Rouge, 1820–1860," *Louisiana History*, 32 (1969); and Clement Eaton's "Slave-Hiring in the Upper South: A Step Toward Freedom," *Mississippi Valley Historical Re-*

view, 46 (1960). *The Other Slaves: Mechanics, Artisans, and Craftsmen*, edited by James E. Newton and Ronald L. Lewis (1978), contains valuable articles relating to skilled slaves in cities.

The best broad treatment of the use of slaves in Southern industry is Robert S. Starobin's *Industrial Slavery in the Old South* (1970). A number of studies focus on slave labor in particular industries, but not all of these deal with industries functioning with African-American labor before 1830. The most relevant of these studies for this book are Ernest M. Lander, Jr.'s "Slave Labor in South Carolina Cotton Mills," *Journal of Negro History*, 38 (1953); Percival Perry's "The Naval Stores Industry in the Old South," *Journal of Southern History*, 34 (1968); Ronald L. Lewis's *Coal, Iron, and Slaves: Industrial Slavery in Maryland and Virginia, 1715–1865* (1979); Lewis's *Black Coal Miners in America: Race, Class and Community Conflict, 1780–1980* (1987); Charles B. Dew's "David Ross and the Oxford Iron Works: A Study of Industrial Slavery in the Early Nineteenth Century," *William and Mary Quarterly*, 3rd series, 31 (1974); and Marcus Christian, *Negro Ironworkers in Louisiana, 1718–1900* (1972). Arguments on control and treatment of industrial slaves are in Starobin's "Disciplining Industrial Slaves in the Old South," *Journal of Negro History*, 53 (1968), and Charles B. Dew's "Disciplining Slave Iron Workers in the Antebellum South: Coercion, Conciliation, and Accommodation," *American Historical Review*, 79 (1974).

A fine introduction to the literature on diseases and health among African Americans is Kenneth F. Kiple's "A Survey of Recent Literature on the Biological Past of the Black," *Social Science History*, 10 (1986). Surveys containing background on the subject include Kiple and Virginia Himmelsteib's *Another Dimension of the Black Diaspora: Diet, Disease, and Racism* (1981), which points out the particular nutritional needs of persons of African descent; *Disease and Distinctiveness in the American South*, edited by Todd L. Savitt and James Harvey Young (1988), which deals with individual diseases, slaves' immunities, and the genetic physiological problems unique to African Americans; Savitt's important *Medicine and Slaves: The Diseases and Health Care of Blacks in Antebellum Virginia* (1978); and K. David Patterson's "Disease Environments of the Antebellum South," in *Science and Medicine in the Old South*, edited by Ronald L. Numbers and Todd L. Savitt (1989). Specific discussion of slaves' diet around the middle of the nineteenth century is found in Sam B. Hilliard's *Hog Meat and Hoe Cake: Food Supply in the Old South, 1840–1860* (1972) and Tyson Gibbs et al, "Nutrition in a Slave Population: An Anthropological Examination," *Medical Anthropology*, 4 (1980). Tieing together issues concerning diet, health, and death rates is Richard H. Steckel's "A Peculiar Population: The Nutrition, Health, and Mortality of American Slaves from Childhood to Maturity," *Journal of Economic History*, 46 (1986).

An insightful overview of recent work on infant mortality in the slave population is Richard H. Steckel's "A Dreadful Childhood: The Excess Mortality of American Slaves," *Social Science History*, 10 (1986). Other articles with useful information on infant mortality and the health of slave children are Steckel's "Birth Weights and Infant Mortality Among American Slaves," *Explorations in Economic History*, 23 (1986); and Kenneth F. Kiple and Virginia H. Kiple's "Slave Child Mortality: Some Nutritional Answers to a Perennial Puzzle," *Journal of Southern History*, 10 (1977). For reasons for the great propensity of African-American slave children to experience sudden infant death syndrome see Todd L. Savitt, "Smothering and Overlaying of Slave Children: A Suggested Explanation," *Bulletin of the History of Medicine*, 49 (1975); and Michael P. Johnson's "Smothered Slave Infants: Were Slave Mothers at Fault?" *Journal of Southern History*, 47 (1981). Effectively connecting the health and working conditions of pregnant women to infant mortality is John Campbell's "Work, Pregnancy, and Infant Mortality Among Southern Slaves," *Journal of Interdisciplinary History*, 14 (1984).

Works on slave medical care include David O. Whitten, "Medical Care of Slaves: Louisiana Sugar Region and South Carolina Rice District," *Southern Studies*, 16 (1977); and Bennett H. Wall, "Medical Care of Ebenezer Pettigrew's Slaves," *Mississippi Valley Historical Review*, 37 (1950). Richard H. Steckel's "Slave Height Profiles from Coatwise Manifests," *Explorations in Economic History*, 16 (1979), complements his "A Dreadful Childhood" in suggesting that the first third of the nineteenth century was a particularly unhealthy time for African-American slaves.

Herbert G. Gutman's *The Black Family in Slavery and Freedom,*

1750–1925 (1976) champions the revisionist position on the importance of the family for African-American slaves and dominates the literature. The argument that Gutman revises—that slavery was such a harsh institution of total control that it made it nearly impossible for blacks in slavery to have viable families—is found in E. Franklin Frazier's *The Negro Family in the United States* (1972). Recent works in basic agreement with Gutman include appropriate parts of the books by Owens, Blassingame, and Genovese, noted above. Mary Beth Norton, Herbert G. Gutman, and Ira Berlin's "The Afro-American Family in the American Revolution" in *Slavery and Freedom in the Age of the American Revolution* edited by Berlin and Hoffman, shows how family connections among many slave families were strong enough by the last third of the eighteenth century to enable kinship and family relations to guide individuals' lives through the chaotic times of the growth of the Cotton Kingdom. Charles Wetherell agrees, showing how a long construction phase of slave-family relations would often result in the linking through kinship of a large proportion of a slave community in "Slave Kinship: A Case Study of the South Carolina Good Hope Plantation, 1835–1856," *Journal of Family History*, 6 (1981).

Excellent overviews of African-American slave religion are found in relevant parts of Boles's *Black Southerners*; Genovese's *Roll, Jordan, Roll*; Blassingame's *Slave Community*; Lawrence W. Levine's *Black Culture and Black Consciousness: African American Folk Thought From Slavery to Freedom* (1977); and Donald G. Mathews's, *Religion in the Old South* (1977). Albert J. Raboteau's *Slave Religion: The "Invisible Institution" in the Antebellum South* (1978) is a thorough study of slave religion that emphasizes activities outside the formal church structure and away from white Christians. John B. Boles's introduction to *Masters and Slaves in the House of the Lord: Race and Religion in the American South, 1740–1870*, edited by Boles (1985), argues that African-American Christianity was not so invisible as Raboteau asserts. A good, concise treatment of the mid-eighteenth-century Great Awakening and its effects on African Americans is Alan Gallay's "Planters and Slaves in the Great Awakening" in *Masters and Slaves in the House of the Lord*, edited by Boles.

Arguments for the 1800–1830 period being one of greatly increasing participation of African Americans in Christian churches are in several studies of the Great Revival. John B. Boles's "Evangelical Protestants in the Old South: From Religious Dissent to Cultural Dominance" in *Religion in the Old South*, edited by Charles Reagan Wilson (1985), is a good, short essay on the rise of the evangelical movement and its broad effects across the South. David T. Bailey's *Shadow on the Church: Southwestern Evangelical Religion and the Issue of Slavery, 1783–1860* (1985) deals more thoroughly with African Americans in the new evangelical churches and points out how white evangelicals had to change their position on abolition before planters looked favorably on slave conversions. Anne C. Loveland's *Southern Evangelicals and the Social Order, 1800–1860* (1980) is another solid treatment of evangelicals' shifting attitudes toward slavery and abolition. The first chapter of Lacy K. Ford, Jr.'s *Origins of Southern Radicalism: The South Carolina Upcountry, 1806–1860* (1988) examines the effects of evangelical Christianity on planters and slaves in one region. Mechal Sobel's *Trabelin' On: The Slave Journey to an Afro-Baptist Faith* (1971) shows how African Americans had little difficulty adapting evangelical Baptism, in this case, to their African world view. And Sobel's *The World the Slaves Made* argues that Africans provided much in general to Southern Christian religious thinking and ceremony.

Herbert Aptheker has long been regarded as the grandfather of the study of slave resistance and rebellion in English-speaking North America. Inspired by an urge to show that American slaves were part of the age-old struggle of the oppressed against their oppressors, Aptheker worked laboriously to uncover evidence of slave revolts. His *American Negro Slave Revolts* (1943) was an effective counter to the existing "myth of slave docility" that such other historians as Harvey Wish in "American Slave Insurrections before 1861," *Journal of Negro History*, 22 (1937); and Joseph C. Caroll in *Slave Insurrections in the United States, 1800–1865* (1938) had attacked not long before. Although Aptheker's book has since received criticism for failing to distinguish between actual insurrections and rumors of the same, his work on revolts and rebellions is correctly regarded as pioneering. For a short discussion of the importance of Aptheker's work see Eugene D. Genovese's "Herbert Aptheker's Achievement and Our Responsibility" in *In Resistance: Studies in African, Caribbean, and Afro-American History*, edited by Gary Y. Okihiro (1986). Herbert Shapiro places Aptheker in a broader context of other historians in "Historiography and Slave Revolt and Rebelliousness in the United States: A Class Approach," in the same book.

Taking the opposite tack from Aptheker is Stanley Elkins, who argues in *Slavery* that the master's power over the slave was so complete and the "closed system" of slavery was so harsh and controlling—like a concentration camp, Elkins argues—that American slaves were rendered child-like and docile. But disagreement with Elkins has been strong. A sample of arguments is in *The Debate over Slavery: Stanley Elkins and His Critics*, edited by Ann J. Lane (1971). Eugene D. Genovese's chapter on "Rebelliousness and Docility in the Negro Slave: A Critique of the Elkins Thesis" is the one most directly related to the issue of slave rebellion.

Genovese has written the best, recent surveys of African American resistance and rebellion. Book Four of *Roll, Jordan, Roll* is an excellent, concise treatment of the subjects, with a particularly useful comparative discussion of rebellions in English-speaking North America and the rest of the Western Hemisphere. Genovese's *From Rebellion to Revolution: Afro-American Slave Revolts in the Making of the New World* (1979) contains his thesis that New-World slave rebellions changed their character after the French Revolution—from being revolts to achieve local autonomy to being revolutionary assaults on the institution of slavery. Arguments in James Oakes's *Slavery and Freedom: An Interpretation of the Old South* (1990) touch on related themes. Merton L. Dillon's *Slavery Attacked: Southern Slaves and Their Allies, 1619–1865* (1990) is a fine new study of slave resistance and rebellion within a larger body of opposition to slavery.

Willie Lee Rose's essay, "The Impact of the American Revolution on the Black Population" in her *Slavery and Freedom*, expanded edition, edited by William W. Freehling (1982), is a good beginning for understanding the effects of changes in the Revolutionary era on African Americans' thought and action. Gerald W. Mullin's chapter on "War, Economic Change, and Slavery" in his *Flight and Rebel-*

lion: Slave Resistance in Eighteenth-Century Virginia (1972) is excellent. Benjamin Quarles's "The Revolutionary War as a Black Declaration of Independence" in *Slavery and Freedom in the Age of the American Revolution* points out how much the Revolution "spurred black Americans to seek freedom and equality." Many of the remaining chapters of the same book describe the far-reaching economic and social changes of the period that so affected African Americans. Sarah S. Hughes's "Slaves for Hire: The Allocation of Black Labor in Elizabeth City County, Virginia, 1782 to 1810," *William and Mary Quarterly*, 3rd series, 35 (1978), is a case study of the evolving nature of slavery in one Virginia county in post-Revolutionary times. Jeffery J. Crow's "Slave Rebelliousness and Social Conflict in North Carolina, 1775–1802," *William and Mary Quarterly*, 3rd series, 37 (1980) is a good addition to this literature.

C. L. R. James's *The Black Jacobins: Toussaint L'Ouverture and the Santo Domingo Revolution* (1938) remains the standard work on the subject. The first volume of Foner's *History of Black Americans* contains insightful treatment of the effects of revolution in the Caribbean on African Americans in the United States.

A good study of Gabriel's plot is Mullins's *Flight and Rebellion*. It is in this book that Mullins sets out most clearly his thesis that relates the level of acculturation to the form and extent of African Americans' rebellious activity—a thesis that has stood up well since the book's publication. A recent study that contains new thoughts on Gabriel's motives is Douglas R. Egerton's "Gabriel's Conspiracy and the Election of 1800," *The Journal of Southern History*, 56 (1990). Egerton views Gabriel as an aware member of his class of artisans, put off with Richmond merchants and conscious of the possibility of taking action to improve the economic position of his class during the hotly contested 1800 election. Other studies that complement these works include Philip J. Schwarz, "Gabriel's Challenge: Slaves and Crime in Late Eighteenth-Century Virginia," *Virginia Magazine of History and Biography*, 90 (1982); and Bert M. Mutersbaugh, "The Background of Gabriel's Conspiracy," *Journal of Negro History*, 68 (1983). Robert McColley's *Slavery and Jeffersonian Virginia* (1964) describes the relaxed state of white control in Virginia on the eve of Gabriel's plot.

Detailed information on unrest and rebellions between Gabriel's in 1800 and Denmark Vesey's in 1822 is spotty. Douglas R. Egerton's "'Fly Across the River': The Easter Slave Conspiracy of 1802," *North Carolina Historical Review*, 68 (1991), is a careful study that shows that the conspiracy was "born of a single source and was not a number of isolated acts of overt resistance." Egerton suggests that the 1802 conspiracy was a "second chapter" of Gabriel's planned insurrection. James H. Dorman's, "The Persistent Specter: Slave Rebellion in Territorial Louisiana," *Louisiana History*, 18 (1977), is the best study of the massive rebellion led by Charles Deslondes in 1811; and Jack D. L. Holmes's "The Abortive Slave Revolt at Point Coupée, Louisiana, 1795," *Louisiana History*, 11 (1970), shows how generally rebellious were Louisiana slaves in the 1790s and 1800s. Frank A. Cassell's "Slaves of the Chesapeake Bay Area and the War of 1812," *Journal of Negro History*, 57 (1972), describes how slaves took advantage of the chaotic times of this war much as African Americans did during the Revolution. John Scott Strickland's "The Great Revival and Insurrectionary Fears in North Carolina: An Examination of Antebellum Southern Society and the Slave Revolt Panics," in *Class, Conflict, and Consensus*, edited by Burton and McMath, is an interesting piece on how rumors of revolt could bring fear and panic to southern whites.

For the Denmark Vesey conspiracy, one should begin with Lionel H. Kennedy and Thomas Parker's *Official Report of the Trials of Sundry Negroes Charged with an Attempt to Raise an Insurrection in the State of South Carolina* (1822). Kennedy and Parker were the presiding magistrates at the trials. They provide the evidence given in each case and information on sentences. William W. Freehling has written two careful studies of the conspiracy, one in his *Prelude to Civil War: The Nullification Controversy in South Carolina, 1816–1836* (1965), which is especially helpful in placing the conspiracy in the context of relevant events of the time, and the other in "Denmark Vesey's Peculiar Reality" in *New Perspectives on Race and Slavery in America: Essays in Honor of Kenneth M. Stampp*, edited by Robert H. Abzug and Stephen E. Maizlish (1986). Marina Wilkramanayake's *A World in Shadow: The Free Black in Antebellum South*

Carolina (1973) contains information on the difficult situation free blacks faced in Charleston in the years before the conspiracy, including discussion of the suppression of the African Methodist church, as well as on the conspiracy itself. John Lofton's *Insurrection in South Carolina: The Turbulent World of Denmark Vesey* (1964) is a thorough and readable treatment.

Richard C. Wade's revisionist article that suggests that the conspiracy was more in the minds of anxious whites than in those of rebellious blacks is "The Vesey Plot: A Reconsideration," *Journal of Southern History*, 30 (1964). *Denmark Vesey: The Slave Conspiracy of 1822*, edited by Robert S. Starobin (1970), is a compilation of materials put together in response to Wade's article. Max L. Kleinman's "The Denmark Vesey Conspiracy: An Historiographical Study," *Negro History Bulletin*, 37 (1974), is a short discussion and refutation of the arguments in Wade's article.

The basis of much that has been written about Nat Turner's rebellion is Thomas R. Gray's *The Confessions of Nat Turner* (1831), an account of what Turner told attorney Gray in his jail cell over several days before his trial. Most authorities believe Gray wrote down and published something close to what Turner told him. Henry I. Tragle's *The Southampton Slave Revolt of 1831: A Compilation of Source Material* (1971) contains Gray's *Confessions* along with the trial record, newspaper stories, and previously published accounts of the episode. Tragle's introduction is an excellent, short overview of the rebellion. Eric Foner's *Nat Turner* (1971) is another useful collection of documents.

Stephen B. Oates's *The Fires of Jubilee: Nat Turner's Fierce Rebellion* (1975) is a gem of a book, carefully studied, reasonably argued, and wonderfully written. Of particular value is the care the author takes to set the rebellion in its place and time, and thus to show its importance in American history through the middle of the nineteenth century.

William Styron wrote a novel entitled *The Confessions of Nat Turner* (1967). The response to this controversial piece of fiction produced more publication over a five-year period than the rebellion did over a century and a half. A good summary of the rebellion, the novel, and the response is *The Nat Turner Rebellion: The Historical Event and the Modern Controversy*, edited by John B. Duff and Peter Mitchell (1971).

Raymond A. Bauer and Alice H. Bauer's "Day to Day Resistance to Slavery," *Journal of Negro History*, 27 (1942), presents the argument that African Americans used a variety of subtle ways to resist slavery. The standard works on antebellum slavery by Stampp, Blassingame, and Genovese further the argument. The short article by George M. Frederickson and Christopher C. Lash, "Resistance to Slavery," *Civil War History*, 13 (1967), argues otherwise—that many of the behaviors regarded as resistance were not conscious efforts on the parts of slaves to resist.

There is a solid and growing literature about the resistance of African-American women to their lot in slavery. Elizabeth Fox-Genovese's "Strategies and Forms of Resistance: Focus on Slave Women in the United States" in *In Resistance*, edited by Okihiro, is a good introduction to the subject, valuable for this study because it examines periods before 1830. Fox-Genovese's *Inside the Plantation Household: Black and White Women in the Old South* (1988) has a chapter on "Women Who Opposed Slavery." Other studies of slave women and resistance include Darlene Clark Hine and Kate Wittenstein's, "Female Slave Resistance: The Economics of Sex" in *The Black Woman Cross-Culturally*, edited by Filomina Chioma Steady (1981); and Gerda Lerner's "The Struggle for Survival—Day to Day Resistance" in *Black Women in White America: A Documentary History*, edited by Gerda Lerner (1973).

Much of the literature on runaway slaves is tied into studies of the Underground Railroad and thus relates mostly to a period past the end of this study. Mullin's *Flight and Rebellion* is the best study of runaways in the eighteenth century, while Genovese in *Roll, Jordan, Roll* and Boles in *Black Southerners* have good, short pieces on escape from slavery with a focus mostly on the antebellum period. McColley's *Slavery and Jeffersonian Virginia* has a chapter on runaways and rebels at the time; its focus is on Virginia's legal efforts to stifle such actions. Ira Berlin's *Slaves Without Masters: The Free Negro in the Antebellum South* (1974) has excellent accounts of fugitive slaves through the early decades of the nineteenth century and of the role the growing free black community played in spurring slaves to run away and helping them do so. Paul Finkelman's "The Kidnapping of John Davis and the Adoption of the Fugitive Slave Law of 1793," *Journal of Southern History*, 56 (1990), explains why northerners voted for a bill they did not like and why southerners soon came to despise the bill and want stronger measures.

Michael P. Johnson's "Runaway Slaves and the Slave Communities in South Carolina, 1799–1830," *William and Mary Quarterly*, 3rd series, 38 (1981), treats African Americans who ran away in groups. Works on the relations between African Americans and Native Americans include Kenneth W. Porter's *The Negro on the Frontier* (1971) and Wyatt F. Jeltz's "The Relations of Negroes and Choctaw and Chikasaw Indians," *Journal of Negro History*, 33 (1948). For maroons in the United States see Herbert Aptheker's "Maroons within the Present Limits of the United States," *Journal of Negro History*, 24 (1939); and John D. Milligan, "Slave Rebelliousness and the Florida Maroon," *Prologue*, 6 (1974).

Two books dominate the literature on free African Americans during the years of slavery. Leon Litwack's *North of Slavery: The Negro in the Free States* (1961) is the book that opened eyes to the prejudice and proscriptions that faced free blacks across the North. Ira Berlin's *Slaves Without Masters* shows how free blacks' circumstances differed from the Upper to Lower South and changed through time. Berlin's book gives the reader a real sense of the hope of emancipation after the Revolution, followed by the failure of freedom by the 1820s. *Free Blacks in America, 1800–1860*, edited by John H. Bracey, Jr., August Meier, and Elliott Rudwick (1971) contains a good selection of articles on the subject. Population figures for free blacks from 1790 are in *Population of the United States in 1860*, published by the United States Bureau of the Census (1864).

There is not a great deal of information on the small free black population that existed before the American Revolution. T. H. Breen and Stephen Innes's *'Myne Owne Ground': Race and Freedom on Virginia's Eastern Shore, 1640–1676* (1980) is a study of several African Americans who were not slaves and who had broad social and economic relations in seventeenth-century Virginia. Winthrop D.

Jordan's *White Over Black: American Attitudes Toward the Negro, 1550–1812* (1968) provides information on the free black population and how it was regulated in colonial America.

The most complete treatment of the ending of slavery throughout the North is Arthur Zilversmit's *The First Emancipation*. Nash and Soderlund explain carefully how Pennsylvania slave owners extricated themselves from the institution without experiencing financial loss in *Freedom by Degrees*. These authors show that ending slavery in Pennsylvania was not easy work, as some have thought, and they provide evidence of the involvement of fugitive slaves in the process.

Robert W. Fogel and Stanley L. Engerman discuss the importance of the growing white labor supply to northern thoughts on gradual emancipation in "Philanthropy at Bargain Prices: Notes on the Economics of Gradual Emancipation," *Journal of Legal Studies*, 13 (1974). Paul Finkelman's "Slavery and the Northwest Ordinance: A Study in Ambiguity," *Journal of the Early Republic*, 6 (1986), is a careful study that suggests that the antislavery section of the Northwest Ordinance was neither clear nor well thought-out. In this, Finkelman disagrees with William W. Freehling, who regards the antislavery effort in 1787 as a designed step by the Founding Fathers toward the end of slavery in "The Founding Fathers and Slavery," *American Historical Review*, 77 (1972). Staughton Lynd's "The Compromise of 1787," in *Class Conflict, Slavery, and the United States Constitution*, edited by Staughton Lynd (1967), explains why southerners accepted the antislavery clause. Merrily Pierce's "Luke Decker and Slavery: His Cases with Bob and Anthony, 1817–1822," *Indiana Magazine of History*, 8 (1989), is about an Indiana farmer and judge who owned and traded slaves in the state in spite of the prohibitions of doing so in the Northwest Ordinance.

Gary B. Nash has two important works on the growth of the free black community in the North. His "Forging Freedom" in *Slavery and Freedom in the Age of the American Revolution*, edited by Berlin and Hoffman, discusses how African Americans broke from their past in bondage and established family and community institutions in several northern cities. Nash's *Forging Freedom* is probably the most important book on free African Americans in recent years. One can see in this book how Philadelphia's black community faced, and was affected by, issues that most free blacks encountered through a formative time. Shane White's *Somewhat More Independent* rivals Nash's work in showing clearly how dramatic was the change, over a relatively short period, from slavery to freedom. Good to read with *Forging Freedom* in particular are Carl Oblinger's "Alms for Oblivion: The Making of a Black Underclass in Southeastern Pennsylvania, 1780–1860" in *The Ethnic Experience in Philadelphia*, edited by John E. Bodnar (1973), which shows the extreme difficulties of African-American life in freedom in a smaller Pennsylvania community; and Emma J. Lapsansky's "'Since They Got Those Separate Churches': Afro-Americans and Racism in Jacksonian Philadelphia," *American Quarterly*, 32 (1980), a good discussion of the established free black community and why lower-class whites resented its existence.

Several books treat mob violence and its effect on free black communities in the North. Paul A. Gilje's *The Road to Mobocracy: Popular Disorder in New York City, 1763–1834* (1987) has a chapter on riots by and against African Americans. John M. Werner's *Reaping the Bloody Harvest: Race Riots in the United States during the Age of Jackson* (1986) contains the most complete study of the Cincinnati riot of 1829. Leonard L. Richards's *"Gentlemen of Property and Standing": Anti-Abolition Mobs in Jacksonian America* (1970) contains related material.

The problem of kidnapping of free blacks as it relates to the personal-liberty laws is treated in Thomas D. Morris's *Free Men All: The Personal Liberty Laws of the North, 1780–1861* (1974). The book is a detailed discussion of the interesting legal problems states faced when they tried to interpose themselves between individual African Americans and the federal government, which had lax requirements governing seizure of suspected fugitives.

The most thorough general study of the experiences of free blacks as they moved to cities is Leonard P. Curry's *The Free Black in Urban America, 1800–1850: The Shadow of the Dream* (1981). Curry's study of the fifteen largest cities of the period provides the sense that, though the process varied widely among urban areas, it was especially in cities during the time of the early republic that free

African Americans developed a sense of community and community organizations.

In addition to the books by Nash and White, there are good studies of free African-American populations in northern cities. Robert J. Cottrol's *The Afro-Yankees: Providence's Black Community in the Antebellum Era* (1982) is more useful for the African-American community in the early years of the nineteenth century than the title suggests. James O. Horton and Lois E. Horton's *Black Bostonians: Family Life and Community Struggle in the Antebellum North* (1979) traces the roots of antebellum religious and social organizations into the time of the early republic. Henry L. Taylor has two good studies of Cincinnati's free black community: "On Slavery's Fringe: City-Building and Black Community Development in Cincinnati, 1800–1850," *Ohio History*, 95 (1986); and "The Use of Maps in the Study of the Black Ghetto-Formation Process: Cincinnati, 1802–1910," *Historical Methods*, 17 (1984). Russell H. Davis's *Black Americans in Cleveland from George Peake to Carl B. Stokes, 1796–1969* (1972) is not strong on the early period. A related study is Jeffery W. Bolster's "'To Feel Like a Man': Black Seamen in the Northern States, 1800–1860," *Journal of American History*, 77 (1990), which describes the importance of the "Atlantic maritime culture" that existed in northern seaport cities for the economic and social growth of African Americans in the first half of the nineteenth century.

Berlin's book dominates scholarship on free blacks in the South, but there are a number of good supplements to it. Chapters three and four of Loren Schweninger's *Black Property Owners in the South, 1790–1915* (1990) deal with "Free Negro Property Owners" and "Affluent Free Persons of Color." One should see the same author's "Property Owning Free African-American Women in the South, 1800–1870," *Journal of Women's History*, 1 (1990), for a discussion of the "remarkable industry and enterprise of the black women living in the middle of a slave society." Larry Koger's *Black Slaveowners: Free Black Slave Masters in South Carolina, 1790–1860* (1985) has related material. The first chapter of Barbara Jeanne Fields's *Slavery and Freedom on the Middle Ground* contains information on the early years of Maryland's free African-American community. Michael L. Nicholls's "Passing Through This Troublesome World: Free

Blacks in the Early [Virginia] Southside," 92 (1984); and Philip J. Schwarz's "Emancipators, Protectors, and Anomalies: Free Black Slaveowners in Virginia" 95 (1987), both in *The Virginia Magazine of History and Biography*, are valuable studies. John Hope Franklin treats *The Free Negro in North Carolina, 1790–1860* (1943); and E. Horace Fitchett deals with "The Origins and Growth of the Free Negro Population of Charleston, South Carolina," *Journal of Negro History*, 26 (1941). Thomas N. Ingersoll's "Free Blacks in a Slave Society: New Orleans, 1718–1812," *William and Mary Quarterly*, 3rd series, 68 (1991); Donald E. Everett's "Free Persons of Color in Colonial Louisiana," *Louisiana History*, 7 (1966); Laura Foner's "The Free People of Color in Louisiana and St. Domingue: A Comparative Portrait of Two Three-Caste Slave Societies," *Journal of Social History*, 3 (1970); and Gary B. Mills's *The Forgotten People: Cane River's Creoles of Color* (1977) describe the unique situation in Louisiana.

Useful studies of free black populations in southern cities include Suzanne Lebsock's *The Free Women of Petersburg: Status and Culture in a Southern Town, 1784–1860* (1984), which points out the real economic problem African-American women faced as heads of households; Letitia Woods Brown's *Free Negroes in the District of Columbia, 1790–1846* (1972), which has more on how many free blacks came to live in Washington and less on what their lives were like; Dorothy Provine's "The Economic Position of the Free Blacks in the District of Columbia, 1800–1860," *Journal of Negro History*, 58 (1973), which adds information on how African Americans in the nation's capital made a living; Henry S. Robinson's "Some Aspects of the Free Negro Population of Washington, D.C., 1800–1862," *Maryland Historical Magazine*, 64 (1991); Leroy Graham's *Baltimore: The Nineteenth Century Black Capital* (1982), which has chapters on the community's origins and early leaders; and the same author's "Manumitted Free Blacks in Baltimore, 1806–1816," *Maryland Magazine of Genealogy*, 5 (1982), largely a listing.

The urban studies, noted above, by Nash and Cottrol are good places to begin investigation of free black mutual aid societies. Daniel Perlman's "Organizations of the Free Negro in New York City, 1800–1860," *Journal of Negro History*, 56 (1971), discusses mutual benefit societies in that city. Robert L. Harris's "Charleston's Free Afro-American Elite: The Brown Fellowship Society and the Humane Brotherhood," *South Carolina Historical Society*, 82 (1981), provides a clear picture of what the societies tried to do for their members. Prince Hall and African-American Freemasonry are the subjects of two studies: William A. Muraskin's *Middle-Class Blacks in a White Society: Prince Hall Freemasonry in America* (1975); and Loretta J. Williams's *Black Freemasonry and Middle-Class Realities* (1980).

Carter G. Woodson's *The History of the Negro Church* (1921) is a classic study, and Milton C. Sernett's *Black Religion and American Evangelicalism: White Protestants, Plantation Missions, and the Flowering of Christianity, 1787–1865* (1975) is a solid, more recent work that treats the early slave churches as well as those of free African Americans. An excellent introduction to the move toward independent black churches in the early republic is Will B. Gravely's "The Rise of African Churches in America (1786–1822): Reexamining the Contexts," *Journal of Religious Thought*, 41 (1984). Gravely makes the point that "the independent black churches stood as institutional symbols for human liberation," much less noticed than white abolitionist activities, but important in the black community for carrying on "a continual struggle to defend, protect, extend, and expand black freedom."

The historical literature on the development of particular independent black churches or of churches in specific locations is out of date. Among good, recent treatments are Carol V. R. George's *Segregated Sabbaths: Richard Allen and the Emergence of Independent Black Churches, 1760–1840* (1973), which can be supplemented by Gary B. Nash's "New Light on Richard Allen: The Early Years of Freedom," *William and Mary Quarterly*, 3rd series, 46 (1989); Nash's "'To Arise Out of the Dust': Absalom Jones and the African Church of Philadelphia, 1785–1795," in *Race, Class, and Politics: Essays on American Colonial and Revolutionary Society*, edited by Gary B. Nash (1986); and George A. Levesque's "Inherent Reformers—Inherited Orthodoxy: Black Baptists in Boston, 1800–1873," *Journal of Negro History*, (1975). W. Harrison Daniel's "Virginia Baptists and the Negro in the Antebellum Era," *Journal of Negro*

History, 56 (1971), makes the point that white southerners' fears of insurrection limited the ability of independent black churches to function in the South.

Good beginnings for study of schools in the early free black community are Carter G. Woodson's *The Education of the Negro Prior to 1861* (1919) and the fourth chapter of Litwack's *North of Slavery*. Charles F. Andrews's *The History of the New York African Free-Schools* (1830, 1969) is the view of the institution by the school's director. Information on the abortive effort at beginning a school in Richmond is in Edmund Berkeley, Jr., "Prophet Without Honor: Christopher McPherson, Free Person of Color," *Virginia Magazine of History and Biography*, 52 (1967). From the first chapter of Joel Schor's *Henry Highland Garnet: A Voice of Black Radicalism in the Nineteenth Century* (1977) one can get a clear sense of the importance of education for the rising generation of African-American intellectuals.

The first two volumes of Foner's *History of Black Americans* contain discussions of the free black elite in the early republic—who they were, what they did, and how they came by their social standing. Julie Winch's *Philadelphia's Black Elite: Activism, Accommodation, and the Struggle for Autonomy, 1787–1848* (1988) shows how Philadelphia became the early center for African-American intellectual life and describes the extensive interaction Philadelphia's black elite had with those in other cities.

Persons wanting an overview of the period between 1815 and 1831 with emphasis on issues relating to African-American history might wish to read appropriate parts of William W. Freehling's carefully written *The Road to Disunion, Volume I: Secessionists at Bay, 1776–1854* (1990). Freehling's focus is on the South, and he shows as well as anyone how slavery influenced much of national politics from the Missouri Compromise to the Civil War. An excellent treatment of African Americans during this period and beyond, which presents a clear, strong argument for the importance of free blacks and slaves in ending slavery in America, is Dillon's *Slavery Attacked.*

Winthrop D. Jordan's *White Over Black* is the standard work on how America came to be the racist society it was by the start of the nineteenth century. Three books by George M. Fredrickson add considerably to our understanding of whites' racist notions of blacks. His *The Black Image in the White Mind: The Debate on Afro-American Character and Destiny, 1817–1914* (1971) has good, early chapters on the relationship between slavery and racism, pseudo-scientific racism, and colonization. Fredrickson's *White Supremacy: A Comparative Study in American and South African History* (1981) is a pioneering work that shows how helpful comparative history can be when it is done well. Fredrickson's section in the book on "Revolution, Rebellion, and the Limits of Equality, 1776–1820" provides a particularly clear assessment of the effects of the American libertarian ideology on African Americans and white concepts of race. And Fredrickson's essay on the "Social Origins of Race" in his *The Arrogance of Race: Historical Perspectives on Slavery, Racism, and Social Inequality* (1988) is good to read along with Jordan's book.

Gary B. Nash in *Race and Revolution* (1990) offers careful assessments of how close the Revolutionary generation came to abolishing slavery, why abolition sentiment waned (with the northern states getting their share of blame), and the role of free blacks in fighting a rear-guard action against the growing racism of the early nineteenth century. The first chapter of Donald G. Nieman's *Promises to Keep: African Americans and the Constitutional Order, 1776 to the Present* (1991) is a concise treatment of the Constitutional compromises involving slavery and how the American political system "worked against realization of the Constitution's antislavery potential" through the years of the early republic and beyond. Paul Finkelman covers some of the same ground in "Slavery and the Constitutional Convention: Making a Covenant with Death" in *Beyond Confederation: Origins of the Constitution and American National Identity*, edited by Richard Beeman, Stephen Botein, and Edward C. Carter III (1987). Robert M. Weir argues that the decision not to limit slavery in the Constitution eventually worked against the liberties of all Americans in "South Carolina: Slavery and the Structure of the Union" in *Ratifying the Constitution*, edited by Michael Allen Gillespie and Michael Lienesch (1989). And Howard A. Ohline shows in "Slavery, Economics, and Congressional Politics, 1790," *Journal of Southern History*, 46 (1980), how special-interest politics during the first session of Congress was instrumental in turning the Constitution into more of a proslavery document than its writers may have intended.

Duncan J. MacLeod's *Slavery, Race and the American Revolution* (1974) is a strong argument for the importance of the Revolutionary Era for the establishment of racism in America. David B. Davis's *The Problem of Slavery in the Age of Revolution, 1770–1823* (1975) sorts out the contradictions between slavery and libertarian ideology. Reginald Horsman ties Anglo-Saxon racism to American expansion in *Race and Manifest Destiny: The Origins of American Racial Anglo-Saxonism* (1981). His treatment of early manifestations of this racism and of the beginnings of "scientific racialism" are useful for this study. Shane White, in a chapter of *Somewhat More Independent* entitled "Impious Rogues," examines magazines, newspapers, and almanacs for the two decades following the Revolution to show how popular culture interacted with elite culture to form white racial opinion.

William S. Jenkins's *Proslavery Thought in the Antebellum South, 1830–1860* (1980) was long the starting point for study of southern arguments in support of slavery, but Larry E. Tise's *Proslavery: A History of the Defense of Slavery in America, 1701–1840* (1987) has proved to be a controversial revision of Jenkins's main themes. Tise views the basic proslavery arguments as being rooted in a New England conservatism that came into existence in the early years of the Republic.

The best overall treatment of African-American emigration schemes and the colonization movement is Floyd J. Miller's *The Search for a Black Nationality: Black Emigration and Colonization, 1787–1863* (1975). For the American Colonization Society, the standard work is P. J. Staudenraus's *The African Colonization Movement, 1816–1865* (1961), but other studies, some more recent, question some of Staudenraus's interpretations. A good, recent work on the origins of the society is Douglas R. Egerton's "'Its Origin is Not a Little Curious': A New Look at the American Colonization Society," *Journal of the Early Republic*, 5 (1985). Stephen L. Cox's "'Polluted With the Blood of Africa': Bigotry, Slavery, and the New Hampshire Colonization Society," *Historical New Hampshire*, 38 (1983), shows how racism was the underpinning of a state colonization society that prided itself in caring for African Americans. Cox criticizes colonizationists for never having "sought to alter society in such a way that would free the black from white oppression."

Much older works on colonization are Henry N. Sherwood's "The Formation of the American Colonization Society," *Journal of Negro History*, 2 (1917); Charles I. Foster's "The Colonization of Free Negroes in Liberia, 1816–1835," *Journal of Negro History*, 38 (1953), which presents a strong argument that racism was behind the society's work; and Early Lee Fox's *The American Colonization Society, 1817–1840* (1919, 1971).

Paul Cuffe's exploits and his role in emigration activities are discussed in Sheldon H. Harris's *Paul Cuffe: Black America and the African Return* (1972), largely a publication of Cuffe's journal and letters, and Lamont D. Thomas's *Rise to Be a People: A Biography of Paul Cuffe* (1986).

Amos J. Beyan's *The American Colonization Society and the Creation of the Liberian State: A Historical Perspective, 1822–1900* (1991) focuses on the society's work in Africa and on Liberia. Thomas Schick's *Behold the Promised Land* (1980) is the best treatment of the ventures of the Americo-Liberians.

Louis Mehlinger's "The Attitude of the Free Negro Toward African Colonization," *Journal of Negro History*, 1 (1916), expresses the general idea that African Americans were opposed to colonization. Marie Tyler McGraw shows that the black response was more complex than previously thought in "Richmond Free Blacks and African Colonization, 1816–1832," *Journal of American Studies*, 21 (1987).

The literature on abolitionism in the United States is considerable, but since nearly all of that literature focuses on the abolition movement between 1831 and the Civil War, it is not directly pertinent to this essay. One has to look much harder to find discussion of antislavery activities in America before the time of Garrison and his "immediatist" approach.

The first half of Dwight Lowell Dumond's thorough study, *Antislavery: The Crusade for Freedom in America* (1961), is a good treatment of most aspects of antislavery before Garrison. Good, but shorter, studies of the same topic are the early chapters of Louis Filler's *The Crusade Against Slavery, 1830–1860* (1960); James Brewer Stewart's *Holy Warriors: Abolitionists and American Slavery* (1978); and Merton L. Dillon's *The Abolitionists: The Growth of a Dissenting Minority* (1974). Alice D. Adams's *The Neglected Period of American Antislavery, 1808–1831* (1908) is long on particulars and short on generalities.

Thomas E. Drake's *Quakers and Slavery in America* (1950) is a good survey of the subject, and Randall M. Miller's "The Union Humane Society," *Quaker History*, 61 (1972), provides a sense of Quaker antislavery activities in the 1820s. John L. Thomas's "Romantic Reform in America, 1815–1865," *American Quarterly*, 17 (1965), ties antislavery into the broader reform movement. For the evangelical strain in early antislavery activities see Gilbert H. Barnes's, *The Anti-Slavery Impulse, 1830–1844* (1933), which deals more with the 1820s than the title suggests; John C. Hammond's, "Revival Religion and Antislavery Politics," *American Sociological Review*, 39 (1974); Donald G. Mathews's, *Slavery and Methodism: A Chapter in American Morality, 1780–1845* (1965); and James B. Stewart's "Radicalism and the Evangelical Strain in Southern Antislavery Thought during the 1820's," *Journal of Southern History*, 40 (1974).

Biographies of some of the major abolitionist figures provide information on their early lives and antislavery activities. See Merton L. Dillon's *Benjamin Lundy and the Struggle for Negro Freedom* (1966); John L. Thomas's *The Liberator: William Lloyd Garrison* (1963); and Aileen S. Kraditor's *Means and Ends in American Abolitionism: Garrison and His Critics on Strategy and Tactics, 1834–1850* (1969). The influence of Baltimore's African-American community on Garrison's ideas is evident in *William Lloyd Garrison, 1805–1879, The Story of His Life Told by His Children* (1885–1889).

Ronald G. Walters emphasizes the importance of events of the 1820s for bringing out a stronger abolition movement in the following decades in "The Boundaries of Abolitionism" in *Antislavery Reconsidered: New Perspectives on the Abolitionists*, edited by Lewis Perry and Michael Fellman (1979). Paul Finkelman examines legal and Constitutional issues in the same decade and shows how the argument over slavery and freedom brought about a breakdown of comity among states—a vital spirit of accommodation gave way to destructive antagonism, he suggests—in *An Imperfect Union: Slavery, Federalism, and Comity* (1981). Though its focus is on the Nullification Controversy and South Carolina, Freehling's *Prelude to Civil War* provides the most complete treatment of the events occurring in the 1820s that related to slavery. As he shows, there were many.

Glover Moore's *The Missouri Controversy, 1819–1821* (1953) is a full treatment of that problem. Merton L. Dillon's "John Mason Peck, a Study of Historical Rationalization," *Journal of the Illinois Historical Society*, 50 (1957), is a brief study of a Baptist preacher who organized forces in Illinois to oppose the effort there to legalize slavery. For a criticism of Freehling's thesis on the Nullification Controversy, see Paul H. Bergeron, "The Nullification Controversy Revisited," *Tennessee Historical Quarterly*, 35 (1976). Freehling tempers his own ideas on the subject in "Paranoia and American History," *New York Review of Books*, September 23, 1971. The best short treatment of the debates over slavery in Virginia in 1831–32 is in Oates's *Fires of Jubilee*. John T. Noonan, Jr.'s *The Antelope: The Ordeal of the Recaptured Africans in the Administration of James Monroe and John Quincy Adams* (1977) is a detailed critique of the legal arguments of the notorious *Antelope* case, which shows how little regard most Americans in high places held for the humanity of Africans.

Benjamin Quarles's *Black Abolitionists* is an important book, for it first made historians examine the role African Americans played in the ending of slavery. Most of Quarles's book deals with the period after 1830, however. Dillon's *Slavery Attacked* makes a strong case throughout for free blacks' growing sense of unity with and responsibility for their fellow African Americans in slavery, and he stresses the importance of free blacks' thinking and action in quickening the pace of abolition. William B. Gravely identifies early manifestations of Du Bois's "twoness" theme in "The Dialectic of Double-Consciousness in Black American Freedom Celebrations, 1808–1863," *Journal of Negro History*, 67 (1982). Bella Gross has a study of *Freedom's Journal* and its successor newspaper, which

Samuel Cornish edited, in "*Freedom's Journal* and the *Rights for All*," *Journal of Negro History*, 17 (1932).

Extracts from David Walker's *Appeal* are in a number of collections of documents. Herbert Aptheker's *"One Continuous Cry," David Walker's Appeal to the Colored Citizens of the World, 1829–1830: Its Setting and Its Meaning* (1965) contains the various editions of the pamphlet. The best study of Walker is Donald M. Jacobs's "David Walker, Boston Race Leader, 1825–1830," *Essex Institute Historical Collections*, 107 (1971). William H. Pease and Jane H. Pease offer information on the dissemination of the *Appeal* in the South in "Walker's Appeal Comes to Charleston: A Note and Documents," *Journal of Negro History*, 59 (1974). Clement Eaton examines the South's reaction to the pamphlet's message in "A Dangerous Pamphlet in the Old South," *Journal of Southern History*, 2 (1936).

INDEX